85-11

Books by Norma Lee Browning

MILLER'S HIGH LIFE (with Ann Miller)
THE HONORABLE MR. MARIGOLD (with Louella Dirksen)
THE PSYCHIC WORLD OF PETER HURKOS
THE OTHER SIDE OF THE MIND (with W. Clement Stone)
JOE MADDY OF INTERLOCHEN
CITY GIRL IN THE COUNTRY

MILLER'S HIGH LIFE

MILLER'S HIGH LIFE

by
ANN MILLER
with
NORMA LEE BROWNING

1972

DOUBLEDAY & COMPANY, INC.
GARDEN CITY, NEW YORK

ISBN: 0-385-03440-7
Library of Congress Catalog Card Number 72-76193

I dedicate this book
to
My Mother . . .
The greatest friend I ever had

ACKNOWLEDGMENTS

Many people helped me as I tapped my way through life, from Texas to Hollywood, where Johnnie Lucille Collier became Ann Miller. I would like to single out some, without whom it would all have been impossible.

First of all my mother, whose Texas strength and courage helped me immeasurably and gave me courage to go on when things were darkest. My mother has been my business manager, cook, chauffeur, seamstress, hairdresser, bodyguard, adviser, and, most of all, my friend.

Benny Rubin and Lucille Ball, who walked into the Bal Tabarin in San Francisco and without whom I would never have been signed to that seven-year contract at RKO.

Hermes Pan, my all-time favorite dance director and dearest friend, the person who brought me my first gardenia corsage, the man who took me to my first Academy Awards night, with Mr. and Mrs. Walt Disney.

The late Bill Morgan, who gave me my first pair of tap shoes, with the special jingles on the heels. I named them Joe and Moe and I still have them.

Willy de Mond, who owns Willy's of Hollywood. He went through hell with me and my long legs and later invented pantyhose because of me.

Bill Tregoe, my drama coach and Harriet Lee, my vocal coach, who always had faith in me and helped me not only as teachers but as friends.

Nat and Valerie Dumont, Margaret and Bill Pereira, John and Alice Tyler, who stood by my side when I most needed them.

Bill Moss, my second husband, who insisted I take singing lessons and who is the man most responsible for my third and strongest comeback in show business—first in *Can-Can* and then on Broadway in *Mame*.

My agent Don Wortman, producer-director John Bowab, and impresario John Kenley, who believed in me and helped me to make important decisions.

I wish to thank Vera Servi and Pam Gallagher, who did endless hours of research on specific facts and dates, which I had long since forgotten.

And most important, warm thanks to Norma Lee Browning for helping me tell the story of Ann Miller.

CONTENTS

MILLER'S HIGH LIFE

Chapter 1

STAR OF DESTINY

I became a Hollywood star on my talent, not on casting couches. If I had gone that route, I could have been a bigger star. That's the name of the game in Filmlandia.

But I could dance. It also helped to have a good-looking pair of legs and a stage-struck ma.

When I was a little girl I had rickets and my mother gave me ballet lessons to straighten my legs. Or at least that was her excuse. My legs were not all that skinny—just a little knock-kneed according to my outspoken Texas mother. And she insisted that I have perfectly straight legs. That's how it all started.

That and the gypsy fortuneteller. The setting was a hot, humid bus depot in Houston, Texas. My mother and I were sitting on a bench waiting for the bus to take us to Chireno in East Texas for a visit with my grandparents. Suddenly a dirty old gypsy woman in a ragged shawl shuffled up to us and said to my mother, "Cross my palm with a coin and I will foretell the little girl's future."

My mother hesitated for a moment, and then placed a silver half dollar in the old crone's hand. The gypsy grabbed my hand in her wrinkled one, gazed at it for a long time, then she looked at my mother and began to speak:

"I see a Star of Destiny here. This child will have her name in lights and she will be a star for many years. I see music and lights and dancing and money. Take her to the West— when your marriage ends—for there she will become a Child of Destiny. You will someday remember my words, when you see her name up there in lights."

Then she disappeared into the milling mass of people in the bus depot.

My dear mother not only remembered the gypsy's words verbatim, she diligently applied herself to making them come true. She nagged me constantly to rehearse, REHEARSE, RE-HEARSE until sometimes I wanted to scream. How I hated those ballet lessons. I found the music too slow and the discipline boring. It was more than occasionally that the dancing master would have to jolt me out of a daydream with a sharp slap on my legs with his cane. My mind was on blowing bubble gum and playing hopscotch—not on ballet. I hated it. Pavlova I would never be!

Looking back now, I realize that my ballet lessons were for more than straightening my rickety legs. My mother was very ambitious for me. How well I remember her words when she took me to see Eleanor Powell in *Broadway Melody of 1936.* And she said it like a command, "Lucille, someday you're going to be a big star like that, just like the old gypsy woman said."

I thought she was out of her head.

But three years later my name was up there in lights, just like the old gypsy said, in *George White's Scandals of 1939,* my first Broadway show. I was fifteen years old and Annie Miller's high life had begun. Walter Winchell came to see me on opening night and he wrote some marvelous things about me in his column. It was Walter Winchell who nicknamed me "Legs," and I've always felt it brought me luck. One of his columns started with "*Orchids* . . . to Annie *Legs* Miller . . ." and that lucky "Legs" tag has stuck with me throughout my career.

I owe a special debt of gratitude to Walter Winchell for nicknaming me "Legs" and making my legs famous nationwide through his column. But even before that lucky break, both in Texas and Hollywood when I first began dancing professionally, I was always known for my long straight legs.

Sometimes it bothered me. I never understood why people stared at my legs—because, well, to me legs were just legs. I thought I was built the same as all the other long-legged kids from Texas. But then, years later, when I met George Petty, the man who drew the Petty girls, he explained some of the facts of life, legs, and female anatomy to me. He said I had a short body with legs that actually *started* almost at my waist, and he seemed to think that was quite unusual.

He said there wasn't any space between my thighs up at the top, and that my knees were flat and a bit dimpled and not bony-shaped. He explained that it is most unusual for a woman's legs to come completely together—with no space or crack in between—from the crotch down to the kneecap; and the larger the space in between, the more unattractive the legs. The closer the legs come together, the nicer they look in a bathing suit or short costume. Mine go completely together, all the way, which is good because I wound up dancing in short costumes, and no one would ever in the world guess that I once had rickets. Thanks to my mom for making me take those ballet lessons, my legs became my fortune.

But as a child I hated my extra-long arms and legs. I felt so awkward at times. I didn't know what to do with them.

In time, my legs turned out to be so straight and so long that all my stockings had to be custom-made, which cost the studios a fortune. And that is one reason why pantyhose were invented, because Annie Miller's extra-long legs wouldn't fit into regular hose But this comes much later.

I keep asking myself, why are you doing this Annie-girl, why are you writing your life story? People will think you're over the hill. Well, I'm here to tell you I'm not over the hill.

First of all, I'm an Aries by birth and Aries people are always optimistic. My love affair with Hollywood has been like a bumpy marriage. It's had its ups and downs but I'm still hanging in there and it may be a while yet before you'll find me on a street corner with a dancing bear and a tin cup. Aries people have lots of energy and ambition.

Also, I'm psychic. Aries people are usually psychic. I believe in things like Ouija boards. And a Ouija board once said to me, "Annie, always push the *Up* button in your elevator of life, never the *Down* button." It was a spiritual message I never forgot.

We all have our own wars within our souls, and special ways of killing our own mental dragons. Some drink, some take dope, some become nymphos, some eat themselves to death. Annie Miller is no better or worse than most people. When she gets scared or frightened or a case of the depressions, she just pushes her UP button, starts humming a song and goes out and buys some new clothes—a purse or a hat or anything to keep her thinking up and not down. Some people are alcoholics. I'm a clothesoholic.

I have a way of hanging onto old things—old clothes, old friends, old memories, old boy friends, even old husbands. My house is crammed with mementos and *things* from everywhere and with literally hundreds of racks of clothes which I have accumulated through the years. It's almost as though I am afraid to let them go because I was once so poor, and perhaps I fear that I shall be again someday. So I hang onto them in case I am faced with being cold and hungry again.

And because I never really had a childhood, I have a collection of stuffed toys in my house in Beverly Hills. I also keep a jar of bubble gum and candy by my bed.

I even have a picture in my wardrobe room of an orphan child—it's one of those Keane prints of a kid with the big eyes—sitting alone on some steps in the moonlight, looking cold and thin and hungry. And when I'm getting all gussied up in my furs and feathers and finery for another opening night, another premiere, or just another Hollywood party, I always remember to look at that picture and say to myself, that was me once, and I thank the Lord it's me no more.

But why am I telling all these things? I find being involved in the writing of a book almost like going to confession. A great purging of the soul.

When I look into the greedy mirror of life in Hollywood, my public image looks back at me and says, "Atta girl, Annie, you're still hanging in there, you're still a star and you're going to continue to be or bust."

As my proud mother would say, that's the Texas in me.

I blew into this world via St. Joseph's Hospital in Houston, Texas, on April 12, 1923. And let anyone who doubts disprove it! Yes, yes, I know, the date on my official Hollywood "bio" (Hollywoodese for biography) is April 12, 1919. How well I know! I'm the one who ordered that phony birth certificate—when I was only thirteen and had to be eighteen.

Anyhow, I'm an Aries and I have Taurus rising, Ram and Bull, the two most difficult signs in the world, but my moon is in Pisces, which means that I have a mystical love for beauty, music, and dancing, though to this day I can't read a note of music.

They say that a girl who will tell her age will tell anything, so first off, I must tell you, as if you didn't already know, that my real name, of course, is not Ann Miller. It is Johnnie Lucille Collier because my father wanted a boy. My father usually got what he wanted, so you can imagine how depressed he must have been when he saw that I was a girl. He insisted on naming me Johnnie anyway, which was three strikes against me right there.

Later on, in Hollywood, I was renamed Anne Miller but then someone at RKO chopped off the *e*, so there you are. Or there I was, Ann Miller.

For some reason I was almost always referred to as "little Annie," even though I was taller than average, or "Little Orphan Annie." I suppose these endearments were due to my tender age and/or the fact that everywhere I went I was always accompanied by my doting mother who hovered over me like a mama hawk.

Sometimes I too thought of myself as Little Orphan Annie because when my mother and father divorced, I assumed the responsibility of fending for myself and my mother. (She was almost stone deaf and unable to hold a job.) So at age twelve, I was experiencing hunger, long, hard hours of work and all the responsibilities of an adult.

But back to little Johnnie Lucille, a name I detested.

My mother had named me Lucille after my great-grandmother Lucindy who was born in Brooklyn, Texas, and who was a medium. I mean she was a for-real, born medium, the kind who could make tables rise up on one leg and objects fly across the room and brooms stand at half angle. She had a force field around her and could tune in on people like a radio receiving set.

I never saw any of these things. I never knew my great-grandmother. But I know it's true because every member of my mother's family, and she's one of eleven children, told me it was true, except one who died. Also my grandmother, my mother's mother, told me.

My great-grandmother could predict the future, and she made a prediction that there would be one grandchild in the family who would inherit her mediumistic or psychic powers. She meant me.

My great-grandmother predicted that I would have the "gift."
She always called it the "gift." But she stopped using her own
gift, I was told, because eventually she began to feel that it
was a gift of the devil. Something evil must have happened
because of it, and she didn't know how to protect herself. It is
very difficult for anyone who is born with this gift to turn it on
and off like a faucet.

There was a time when my mother and I began working
the Ouija board together. We started it in fun, but it soon got
to be very serious—so serious, in fact, that we had to ask a
minister of the Spiritualist Church to come over and exorcise
our house. He said I had true mediumistic ability and suggested
that I stop doing it because I did not know how to protect
myself from the earthbound spirits. I have not worked a Ouija
board since then and my mother to this day is frightened to
death of them.

Can you blame her? We both knew what that preacher meant
when he said I didn't know how to protect myself from the
earthbound spirits. Hadn't the Ouija board told me always to
push the *Up* button? And for me this meant going on a buying
spree. Trying to be a star and *look* like a star is a full-time job.
These are the mental sandbags one uses to hold back the surging
tides of time, to preserve the great monument one has built to
the Image that Hollywood demands. But only *material* things
are laid at the feet of the Altar of Fame that the great God of
Hollywood demands of you. And material things cost money.

I have piled up bills like rocks heaped upon a beach and I've
gone deep into debt much to my poor mother's grief when I
feel depressed and push the UP button. I suppose it could be
said that in some ways I'm just a sucker for those materialistic,
earthbound spirits.

It is true that most of my signs are water signs—Jupiter in
Scorpio and Uranus in Pisces—and a lot of water signs in
anyone's horoscope means that you're very psychic. I pride

myself on this distinction. But it has often puzzled me why I wasn't psychic enough to pick the right kind of husband for myself.

I could have married movie czar Louis B. Mayer and been the Czarina of Hollywood. But no, I blew it and fell in love and married a handsome multimillionaire. That was number one, it was traumatic and ended in a divorce. It should have taught me a lesson. But twelve years later I married number two. It was a marvelous marriage part of the time but that one didn't work either.

Then there was number three. He thought he was a Beverly Hills Maharajah and he lived like one! It turned out he had five ex-wives and sixteen mistresses.

All of my three husbands had quite a lot in common. Texas is oil country and maybe subconsciously that's why I was attracted to men who made their living in oil. All three were oillionaires. Two were Texas oil men. The other was from an old pioneer California family. All of my husbands were handsome, rich, and utterly charming when they were sober. They were all basically playboys and quite spoiled. All my husbands wanted to be married bachelors, and I was too dumb to catch on.

Talk about mistakes! I can understand making the same mistake twice, but three times is one too many.

My three marriages represent only five years of my life. Not a very pretty picture, is it?

Out of life's experiences we are supposed to gain wisdom. I hope I have. But I still feel there's a lot I don't know and a lot I must learn. I still don't know anything about men, nor how to handle a man.

I was a virgin when I married my first husband. And that's something you can't say of many Hollywood star ladies.

But after three marriages and a couple of romances, I still feel like a virgin. That's how much I know about men.

Strange, I never really wanted a career. I wanted a happy marriage. Three times I have retired from my career. Three

times I ran back to it. But there will be no running back next
time, for the sands of time are running out for Lucky Legs
Miller. That's what I'm faced with when sometimes I forget
and push that damn' *Down* button.

So then I stay in bed and pull the covers up and sink deep
into them, and they act like my security blanket, and I feel
safe and warm inside them trying to think things out.

How does one put into words the hopes and heartbreaks,
the dreams and disappointments that span a time zone of thirty-
five years? How do you make people understand that somewhere
behind-stage there is very often a scared-to-death little girl who
is anything but the star image she appears on stage?

My love affair with Hollywood started in 1937 with the film
New Faces which won me a seven-year contract at RKO Radio
Pictures. My real age was thirteen but I fibbed and said I was
eighteen and got by with it. By the time I was fourteen, I was
a star in big RKO musicals. It was exciting. But also weird. It
was like attending the biggest and longest Halloween party on
record because I had to dress in grown-up clothes and wear
high heels and lipstick and bust pads.

And I had to constantly lie about my age. It worked as long
as I kept my big mouth shut and didn't laugh or giggle too
much. I don't remember exactly how many years I stayed
eighteen, but I know that in later years I wound up choking on
this Big Lie of my youth. Who needs an extra five or six years
tacked onto your age when you're over forty?

But because of the Big Lie I did have the opportunity to
grow up in Hollywood's Golden Era, and I'm glad I did. Those
were the days of the "star system," when the big studios created
stars and took care of them and saw to it that the stars lived
up to their star image. I still think the public expects a movie
star to look and act like one. I remember vividly one of the
first stars of that Golden Era I ever met, Jean Harlow, and how
beautiful she was. Mother and I happened to meet her on the
street, soon after we moved to Hollywood, and we stopped her

and asked for her autograph. She was most gracious, not at all uppity or condescending, as one might expect of a really big star lady like that. I remember her looking me up and down in an approving way and then encouraging Mom to put me into films. I am sure my mother was already hell-bent in this direction. But there were some rough times in the beginning . . .

Looking back over that long span of time is not easy or too clear. Actually, it is closer to half a century when you start with Johnnie Lucille Collier in Texas. When you're trying to tell it in a book, it's like trying to relive it all by playing it back on a tape recorder, and hoping your brain has recorded everything accurately. It's also like looking at a television screen and you see people moving and you know it's you but you're not sure . . . almost as though it's all happening to someone else.

Life is like roses in a vase, watered by tears. The roses die but the scent lingers on. And memories come flooding back to haunt your waking moments, for you to analyze and try to dissect as with a surgeon's scalpel . . .

I remember that little girl, Lucille Collier, standing up against a lamppost in an apache outfit singing "The Boulevard of Broken Dreams" at a Big Brothers Club kiddie show back in Houston, Texas. Little did I know then that I would one day be literally living on the Boulevard of Broken Dreams in Hollywood.

Sometimes I wonder whatever happened to Lucille Collier from Texas. And I know the answer. She's trapped inside the Ann Miller image, the dancer from Hollywood who was teethed on caviar and champagne, orchids and furs, parties, limousines and spotlights. Little Orphan Annie Miller, they called her, with her protective stage mother hovering over her, and poor Lucille Collier is stashed away in a barrel with the top nailed down, discarded like a broken doll and locked up when she was ten years old.

But there's a part of me that will always be Lucille Collier from Texas, and she's just waiting for this long-winded Hollywood love affair to end with the Ann Miller creature so she can once again take over her own body . . .

It's really Lucille who is writing this book. And I suppose one reason she decided to do it is that in some ways Lucille Collier's story is the kind of fairytale that all girls, in their childhood dreams, would like to have happen to them. On second thought, oh no! Forget all those marriages.

But the rest of it, the Hollywood part—what girl hasn't dreamed deep down of someday becoming a movie star or a stage star or a television actress?

Lucille Collier's story is really a Hollywood Cinderella story.

Any woman who can buck this town on her own and still keep her legs crossed, as my mother always admonished me, can't be all stupid or bad. And at least I didn't wind up on dope, booze, or pills, or slashing my wrists like poor Judy Garland.

It's not easy to keep your eyes on the stars and your feet on the ground in this lotus land of milk and honey, which is ruled by the box-office jingle. But don't believe everything you hear or read about our town. In recent times it has become popular and chic to give Hollywood the big put-down, but I for one am grateful for what it has given me and I would like to help revive and perpetuate that wonderful feeling that Hollywood still is or can be a land of dreams come true. It is still the fabled land that can bring instant wealth and fame overnight. For me, the "Golden Era" is still here; it's just dormant for the moment. But the gold is there.

I think it was a very daring thing my mother did, bringing me to Hollywood and putting me to work in that "jungle out there," as she called it, at such a young age. But I survived the jungle with a sense of values and ideals, which is the best thing that can happen to you in this town. If you come out of it with ideals, you have a handful of gold.

People like Hedy Lamarr do our industry a great disservice by publicizing their sexual conquests. Sure, a lot of stars have made it that way, but not all.

I made it with my lucky legs, my mother, and a lot of backbreaking hard work.

My legs have earned me many high compliments and tributes in my dancing career, but one I cherish the most came from that late great French showman who oozed Gallic charm, Maurice Chevalier. It happened during a party which my husband (number three) and I gave for him on October 16, 1965, to celebrate his sixty-sixth anniversary in show business. We took over the entire top floor of the Beverly Hilton Hotel, served a menu of all French foods and vintage wines, and presented him with a huge cake in the shape of his straw hat. The head man at Dior in Paris flew in and presented each of the ladies at the party with a little bottle of Dior perfume.

All the great and near great of show business came that night to pay honor to Maurice Chevalier. The party cost my husband in the neighborhood of $25,000, but it was worth it if for nothing more than the great compliment Chevalier paid me when he said, "Annie, you have legs just like Mistinguett's." She was the French musical star who made him her dancing partner and became the one big romance in Chevalier's life. (She died January 5, 1956.)

What a thrill to have Maurice Chevalier himself tell me I had legs like his Mistinguett's. It was the ultimate compliment. My mother had done her job well.

Chapter 2

WINGS ON MY FEET

My earliest memories are of my mother standing over me making me practice my ballet steps. I resented it because it took me away from my dolls and bubble gum and hopscotch and all those normal pastimes of little girls growing up.

My poor dear mother also tried me on piano lessons but she finally gave up on that. Piano lessons bored me. I played better by ear. Then she bought me a beautiful violin and sent me to the best violin teacher in Houston.

My lessons were at four o'clock in the afternoon, after school, and at four o'clock I always got hungry. I still do. I'm like the British, at four o'clock in the afternoon I have to get something in my stomach—a cup of tea, a piece of candy, or something, because I have that kind of stomach.

Well, my violin teacher used to make peanut butter fudge and she would eat it right in front of me and never offer me a bite. It wasn't just any old candy. It was real homemade peanut butter fudge. She really made it herself and it was fresh and hot and it smelled divine. But never once did she give me a piece of it. I was so hungry that my stomach would even start to make loud noises but she pretended not to notice. I got through four violin lessons with my teacher eating her peanut butter fudge while I suffered my hunger pains. Then during the fifth lesson it happened. I exploded. I told you I'm Aries and I have Taurus rising, Ram and Bull, the two most difficult signs in the world. When stepped on I have a bad temper. Aries people don't like to fight but when they're backed up against a wall, brother, watch out! They explode. Even at this young age . . .

This one afternoon I was so hungry that I simply couldn't stand it any longer, so I said to my teacher when she continued stuffing her mouth with fudge, "Please, Miss Morrow, could I have a piece of your fudge?"

My stomach was growling. I'm sure she could hear it.

Would you believe what she did? She said to me, "No, Lucille, you are here to do your violin lesson, not to eat candy. Continue with your lesson."

So little Lucille Collier raised her brand new violin as high as she could and hit her teacher on the head with it as hard as she could and ran out.

And that was the end of my violin lessons. My mother spanked me hard as the devil. I couldn't sit down for a week. I have never touched a violin since. Nor peanut butter fudge!

With both my piano and violin lessons I was nothing but total disaster. I hated anyone standing over me with a stick.

And ballet was almost as bad. I just felt like a big crow flapping with those long legs and arms. My mother tried her best to make me into a great ballerina but I could never really do ballet the way it should be done. I just always flapped. (This is why my choreographer friend Hermes Pan always called me Annie–Crow.)

It was the great Negro tap dancer Bill Robinson, Mr. "Bojangles" himself, who gave me my first tap lesson and changed the course of my life. Mr. "Bojangles" came to Houston once for an engagement at the Majestic Theatre, and my mother took me to see him. Something in the way he danced turned me on. After the show, my mother took me backstage to meet him and she insisted, much to my embarrassment, that I do a little dance for him. She wanted him to tell her if I was doing my steps properly. Poor Mother . . .

I'll never forget how nice and kind and patient Bill Robinson was with us. He watched my little ballet number. Then he did a few taps for me and asked me to try to tap along with him. He sang "Bye, Bye, Blues" and clapped out the rhythm with his hands, and there I was doing my first tap dance with Mr. "Bojangles" in his dressing room. I took to tap dancing like a duck to water. I seemed to have a natural rhythm. Mr. Robinson complimented me on this and told my mother to buy me some tap shoes with wooden soles instead of steel taps. Wooden soles were all he ever used, he told us. I learned to dance quite well with the wooden soles. Many years later when I met Eleanor Powell, she told me that she too had used only wooden soles at the beginning of her career.

After that session with Bill Robinson, I somehow knew that Mother was right and that someday I was going to be a dancer. But I knew that I would never be a ballerina or an acrobatic dancer. There was too much rhythm in me—which is probably why I never took to ballet.

But tap dancing was something else. I'll never forget the thrill and excitement of that backstage lesson from Bill Robinson. It was as though that little girl Lucille who loathed ballet had suddenly and magically sprouted wings on her feet. And also stardust in her eyes. Now, at last I could dance up a storm for my mother. Now, at last I didn't mind rehearsing, rehearsing, rehearsing because the wings on my feet seemed to lift me up and fly me away on some magic carpet. It is still like that with me to this day, a wondrous, exhilarating kind of magic when I'm dancing that simply flies me out of the here-and-now of reality . . .

My poor dear stage-struck mother of course was ecstatic that her little girl was finally beginning to take to *something* musical. I learned easily and fast. Later on, I developed my own style of tap dancing. I don't know where it came from—just out of the air, I guess, and from watching movies, especially movies with Fred Astaire, Eleanor Powell, and Ginger Rogers. I became mad about movie musicals, which to my mother was another encouraging sign for her dancing daughter.

I remembered the old gypsy fortuneteller's words in the bus station. "I see a Star of Destiny here. This child will have her name in lights and she will be a star for many years. I see music and lights and dancing and money. Take her to the West—when your marriage ends—for there she will become a Child of Destiny. You will someday remember my words, when you see her name up there in lights." I had a strange feeling it would come to pass.

And, when I went to visit my grandparents in Chireno, Texas, I would sit there on the front porch in the big swing they built for me and I would watch the millions of fireflies flicker on their little taillights—and I would pretend that they were beautiful twinkling lights on a stage and I was out there somewhere dancing.

Yes, I used to sit there in that swing and pretend that I was a great star singing and dancing in Hollywood, like Eleanor Powell and Ginger Rogers. Could it be that a little of my mother's ambitions were finally rubbing off on me? I don't really think it was that as much as it was the inborn talent for tap and rhythm that Bill Robinson had discovered in me— and for me.

From then on you couldn't stop me from dancing. The way I danced, however, didn't always set too well with my dancing teachers in Houston. I was always tapping like a whirl-wind and jumping with rhythm and inventing my own steps instead of following the instructions of my teachers. Rhythm dancing seemed to come natural for me. I seemed to have a throbbing, primitive kind of rhythm. And I had an affinity for drums. I loved drums. Just dancing to drumbeats without any music at all was exciting to me.

I don't know how many thousands of miles I have tap-danced in my lifetime—probably several times around the world —but a Hollywood press agent once put a speedometer on my feet and it recorded that I was dancing 500 taps a minute, which he said established me as the fastest tap dancer in the world. If anyone wants to refute this, go ahead.

All I know is that some people are born to dance and I was one of them. I'll tell you why I know this. I believe in Reincarnation and every seer I've ever been to has told me that in most of my previous lives I have been a dancer. Most of them also have told me that I was Egyptian in my other lives, and I firmly believe this.

When I was about seven or eight years old, my mother sent me to my first real dancing school. This was in addition to my private ballet lessons.

My dancing-school teacher put me in my very first musical show for the Big Brothers Club. My hair was jet black and absolutely straight, and I used to wear bangs. My dancing teacher said I didn't look like an American child, that I could be French or Italian or Spanish—or Egyptian. So she picked out a number for me called "Egyptian-Nella" and taught me how to sing it. It had a primitive beat.

My parents were so proud, and they spent a lot of money on an Egyptian costume for me. It was beautiful—breastplates done with round circles of beading in colors of emerald green, blue, red, and gold on a gold lamé base. Below the navel there was a waistband of solid beading and attached to it was a long gold fringe which hung to the floor. I had marvelous big wide bracelets of beading in stripes of all colors, and an exotic gold headdress which my parents rented for me. The cobra had emerald eyes. I had cymbals on my fingers and I was supposed to come out on stage and all the other kids were to come out behind me like a chorus and do a little Egyptian folk song with poses while I sang "Egyptian-Nella."

I remember how excited my dancing-school teacher was about it. Miss Halli Preachard, that was her name. "Egyptian-Nella" was a hit tune at that time and Miss Preachard was pleased with the way I had learned to sing the song. She had planned this entire number as the highlight of our Big Brothers Club show.

While the rest of the kids did their little Egyptian folk dance, based on their beginning ballet steps, I was supposed to stand still and pose and just sing and rattle the cymbals on my fingers.

But when the curtain went up and I heard the drums, something happened and I just automatically went into a dance, a real authentic Egyptian nautch dance. That's the authentic word for a belly dance.

The cymbals on my fingers were clicking furiously and as the rhythm got faster, I whirled and whirled and whirled . . . and when the music ended, I did a deep salaam.

My father almost fainted and my teacher was furious. "We didn't teach her like that. Where did she learn *that?*" she screeched She had taught me to sing it but she didn't teach me how to dance it, she kept on reassuring my astounded parents, and I didn't know why they were so angry . . .

Naturally, I was a hit with the Big Brothers Club—a seven-year-old girl doing a belly dance and out there wriggling to just drums and tinkling cymbals. I never did a dance like that again until I grew up and played in a picture called *Hey, Rookie*. I did a number called "Streamlined Sheik" with a comedian named Joe Besser in an Arab tent, and then I danced him out of the way and went into my Egyptian nautch dance.

I did it again just to drums, a wild and furious rhythm played by Thurston Knudson, who was once considered the world's greatest living authority on primitive drums. It's one of the best things I ever did. And I danced the number in a costume like the one I wore when I was seven years old. I had it designed exactly the same. To this day my "Egyptian-Nella" costume is the only one I can remember from my childhood dancing days.

Years after the movie *Hey, Rookie,* I went to Cairo on a trip and all the Egyptian fans asked me about that number in the tent and begged me to dance it for them, which I tried to do. I think it could be a sensational number to do in Las Vegas some day.

Not long ago Jess Stearn, the author of many books on psychic phenomena, took me to see a medium he had discovered. Her name is Maria Moreno. She went into a trance and told me that I was an "old soul" and that I had been reincarnated many times.

She said that in past lives I had been Egyptian three times, had lived in Babylon once, and in Arabia. She said that once I was Jewish and that I had a very warm feeling for the Middle East, which is true.

She told me, "You have lived all your previous lifetimes in the Middle East, and you could go and build a home there and probably be very happy."

It's true. I've been there, I feel very much at home there, and I could be very happy there if it were peaceful and there were no wars. I know I could be happy living in either Morocco or Tangier or Beirut or in Cairo.

When I was a little girl, four or five years old, one of my favorite pastimes was drawing. For some peculiar reason I always drew camels and pyramids and palm trees. My mother and father were amazed and puzzled. I wasn't in school yet, I was too young, and I was too young for movies then also. So how did I know about camels and pyramids and palm trees? Often I would get out my Crayolas and paint these things in colors. I remember trying to draw a camel with the humps on it and I wasn't very good at it. There were no palm trees or pryamids or camels in Houston. How did little Lucille Collier know about them?

It's spooky when all these mediums tell me I was ancient Egyptian in previous lives because even my bedroom is done all in Egyptian Pharaonic décor—and one medium, Maya Perez, described my bedroom without ever having seen it.

"You have always loved to dance and you have been a dancer through most of your reincarnations," she said. Could that be the reason I was able to do an authentic Egyptian nautch dance when I was only seven years old? How else can you explain it?

Some years later, when I was in New York doing *George White's Scandals*, my mother took me to the Metropolitan Museum. We went to see the Egyptian collection and we were just ambling around when all of a sudden I stopped dead cold in front of a huge lioness sphinx with the face of a woman on it—but the woman's face had a beard. I stared into her eyes, paralyzed with a strange fear, for she reminded me of me. Her face looked too much like mine for comfort.

A plaque identified her as Queen Hatshepsut of Egypt, and a Pharaoh—the first woman Pharaoh of Egypt, and the last. As I stared at her bearded face I felt trapped with the strangest sensation, one that I now know was true *déjà vu*, the feeling of having been there before.

Many years later while I was in Cairo on a promotional trip for M-G-M, a famous Egyptian seer told me that I had been an Egyptian queen in another lifetime and that I had been responsible for having many men killed. She said that I would be repaid in this lifetime with much suffering and emotional unhappiness from all the men in my life. This is called karma. And it has come to pass.

Chapter 3

MY KARMA BEGINS

I suppose you could say that my karma started with my father, John Alfred Collier, who became a very successful criminal lawyer in Houston. Some of his more notorious clients, I recall, were "Baby Face" Nelson, and Bonnie Parker and Clyde Barrow, the original "Bonnie and Clyde."

But my father was an Irish playboy at heart and success went to his head. Almost as far back as I can remember, I knew that there was something wrong between my mother and father. I saw my mother crying a lot and somehow I knew instinctively that my father must be the cause of it. Then later came the arguments and battles which they could no longer keep from me.

But my very first recollection of my distrust of my father came through a psychic experience I had as a small child. I could not have been more than four or five years old. We were then living in a small upstairs apartment in Houston. My mother left the apartment to go downstairs for something, and I was left alone. I remember I was playing with my doll in the middle of the living-room floor, and I heard somebody calling, "Lucille." I turned around and there was no one in sight, but the voice came closer and said again, "Lucille, Lucille." Again I turned around and looked and looked. Still nobody there. The voice said, "Remember, you'll always hear me." I was frightened.

When my mother came back in, I asked, "Mother, were you in the kitchen, calling me?" She laughed and said, "You're imagining things. There's nobody here."

I didn't argue with her but I knew that I had heard a voice and for a moment I was terrified and confused.

My father came home late from work that day, and walked in the door pretending that he had come straight from the office. When my mother asked him why he was late, he told her he had to finish something at the office. I knew he was not telling the truth. I didn't say anything in front of my mother but I followed him into the bedroom and said, "Daddy, you were not at your office, that's not true. You were out with a dark-haired lady in the park, in a boat. Why did you lie to Mother?"

At that time I did not know that my parents were having trouble. I was still too young to realize the significance of his being out in the park with another woman. In my innocent child's mind, I supposed she was merely a friend of my daddy's. I did not attach anything sinful to their being together. What disturbed me simply was that he had not told my mother the truth, and I didn't know why. Puzzled and hurt, I looked up at him, waiting for his answer. Then I asked again, "Why didn't you tell Mother the truth?"

He was terribly angry with me. For a moment I thought he was going to strike me.

"How did you know that, Lucille?" he asked hoarsely.

I was so frightened I just stood there shaking my head.

"Answer me, Lucille. How did you know that? Were you watching me? Where have you been? Who took you to the park?"

I started to cry.

He softened a little and said, "Lucille, listen to me. I want you to promise me something. You must not tell your mother, you understand?"

No, I did not understand but I promised not to tell. What else could I do?

He looked at me strangely and asked again, "Lucille, please tell me, how did you know that?"

"I just know. I saw it," I said. "I don't know how."

How does anyone explain a psychic flash? We "see" it visually or hear a "voice" or somehow sense it intuitively. It has happened so often with me.

I must say my psychic flashes didn't do much to cement relations with any of my husbands. I was on my honeymoon with number two when I suddenly sat bolt upright in bed one night and screamed, "He's dead! I'm packing my bags and going home." Sure enough, I learned later, the man I had been deeply in love with for twelve years had died of a heart attack during the very hour that my psychic antenna flashed the word to me. My marriage was doomed right then. Nor was it helped any by the long-distance telepathic "vision" I had in Honolulu of my husband being out with a blonde in Dallas. But that came much later . . .

My great-grandmother Lucindy, for whom I was named, had predicted that I would have the "gift," but looking back now, I feel certain that whatever psychic sensitivity I may have been born with—and I am convinced we all have it, some more than others—was honed and sharpened considerably by the unhappiness and loneliness of my childhood caused by my parents.

I *knew* there was something wrong between them long before it came out in the open. I *knew* that something awful was going to happen to Mother and Daddy. I sensed it long before it ever happened. And I didn't want it to happen. But I knew that it would.

My first impression of trouble came during those weekend

trips to my grandmother's house in Chireno, in East Texas. It seemed that my mother was always yanking me off to my grandmother's, and I could not understand why my father didn't come with us. Then sometimes in the bus on our way to Grandmother's, I would catch Mother crying. When I finally asked her why she was crying and why Dad didn't come with us, all she would say was that he had work to do.

Later on, they began to have terrible fights and arguments, right out in the open. These always upset me terribly because I loved them both so much.

With the growing realization of the serious breach between my parents, I became more withdrawn and lonely. I hated to go home after school because I couldn't stand to see what was happening between them, so instead of going home I would go off by myself in the little wooded area of pine trees which I called my enchanted forest behind Sutton Elementary School, and I would sit there and daydream and cry and pray for Mom and Dad to stay together . . .

It was a small forest behind my school, but a real one, and sometimes the deer and the squirrels and the frogs would come out and stare at me. I used to talk to them. I carried on real conversations with them. I felt they understood me and it always cheered me up to be with them. It was my retreat, a world of childish fantasy, but so real to me then because I was much happier there than anywhere else.

I never cared much for school. I didn't feel close to the other children. Somehow, I never felt that I was one of them even though my mother and I were always well dressed, and I had a bicycle and toys and dolls and all the things most of the other children had—plus my dancing lessons, of course.

I was soon to realize what my mother meant when she kept nagging me with the words, "Now, Lucille, you must rehearse your dance lessons because someday you may have to take care of your mother."

I do not wish to leave a totally bad impression of my

father. In fact he was an absolute charmer, with reddish blond hair and blue eyes and beautiful teeth. He loved to dance and he had a fantastic sense of rhythm. He never danced professionally but he was a marvelous ballroom dancer. I suppose I might have inherited some of my sense of rhythm from him.

Neither of my parents nor anyone on either side of our family was ever in show business, though I think my mother harbored a secret ambition to be an actress. And she was beautiful enough, too. She had long legs—almost as long as mine—and a beautiful body and dark rich mahogany hair. I remember how beautiful she used to look as she sat in a chair brushing her hair, and it was so long that it touched the floor.

My mother loved my father very much. Even as a small child I knew this and that is why it was so painful to me to watch their marriage breaking up.

You see, my mother came from a very small town, Brooklyn, Texas, and my father married her and took her out of that small town. I think he always thought he had done her a great favor by taking her out of Brooklyn, Texas. He started out as a barber but went to law school at night after he was married. He paid his way through law school by being a barber. So he was a self-made man, he deserves credit for that.

But my mother helped him. She was always behind him and helped him in many ways with her penny-pinching and make-do homemaking in their early married life. She loved Dad, and she scrimped and saved when he was a barber to help him become an attorney. It was only after he hit it big that he started all his Irish shenanigans. He was a gregarious person—he loved people, he loved life, he loved boozing, he loved beautiful women. All the things he probably never had as a young man, he tried to have later in life. And this just doesn't work when you're married and have a child. He became a *nouveau riche* Texan, a show-off, and girl crazy. With success came money and with money came liquor and women, and with women came their divorce.

I must have been about seven or eight years old when I first became really conscious that my father had other women besides my mother. And now I also knew it had been going on a long time. I remembered that woman in the park, and now I knew she was something more than a psychic vision, she was real, and so were all the others. Something inside me just more or less died. I no longer had any feeling for my father.

He never had much time for me but in his own way he tried to hang onto me. Sometimes he would take me away for a weekend, usually on fishing trips. Maybe if I had been a boy, like he wanted, things would have been different. He used to take me fishing with him near a town called Kemah, Texas, where there's a river with lots of catfish, and Dad used to love catfish. He tried to teach me how to fish but I didn't take to it. He would catch these horrible-looking creatures and then fry them and eat them.

I couldn't bring myself either to catch them or to eat them. I must have been a massive disappointment to my father. I hated catfish. I still do, though I do not recall ever having seen any outside of Kemah, Texas.

There was one weekend outing with my father which I shall never forget, and which made me distrust him forever, even more than the time he lied to my mother about being at the office. He took me to Galveston for the weekend and he was going to teach me how to swim. I had a tremendous fear of water, as any child does until he knows what it is, and we didn't have a swimming pool. So, he made the grave mistake of taking me way out beyond the breakers in the Gulf of Mexico at Galveston—he was trying to show off his teaching ability, I'm sure—and he said, "Now, Lucille, don't be afraid because I promise I won't let you go." He held his hand under my stomach and tried to make me paddle my feet and hands.

I was terrified, and I clung onto his arm, begging, almost hysterically, "Please don't let me go. You promised, Dad."

"I promise. Don't be afraid. I won't let you go." He reassured me, and with his hand still under my stomach he was teaching me to paddle around. Then suddenly he jerked his hand away and ordered, "Swim!"

I sank, paralyzed with fear, and the undertow got me. I blacked out. The last thing I remember is my father calling for help. And the next thing I remember was lifeguards and people all around me trying to pump the water out of me. I had barely escaped drowning. My mother, of course, was not there, and the first thing my dad said to me when it was all over and I was safe again, was, "Lucille, please don't tell your mother."

My father meant well. He was only trying to teach me how to swim. But when he promised not to let go of me, I believed him. From that day on I never trusted my father again.

I think I was about eight years old at the time. I never did learn to swim. I've had swimming lessons from professionals but I am still petrified of water. All I can do is go in and paddle around like a ruptured duck. But I love to sail, and I have no fear in a boat, which seems peculiar, I must admit. In Hawaii I even went sailing in outrigger canoes—until one day I saw one turn over and I realized the great danger of it because I couldn't swim. After that I would always manage to sit behind a big strong Hawaiian, and I would warn him, "Look, I can't swim, so if this thing turns over, you've got to grab me, okay?" I would give him an extra tip to keep an eye on me, but fortunately we never turned over.

It's strange how an incident like the one with my father can affect a whole lifetime. In my heart I knew I shouldn't hold it against my father. Anyone can make a stupid mistake . . . And he paid for it, he really did. For a few minutes there he thought he had lost me forever and even if I wasn't a boy, I'm sure he must have felt pretty bad. I can remember being pulled under and my chest filling up with water . . . and then the artificial respiration with the water coming out. It was a very frightening thing for a little girl . . . I was hurt and angry for a long time and my trust in my father was destroyed.

Allegorically, the incident might represent an omen of my ill-fated marital adventures. I put childlike implicit trust in each of my three husbands. They violated this trust as surely as my father did when he turned me loose beyond the breakers and said, "Swim!"

I often wondered if I had died would my father really have cared?

After Dad became successful as an attorney we moved from our apartment into a pretty little red brick house in Houston. It was by no means ostentatious but it was comfortable. It had a big fireplace in the living room, and beautiful Cape jasmine bushes all around the house. I liked my home very much and when we moved there, I remember I prayed harder than ever that my mother and father would stay together. I didn't want them to break up. I didn't want to be taken away from the only home I ever loved as a child.

In the summer of 1934, after school was out, my father sent us, Mother and me, on a vacation to Hollywood. I am sure it was my mother's idea to spend our summer vacation in Hollywood, and my father must have approved. At least he paid for it. Looking back now, I assume he was happy to be rid of us for the summer.

We stayed at a small hotel on Hollywood Boulevard, and Mother promptly enrolled me at the Fanchon & Marco Dancing School, the best one in town, and also registered me at Central Casting.

It was at the Fanchon & Marco Dancing School that I first met Rita Hayworth, whose real name was Marguerite Cansino, and her Spanish father, José Cansino. They did a dancing act together and he also taught at the school.

It was also at the Fanchon & Marco Dancing School that I first met Jane Withers, one of whose husbands later became one of mine. And Judy Garland and her mother, Mrs. Gumm. When we did children's programs at the dancing school, it was Mrs. Gumm who played the piano for me. That's also where I met the now famous designer, Helen Rose, who fitted me for costumes for our kiddy shows at dancing school.

During that summer I also got calls from Central Casting for child extra parts in two movies. One was with Margaret Sullavan and Herbert Marshall in *The Good Fairy* and the other was in Anne Shirley's movie, *Anne of Green Gables*. My mother was very proud of me. I'm sure she was remembering the old gypsy's words in the bus depot.

The summer was almost over when I did a revue called *All Aboard*, produced by Francis Lederer and Frederick Hollander. It was a grown-up revue, and though I was only eleven, I said I was fifteen and got into the show. I did a couple of dramatic scenes and as a result of this I received offers from two talent scouts for screen tests. I made two tests, one at Warners and the other at M-G-M, but at both studios I was told that I was too young. So when the summer was over we went back to Houston and to Dad. And I went back to school.

For a little while things seemed to be running more smoothly between my parents, and I was praying with all my heart for everything to be all right. But it was merely the calm before the storm.

One weekend my mother and I went to see my grandparents in Chireno but came back to Houston sooner than we had planned because Mother was not feeling well.

I bounced into the house ahead of her and sailed into the bedroom with my little satchel of clothes, and was stopped dead in my tracks by a nauseating sight that is seared in my memory; my father and his lady of the day nude in bed in the middle of their passionate lovemaking. And in my mother's own bedroom.

This is the kind of scene that can turn little girls into old women fast.

My mother, of course, walked in on it, also, right behind me. Things were a bit chaotic for a few minutes.

I remember the creature on the bed screaming at my father, "Get that damn' kid out of here."

There was a lot of loud commotion and then my mother and I were in the living room crying with each other. Finally, I patted her on the cheek and said, "Don't cry any more, Mother. We're going to leave. We can't stay here. Don't worry about him, he isn't worth it, he only brings you heartbreak. We'll just leave and from now on I will take care of you, Mother."

Later my mother told me she knew by looking into my eyes that she wasn't talking to a little girl any more, she was talking to a fifty-year-old woman. She said that looking into my eyes was like looking into a dark mirror of time.

Before we left the house I told her, "He's not my father any more, and you don't need him. He doesn't respect us and he doesn't love us. Just let him do what he wants to do and we'll make a new life for ourselves."

It was a shattering experience. My memories of the details of this sordid episode in my life are a little hazy. I think my father took that creature away and deposited her somewhere and then came back to find us gone.

We packed a few clothes and walked out—lock, stock, and barrel. I vaguely remember spending the night at the house of one of Mother's friends who had a daughter my age. And we talked about going back to California. The old gypsy woman's words again rang in my ears. She had told us exactly what to do—"Take her to the West—when your marriage ends—for there she will become a Child of Destiny . . . her name up there in lights."

So my mother and I set out for California again, almost no sooner than we had returned, only this time under quite different circumstances. I remember that I never cried once from the moment we left my father's house, because somehow I knew that this was what must be done. It was the best way. Or, as the Arabs say, "It was written." So be it.

Within an hour's time my whole life changed, I had grown

up suddenly from a little girl into a woman who had promised
to make a living for my mother. When I said to her, "I will
take care of you, Mother. You don't need my father," I meant
it and she believed me. I was eleven years old at the time. I
have kept my promise to her all these years and it's been a
pleasure. My stage mother is a lovely lady.

It hasn't always been easy. We drove back to California with
the other woman and her daughter, in our car. About all I
remember of that long ride are the mountains and the narrow
winding roads as we drove over the Apache Trail. It was frightening. But we finally made it.

Mother and I found a tiny one-room kitchenette apartment
in Hollywood with a sofa that converted into two beds. We
each had our own little pull-out bed, so narrow that I used
to roll off mine all the time. I hate twin beds. To this day
I've never had another twin bed in my house. I've always had
nothing but king-size beds in all my bedrooms. How I hated
that little narrow pull-out bed in our first apartment in Hollywood.

My mother had some money which she had managed to save
out of her grocery allowance and other housekeeping funds which
my father gave her. But this did not last long. And since
Texas pays no alimony, we had no source of income. My
father, in fact, tried to force my mother to come back to him
by not sending her even a penny to help us.

I guess he wanted to eat his cake and have it, too. I'm sure
he wouldn't have given up his other women, but he wanted
us to come back because a successful attorney needed the
window dressing of a wife and child in Texas. He liked to look
good.

I'll never forget my first Christmas in Hollywood in that
dinky little one-room apartment. We had no tree, no presents,
and nothing to eat. My mother had sold the car to pay our
room rent and we had lived on crackers for two days. Our

landlady came by and brought us a chocolate cake she had
baked as our Christmas gift. I am sure she was not aware that
we had no food in the house. But that was our first Christmas
dinner in Hollywood, our landlady's home-baked chocolate cake
and nothing else.

I remember going out to the trash can behind our apartment
and rummaging through a stack of papers and magazines. I
don't remember what I was looking for but I picked up a little
book at the top of the heap in the trash can—I think it caught
my eye because it had a bright yellow and white cover, and
to this day yellow and white are my favorite colors. For when
I picked it up the book fell open to one page with a corner
turned down and a short passage underlined in ink.

It was one of those inspirational or Science of Mind books
that I didn't know much about at the time, and the passage
that was underlined where the book fell open was from the
Bible. I have forgotten the exact wording and I do not know
whether it was an exact word-for-word quotation from the
Scriptures, or a paraphrased version. But I definitely remember
the feeling I had when I read the underlined passage, for it
was like an omen. I knew its message was meant especially for
me. It was: Have no fear. Have faith. Because I am with you
always. If you have the faith of a mustard seed, you can move
mountains.

I started to cry. Then I took the book in to my mother and
laid it on her lap. She was crying, too, because it was Christmas,
our first Christmas away from our home in Houston, and because we were sad and homesick and broke and had nothing
to eat after that chocolate cake was gone, and because it wasn't
as easy for an eleven-year-old girl to take care of her mother
as she thought it would be. My mother was ready to call my
father and tell him to come and get us. But I begged her not
to.

"We can't go back to him, Mother, please don't. He doesn't
love us. We'll find a way."

Finally she looked at the yellow and white book I had placed in her lap, the book I had found on top of the trash can. I pointed to the passage that was underlined. She read it slowly, then looked at me and said, "I think that's what's wrong with us, Lucille. We don't have enough faith. I feel this is an omen and things are going to be all right for us—if we have *faith*." She emphasized the word. And then we both said it together, and we felt better.

That first Christmas Day in Hollywood, when I was eleven, was the turning point in my life. It marked the end of my childhood, if I ever had one, the beginning of adulthood long before I was ready, and my introduction to the dream factory of Tinseltown.

Thank the lord for those rickets I had as a kid, and the ballet lessons Mama forced on me, for by now little Lucille Collier's legs were in pretty good shape for all those thousands of miles of dancing that lay ahead of her.

Chapter 4

HOLLYWOOD, HERE I AM

In case you're wondering why it was up to me to earn a living and take care of my mother instead of the other way around, I should clarify it right here and now. My mother was never able to work because of a hearing impairment. She was quite deaf in both ears and could not hold down a job even as a saleslady or secretary. In those days, doctors did not—or could not—operate on the ears to restore one's hearing as they do today. So my mother was handicapped, and I always somehow knew that it would be up to me to provide for her.

But the day after Christmas, Mother went to see our landlady and just plain told her the truth, that we were in desperate circumstances and needed work. Did she know where I might get some dancing jobs after school or on weekends? That wonderful woman lent us some money, I'll never forget that; and she told us to go and see a Mr. William Morgan at a little tap shoe shop called Morgan's Dance Shop on Sunset Boulevard. It was just a few blocks from our apartment and across the

This photograph was taken when I was four years old in Houston, Texas, in 1927.

Below, at seven years old I was a smash hit dancing for the Big Brothers Club in Houston.

Christmas, 1934, when I was eleven years old. I wore bangs as a child until I was twelve years old. Without them I looked much older.

Below, in 1936 I played a chorus girl in *Devil on Horseback* which starred Lili Damita (That's me, second from the left). Even then I was tall for my age (twelve years old).

Above, photo taken at the
Bal Tabarin in San
Francisco, prior to my RKO
contract in 1937. Benny
Rubin, talent scout for the
studio, came in one evening
with Lucille Ball—and that's
how it all started!
(*Photo by Romaine*)

Left, a holiday in California's
Palm Springs when I was
fourteen (1937–38) and
under contract to RKO.
Little did I realize then that
a horse and I had something
in common!

My first real publicity glamour photographs taken at RKO in 1937
when I was almost fourteen years old. (*RKO photo*)

street from the Fanchon & Marco Dancing Studio where I had taken lessons the previous summer. Since my father was not sending us any money, we could no longer afford for me to take dancing lessons at Fanchon & Marco.

But we went to see Mr. Morgan across the street and he was a saint. He lent us some money too, and then he gave me a pair of tap shoes and asked me to show him what I could do. I did a little dance for him and he was so impressed that he gave me the shoes to keep and told me that I could rehearse in his shop on a special tap board which he would set up whenever I wanted to use it.

So that's where I really started as a tap dancer, in Mr. Morgan's little tap shoe shop, and with my very first pair of professional tap shoes with steel toes and heel taps. That marvelous Mr. Morgan made special taps for the toes and special jingles on the heels, and I loved those shoes. I named them Joe and Moe and I still have them and cherish them. I have always felt that they brought me good luck. Every day after school I would race down Sunset Boulevard to Mr. Morgan's shop and spend hours rehearsing on the little tap board which he set up for me right there in the showroom where they showed the shoes. This was where I learned to develop that quick machine-gun-style tap that I later became known for, and that was to help me get started in movies.

My mother always went with me to Mr. Morgan's. One day he told us that if we could just get a little routine together, he would find a piano player for me and maybe I could get some luncheon jobs entertaining at the Elks, Rotary, and Lions Clubs. The piano player he found for me was a young man named Harry Fields and I'll never forget him because he's the one who changed my name to Anne Miller—spelled with an *e*. He did not like the name Lucille Collier.

"You need a name that's simple, something people can remember," he said. "Like Jones or Smith or Miller . . ."

Mother and I didn't much like the idea of changing my name,

but as long as our luck seemed to be changing, too, we were willing to go along with it, if it would help keep the wolf from the door. Mr. Fields also kept telling my mother, "She's so tall, you know, that she could easily pass for an older girl if you're willing to fib about her age. She could get by with it and probably get lots of work." We were practically starving to death and really desperate for work.

So that's how Anne Miller was born, by now a twelve-year-old trying to pass for eighteen. And it worked. I had fibbed about my age that summer, when I was only eleven and said I was fifteen and got into the revue, *All Aboard*. I was about to embark on a very long binge of fibbing about my age, which created problems that still hound me.

But at the time, the thing uppermost in my mind was paying the rent and bringing home the bacon. I created some little dance routines—don't ask me how, I just did it. I didn't really have all that much formal training in music—dancing, singing, or anything else. But I knew I *had* to do it. And that little yellow and white book I had found in the trash can on Christmas Day helped. I had faith—in something, I didn't know quite what. Maybe it was just faith in my ability to take care of my mother so she wouldn't go back to my father.

Soon I began to get luncheon jobs, as Mr. Morgan had said I would, at the service clubs—Eks, Rotary, Lions, and American Legion. They paid a pittance, anywhere from $5 to $10 per performance, but these little handouts kept us going.

Once I took a job that turned out to be so humiliating I'll never forget it. Actually it was a Sunday night amateur contest at a cafe-bar on Vermont Street. I didn't have a costume and we had no money to buy one, so I wore a pair of fancy pajamas. But they were quite attractive pajamas with wide bottoms, big puffed Russian sleeves and a big white bow, like a jumper suit. That's what I danced in because that's all I had that even resembled a costume. And I won the contest.

I was thrilled, of course, but terribly embarrassed when the customers began throwing money at me. It was the first time that had ever happened and I think the reason I felt humiliated was that I assumed the audience must know how hard up we were, and I got down on my hands and knees and started scooping up the money like a greedy little monkey.

There was a man's hat lying on a table and I asked the owner if I could borrow it to put the money in it. I remember there was one one-dollar bill. The rest were dimes, nickels, and quarters. I scooped them all from the floor and into the hat. Then I took it to my poor mother who looked horrified as I dumped it all into her lap. She was humiliated, too. I took the borrowed hat back to the fellow and thanked him. There was nearly $6 in the hat—a real bonanza for us. And besides this I was paid $5 just for being in the contest. There was a prize, too, which must have been presented to me, since I won the contest. But for the life of me I can't remember what it was. And I'm positively certain that the reason I can't remember is that it was not food. I do remember that while I was picking up those coins, all I could think about was the food they would buy for my mother and me. I won't swear that we were starving but we did go hungry a lot. So whatever the prize for that contest was, I know it was not money or food, or I would have remembered it.

Soon after this, Mr. Morgan told me about another amateur contest at the huge Orpheum Theatre in downtown Los Angeles. Again I entered, with no costume and no musical arrangements. I had only a piano and sheet music and I danced in slacks. But I also won that contest and the prize was a two-week engagement at the Orpheum. The theater manager, Sherrill Cohen, knew that I really was an amateur since I didn't even have a costume. He bought two costumes and also paid for a couple of small musical arrangements—special orchestrations for me—and I was put on the regular Keith vaudeville bill at the theater for two weeks.

This was my first break as a professional dancer. An agent,

Arthur Silber, saw me at the Orpheum and booked me into the Casanova Club, which in those days was one of the famous night clubs on the Sunset Strip.

It was illegal, of course, for a minor to be working in a night club, but by now it seemed natural for me to say I was eighteen, and I was getting by with it. Nobody yet had asked to see my birth certificate. Remember, as I said, I've always been one of those very tall, very long-legged Texas gals. And by now I was beginning to appreciate those legs because they helped me look older than I was. And as long as I remembered my mother's advice to keep my mouth shut, I was doing all right.

Out of that Casanova engagement I was booked into the Bal Tabarin in San Francisco, my first big dancing job. I was hired for only three weeks but stayed sixteen. The owners, Frank Martinelli and Tom Gerun, apparently felt that they really had a new star on their hands because there was no one around at that time who could do the machine-gun taps the way I could —except, of course, the great Eleanor Powell and her price was high. She was getting anywhere from $150,000 to $200,000 a film.

The owners of the Bal Tabarin decided they had made quite a discovery with me. I was younger and newer and how I could tap! They changed the show every four weeks and I had to create new dance routines, but as long as they furnished me with new arrangements and new costumes, it was fine with me. I was having a ball.

I still have those original costumes and I keep them in a trunk along with Mr. Morgan's tap shoes, my Moe and Joe.

During the day in San Francisco I would do my school lessons and then take a nap in our hotel room. We had to eat out because we did not have enough money for a suite with a kitchen. We lived mostly on hamburgers and hot dogs. Sometimes my mother would take me to a movie in the afternoon, or for a ride on the cable car, or down to Fisherman's Wharf for a little snack overlooking the Bay. But my schoolwork always came first, and at

the end of the week we would mail my lessons in to the Hollywood Professional School.

Sometimes I would see mother crying and I worried so about
her but I tried my best to keep her thinking happy thoughts.

The Bal Tabarin wasn't really a night club. It was considered
a theater-restaurant, and people brought their children there to
have dinner and watch the show. I had two big numbers in the
show, and two changes of costume. I'll never forget the Bal
Tabarin. My mother naturally was with me all the time, waiting
for me to come off stage, and she would wrap me in a big robe.
She never let me out of her sight all the time we were in San
Francisco. Sometimes after the show we would have another
hamburger at a small restaurant, and then she would take me
back to our hotel room. That part of it was depressing, the way
we had to live and eat and work and do my school lessons, too.

Sometimes I was very tired. But no matter how tired I was,
when I got up there on that stage I always perked right up,
like a race horse at the sound of the bell. He's out there to
win, and so was I. Once I got on stage I always knew there was
a job to be done and I did it. Strangely enough, when those
spotlights hit me I brightened up and sort of magically came to
life as another personality took over. That other me, Anne
Miller, popping out like a jack-in-the-box and clamping the lid
on Lucille Collier. It has always been that way with me and
still is even today. I'm a true split personality.

I danced by night and did my schoolwork by day, and never
really had time for a normal childhood. And I'm afraid my
formal education was rather splotchy. It wasn't until long after
I had done *George White's Scandals* in New York that I finally
finished high school at the Hollywood Professional School. And
I finished on a wing and a prayer. Fortunately, through the years
I've done a lot of reading and traveling to compensate for my lack
of formal schooling. But my spelling at times is peculiar. And
so is my check book. How I hated math!

When I first came to Hollywood from Texas in the fall of

1934, I had enrolled in LeConte Junior High School. I remember it mainly because that is where I met Bonita Granville. She was very big as a child star at the time. She had just finished a picture called *These Three*, in which she played the role of a mean little brat. She was a tremendous hit in this film and a big celebrity in my school. In other words she was a Big Shot and the center of attention because she was a Big Movie Star. I secretly admired her very much.

I was Captain of the Commissary at my school, which meant that it was my job to help patrol the commissary and see that only those children who bought and paid for their own hot lunches had seats inside. Children who brought their lunches from home were not permitted to sit inside the commissary because there were only enough chairs and tables for the children who were paying for their lunches. There were tables outside for the lunch-bringers, and my orders as Captain of the Commissary were not to let any child come in with a lunch brought from home. Well, Miss Big Shot Bonita used to bring her lunch from home and sneak into the commissary with her chums and sit there and eat with them while they were eating their hot lunches.

I went over to her one day and said, "I'm sorry, Bonita, but you can't stay in here." I explained to her that she was taking up a seat that rightfully belonged to someone else who had bought a hot lunch in the commissary. She told me she was almost finished. She just sat there and laughed and then she walked out with her chums.

We went through this routine twice. The third time she got snippety with me and snapped, "I'm going to sit here whether you like it or not."

I was so angry I couldn't control my Aries temper so I just hauled off and slapped her, and we had a terrible cat-and-dog fight right there. The teachers broke us up and we were both taken into the principal's office and reprimanded and sent home from school. The principal said I was right in trying to keep her out of the commissary but that I should not have slapped her. That temper of mine was bad.

We're good friends today and Bonita and I reminisce and laugh about it quite often. We have something else in common also. We like oil men. Bonita is now married to a very wealthy and handsome oil man from Texas, Jack Wrather. She obviously has had better luck with her oil man than I had with my three. They own several television stations, and Bonita is also a successful TV producer. She produces the *Lassie* show.

One night while I was dancing at the Bal Tabarin in San Francisco, I was surprised to see Lucille Ball come into the room. She was with a man I didn't know then but who was to change the course of my life. His name was Benny Rubin and he was a talent scout for RKO. I recognized Lucille Ball, of course, because I had seen her in movies. She wasn't really a big star at that time, but I knew who she was and I had read that she was in San Francisco for the premiere of one of her films.

I was later told that during my show she said to Benny Rubin, "That girl is a marvelous dancer, and you ought to get her a screen test. She could give Eleanor Powell a run for her money."

After my show, Benny Rubin came backstage and then took my mother and me over to the table and introduced us to Lucille Ball. I was thrilled to meet a beautiful film star.

I remember Mr. Rubin telling my mother, "We think your daughter is absolutely terrific, the greatest dancer we've seen in years. But"—and we both knew it was coming—"how old is she?"

The Bal Tabarin owners, Frank Martinelli and Tom Gerun, had already prepared my mother for that question. I'm sure they were onto our little fakery, those two, but I think they believed I was at least fifteen or sixteen, and though even at that age it would have been illegal for me to be working in a theater-restaurant, they employed me anyway because they knew we

were desperate for work. And besides the audience *did* like
me. They were very popular men and their Bal Tabarin was the
biggest place of its kind in San Francisco and played to top
stars. They had already warned my mother that if anyone ever
asked to be *sure* to say that I was eighteen, otherwise no one
could hire me and I might even lose my job at the Bal Tabarin
and get them all in trouble with the union.

So when Mr. Rubin asked my age, my mother said without
batting an eye, "Anne is eighteen." He and Miss Ball cast
knowing glances at each other and said, "We don't believe it."
My mother insisted, but they knew better.

"She's much younger than that, Mrs. Collier," they said. "We
can get her a screen test but you'll have to bring in her birth
certificate."

(Although I was called Anne Miller then, my mother had kept
her name Collier. She later changed it to avoid confusion;
it seemed much simpler for both of us if she were known as
Mrs. Miller.)

Mr. Rubin and Miss Ball were very nice about the whole
thing. They explained to my mother that although I did look
much older on stage and possibly could pass for eighteen in some
places, I really looked very young off stage and they were sure I
could never get by with it in the movies. There was a child
labor law the studios had to contend with and so they probably
would demand to see my birth certificate.

Mr. Rubin said he was sure that he could get me a screen test
and a contract. In fact, he guaranteed me a contract, with or
without a test—but he said, "They're going to ask her age,
Mrs. Collier, and you'll have to bring in her birth certificate
to prove it. A contract won't do her any good if they won't
let her work, and they won't let her work if she's under age."

He explained that as a talent scout for RKO, he could only
consider those who had reached the age of eighteen, the legal age
for employment. The studio was not interested in building
child stars, he said, because it cost too much money to employ

them. If you were under eighteen, the studio had to pay for a teacher on the set and you couldn't work a full eight-hour day.

I knew I was sunk. My birth certificate from St. Joseph's Hospital in Houston definitely said that Johnnie Lucille Collier was born on April 12, 1923, which at the time of our confrontation with Mr. Rubin and Miss Ball would have made me still only thirteen years old, going on fourteen.

I could hardly believe my ears when I heard my mother calmly say, "Don't you worry about a thing, Mr. Rubin. I'll bring Annie's birth certificate with me when you arrange the screen test."

Mr. Rubin and Miss Ball exchanged more raised-eyebrow glances, but smiled sweetly at me, and told Mother they would be in touch with her. Then they bade us good night.

Back in our hotel room Mother explained to me calmly what we had to do. Somehow we must obtain a fake birth certificate that would make me eighteen years old. The only person we knew who could do this for us was my father. He could, but would he?

He was a criminal lawyer. He ought to know how or where to obtain a forged birth certificate for his daughter. So my Texas mother reasoned. And she figured we would have better luck if I asked him for it. He wouldn't do it for her. So together we composed a frantic telegram to my father in Houston, appealing to him in desperation as if my life depended on it (well, maybe it did) to somehow produce for me a fake birth certificate that would make me eighteen years old.

I hoped and prayed with all my heart that he would do this for me. And he did! He sent it special delivery. It said I was born in Chireno, Texas, on April 12, 1919. And my new name was Lucy Ann Collier, a name Mother and I dreamed up as a combination of Lucille and Ann Miller.

It was that fake birth certificate which got me my first movie contract. I sometimes wonder what course my life would have taken without it.

My father is dead now, so they can't put him in jail. And I think it is time to set the record straight. Besides, at this stage of my life—and my career—I do not need extra years tacked onto my real age.

Anyone who bothers to look back through the "official" Hollywood biographies or the early press clippings of Ann Miller's rise to fame as a tap dancer will invariably find it noted that Ann Miller's real name is Lucy Ann Collier, born April 12, 1919, in Chireno, Texas.

That added four years to the real age of Johnnie Lucille Collier, born in Houston on April 12, 1923.

Chireno was in the red clay county of Nacogdoches in East Texas, where my grandparents lived.

Now it can be told.

Don't ask me how he did it, but getting me that fake birth certificate is the only kind thing my father ever did for me.

Ironically, the night after Benny Rubin and Lucille Ball saw me at the Bal Tabarin, another talent scout, Joe Rifkin from Columbia, came in and also offered me a screen test. When it rains it pours. But it was Benny Rubin from RKO who saw me first and Mother and I felt that we should let RKO test me first. In fact, I've always felt that it was Benny Rubin and Lucille Ball who really "discovered" me for films and started me on my career.

We came back to Hollywood when my booking at the Bal Tabarin ended in early 1937 and Mother took me over to RKO for my test. She reminded me to tell them if they asked, that I was eighteen—as if I needed to be reminded. And as usual she warned me, "Now just keep your mouth shut and don't talk too much and they'll never know." I was so scared, and she was trying to reassure me. Of course she had the birth certificate to prove that I was eighteen tucked away in her handbag, just in case they should ask for it.

The screen test was directed by a man named Billy Grady, then casting director at RKO. He was testing dozens of girls, running them through like hamburgers on an assembly line. When it came my turn, Mother told him I had to have my hair and make-up done. I was trying to look very grown-up in my high heels and bust pads. He said there was no time to do my hair and make-up and that they were only going to photograph my feet anyway.

He fibbed about that. They showed my whole body. But it was quite a thrill walking out there on that sound stage for my first grown-up movie screen test. True, I had had two quickie screen test that first summer of 1934 when Mother and I were vacationing in Hollywood. I was only a child extra then. This time it was different. I was a make believe grown-up now!

I did one of my dance numbers from my show at the Bal Tabarin. Mr. Grady seemed somewhat impressed. At least he didn't dismiss me as fast as he did some of the girls. He asked me to walk back and forth across the stage a couple of times. Then he interviewed me, but fortunately he didn't ask too many questions. I remembered my mother's advice to keep my mouth shut and I made my answers as brief as possible.

Fortunately, he did not ask my age. I was over the first hurdle. The crisis was yet to come.

Mother and I returned to RKO and saw my test in a screening room. Several producers were present and one of them came up to us as we were leaving and stopped me and said, "Hey, you! I just saw your test, kid. I'm doing a picture—*New Faces of 1937.* How would you like to be in it and do your tap number?" I said, "Yes, sir, I'd be thrilled!"

I was practically tongue-tied, I was so elated and excited. Not only had I passed my screen test with flying colors, but the studio was offering me a seven-year contract and I had a part in my first film. I was going to be a real movie star.

It was quite an adventure and a thrill, signing a seven-year contract—something every girl who comes to Hollywood dreams of. At least in those days they did.

True, I had worked as a child extra in those two movies, *Anne of Green Gables* and *The Good Fairy*. And just before I went to San Francisco to work at the Bal Tabarin, I was cast as a chorus girl in a "B" picture called *The Devil on Horseback*, starring Lili Damita. I still have photographs of me in my rhumba costume, and they show that my legs looked about the same then as they do now.

This tiny taste of Tinseltown was just enough to make me want more. And now here I was with a real contract with a big Hollywood movie studio. I was on my way at last. I felt like— Hollywood, here I am!

My manager-mother, of course, was ecstatic. She was certain that my name was soon going to be up there in lights just as the old gypsy woman in the bus station had told us it would be.

I was put under contract for $150 a week, my first steady income, the most I had ever made, and a rather phenomenal contract salary for a starlet in those days. My mother and I moved out of our dinky apartment and into a better one. What a big thrill *that* was! Matter of fact, RKO found the apartment for us. Sam Briskin was head of the studio at the time and he told us that a young upcoming star should have a nice address. We moved into the St. Francis Apartments on Vine Street for a while and then into the Hermoyne Apartments on Rossmore. We had a doorman and a big indoor pool there. Yes, a real Hollywood swimming pool! And it made me feel like a real "movie star" when the doorman tipped his hat and said, "Good morning, Miss Miller."

But one thing constantly bugged me—my age. Sure, I had my father's fake birth certificate to "prove" my age all right, but I now lived in constant fear that someone would find out my real age and overnight little Cinderella-girl Orphan Annie would be changed back into a hungry urchin scraping up nickels and dimes from the floor . . . Or even worse, my mother and I both might be put in jail.

One reason for all the interest in me, I knew, was that Eleanor Powell was so big at the time. I was young but not all that dumb. I was the only one around who could do those machine-gun taps, and I was fourteen years younger than Eleanor. It naturally followed that I would be given the big build-up as her competition. Eleanor Powell was my idol and I couldn't have dreamed in a million years that I would be any threat to her. My $150 per week was peanuts compared to her huge salary per picture, but it seemed like a fortune to my mother and me.

And best of all, RKO did put me in a picture right away— *New Faces of 1937*, in which I was featured in a specialty taps number.

I wore a beautiful costume of silver and solid-beaded pajamas, and for my entrance I tapped down a high shiny black ramp, all around a huge orchestra and onto the main floor. Sam Briskin, the head of RKO, came on the set to watch me. Pandro Berman, Lucille Ball, Benny Rubin, and Billy Grady all came in to see me do my number. And of course my mother was there. It was all terribly exciting and a big thrill for me—my first day on a big sound stage doing my first picture.

I felt as though finally I had really arrived in Hollywood!

Actually, Mother and I had been in Hollywood about two years when I signed my RKO contract.

But I have always counted my RKO contract and *New Faces* as really the beginning of my Hollywood career. It was my first chance in a rather important picture, and the first one in which my name, Ann Miller, received billing.

Joe Penner and Milton Berle were the stars of the picture. It was a thrill for me to be in a picture with them. I was surprised to discover that Milton Berle also always had his mother with him. I later learned that he would never do a show on the stage without his mother sitting in the back row applauding him. She was his devoted fan and friend and her being there brought him luck, he said.

We rehearsed my number in the morning and shot it that afternoon. It took only two hours to do it. They had three cameras on me, and again, as with my singing and dancing, I seemed to know intuitively, with no previous training, how to pose for the cameras, how to angle my tap dancing routines so that my body would look right from certain camera angles. I did it all by instinct. It was as though an invisible force was guiding my every move. And I did it right. Everyone seemed pleased.

The picture came out within three months, in the middle of 1937, and my dance number was a big hit. It got very good reviews, created quite a stir, and focused a lot of attention on "Little Orphan Annie" Miller, as Benny Rubin had nicknamed me.

I was a hit. A new star was born. Or maybe I should be more modest and say starlet. Anyway people were suddenly aware of a long-legged brunette Texas tap dancer named Ann Miller, age eighteen.

One nice critic said, "If you would close your eyes and just listen to the tapping feet of Ann Miller, you'd swear there were two people dancing—so rapidly does she clack agile toes."

And so terrifically did I score in my screen bow in *New Faces* that I was immediately cast in two more pictures, one called *Life of the Party* and the other *Stage Door*, the film version of the Broadway play by Edna Ferber and George S. Kaufman. Ann Miller was definitely in pictures.

In *Life of the Party* I had two dance numbers and one line of dialogue. I had to say, "Get hot! Go to town!" That was it. But at last I was also an actress—or so I thought—as well as a dancer.

My first real acting role, though, was in *Stage Door* with Ginger Rogers, Katharine Hepburn, Constance Collier, Adolphe Menjou, Gail Patrick, Andrea Leeds, and Lucille Ball . . . What a cast!

Pandro S. Berman was the producer and Gregory La Cava was the director of the picture. They were a great combination. I played the part of "Annie," or Ginger's pal, "String Bean." The part was written in especially for me, but for a while it was touch-and-go whether I would actually get to do it, because it turned out that I was too tall for Ginger.

I think the only reason I was considered in the first place was that Lucille Ball put in a good word for me and she was Ginger's dearest friend. When it came time for my dance number, we all met in Pandro Berman's office to discuss it, and suddenly Ginger said, "Well, I really don't know . . . I think Ann is too tall for me." My heart sank. I wanted so badly to be in this picture with Ginger Rogers. She was another of my childhood idols.

I said, "Oh, please, Miss Rogers, couldn't you wear higher heels and a higher top hot and I could wear lower heels and a shorter top hat. Mine doesn't have to be as tall as yours."

The nerve of a neophyte talking like that to a big star like Ginger Rogers. But it struck her as funny. And also Greg La Cava. They started laughing. I didn't understand why. I thought they were laughing at me, and I dissolved in tears. I especially didn't want Ginger Rogers laughing at me. She had been my idol for a long time. I adored her. In school I collected photographs of her, and I would trade twenty pictures of anyone else for one of Ginger. To me she was the epitome of glamour and sophistication as a musical performer.

I had even plucked out most of my eyebrows, trying to look like her. They never did grow in again! And the anticipation of working with this wonderful star lady, my very own long-cherished childhood idol, and then to have her laughing at me—it was almost too much to bear.

Apparently Ginger sensed my feelings and she was marvelous about it. She said to Mr. La Cava, "Well, I think maybe we can work it out, Greg. I'll do it with little Annie." I don't know why everyone always referred to me as "little Annie" when

I was so tall. Even columnists like Hedda Hopper and Louella Parsons always called me "little Annie."

Stage Door gave me my first really important role. Also it was important to me personally because it introduced me to Ginger Rogers, who has remained a good friend to this day, and to Hermes Pan, who was to become one of my longtime dearest friends, as well as my dance director. At one time he was Hollywood's highest paid choreographer. Fred Astaire and Ginger Rogers never made a movie without him.

The number he did for us in *Stage Door* was called "Put Your Heart into Your Feet and Dance." It was quite difficult to do because there had to be dialogue between us while we were dancing together, and Greg La Cava was writing the dialogue right there on the set as we went along which was very unusual in those days. Ginger and I had to talk and dance at the same time. It wasn't easy, at least not for me. But I did it. And Ginger was a darling to go along with my suggestion—I mean, she wore higher heels and a higher top hat and I wore lower heels and a top hat that wasn't quite as tall as hers. Everyone agreed that we looked quite well matched.

The picture originally was planned to be finished in two months but ran to nearly three.

There was great tension between Ginger Rogers and Katharine Hepburn then. Greg La Cava wrote the script right on the set, which contained the machine-gun barrage of dialogue and humorous quips that the girls shot back and forth, and neither one of them knew who was coming out ahead. Also, I think it irritated Ginger that Katharine had to have tea served on the set every afternoon at four o'clock.

And that awful dreaded thing happened. I let it slip about my age. It was my own fault. But I did it through sheer embarrassment and anger in the wardrobe department where the wardrobe ladies had to keep stuffing me full of bust pads to make me look sexy. I was thin, but they couldn't understand why I wasn't more developed for an eighteen-year-old girl.

They laughed at me. At first I said I just dance them off. But they kept making jokes about my bust every time they stuffed me with more and more pads. This went on day after day and week after week. Finally I could take it no longer and I burst out in tears, "I am *not* flat-chested. The reason they're not any bigger is that I'm not as old as I'm supposed to be."

I couldn't stop crying, and they felt sorry for me and were nicer to me after that. They never teased me again.

But the word was out. The wardrobe ladies told Somebody Else, and Somebody Else told Somebody Else until it finally got back to Ginger and to Pandro Berman, and he was fit to be tied. He said, "Oh, dear God, we could all be put in jail. This girl is working adult hours and she's only a baby. She should have a teacher on the set . . . I don't know what we're going to do, how we're going to hush this up until the film is finished."

He was practically petrified at what could happen to him if the higher-ups got wind of the situation. But at the same time he was not about to hire a teacher to sit on the set with me and only work me four hours a day. The film was way over budget and that would have delayed production even more. And God knows the picture was being delayed enough already with Greg La Cava tearing up the script and rewriting it, scene by scene.

I had heard about Mr. Berman's dilemma via the studio grapevine, which carries news fast. When he finally came on the set and asked me point-blank if what he had heard was true I violently denied it, of course. I had to. I felt it was a matter of life or death for my mother and me. I told him that I was eighteen, and that I had a birth certificate to prove it. I could tell by the glances exchanged between Mr. Berman and Ginger that neither of them really believed me. But Ginger helped me out of the jam by saying, "Leave her alone, Pan."

I'm sure Ginger knew the truth, but I'm also sure she knew how desperately I needed work to support my mother. She adored her mother too. Anytime the subject of my age was even hinted at on the set or at the studio, Ginger Rogers and Lucille Ball would never discuss it. I'll always bless them for that. But I'm sure everyone knew.

The casting director finally asked for my birth certificate. Mother produced the fake one that my father had sent and I am positive that everyone knew it was a fake.

I think Pandro Berman* and Greg La Cava fully expected to be dragged off to jail any moment on my account, and I breathed a sigh of relief when that picture was finished.

It taught me a lesson. I did not tell my age to any more wardrobe ladies.

* When I checked producer Pandro Berman (now retired) for his side of this story, he said, "I am very vague about the details. I knew she was under age and lying about her age but she was very big for her age, so she got by with it. I remember there was a lot of talk about the trouble we could be in for. I suppose someone from the studio had to go and report to the city and apologize and explain the situation. But I don't remember the details. Hell, I don't remember who I was married to then."

                                                                    N.L.B.

Chapter 5

SWEET FIFTEEN

All the time I was under contract to RKO, I was working a full eight hours a day. Evenings I spent learning my lines—and doing my schoolwork! I usually didn't get to bed until one in the morning, and was up again by six to go to work. During this period, too, I was still mailing my lessons in to the Hollywood Professional School. I was still enrolled there under my real name, Lucille Collier. But they now knew that I was Ann Miller.

After I did *Stage Door*, RKO gave me my first big break—a starring role in a daffy, tuneful film called *Radio City Revels*. It was a big-budget picture—over $2,000,000, an enormous sum in those days.

The cast included some pretty high-powered names—Bob Burns, Jack Oakie, Kenny Baker, Victor Moore, Milton Berle, Helen Broderick—and right up there with them, Ann Miller. Also Hal Kemp's Orchestra. At least I was in good company.

And again my dance director was Hermes Pan.

If for nothing else, the picture was memorable for me because in it I had *my very first kiss*. Period. And I don't mean only my very first screen kiss. I had never even been kissed before, except by parents and relatives. Never by a boy.

My leading man was Kenny Baker, who once sang on Jack Benny's radio show. He later became quite well known as an actor, singer, and leading man. He was the unlucky one destined to bestow upon me—though he didn't know it at the time—my very first kiss. I was petrified. The day we were to shoot the scene I felt almost ill, as though I was about to faint. Finally, I told the wardrobe lady as she was fixing my bust pads. Always the wardrobe lady. But I had to tell someone.

"I just don't think I can go through with it," I wailed. I knew when he pressed me to him that he was going to feel those awful pads. "What am I going to do? I'm scared. I don't know how to kiss."

My second big fat mistake.

The wardrobe lady gave me a peculiar look and said, "Well, just close your eyes and relax and let him lead you."

Some wardrobe ladies apparently never keep their mouths shut. Soon everybody on the set knew that this was going to be little Annie Miller's very first kiss.

When the time came for the big kiss, which was at the end of the scene, we went through rehearsals and everyone knew I was petrified. I was shaking like a leaf, with everyone watching me. The director, Ben Stoloff, knew I was scared, and he would never let Kenny kiss me during rehearsals.

Finally, just before we were to do the actual take, the make-up man came and powdered me down with a thick powder all over my lipstick, and he asked me to lick my lips. I said, "But I'm going to look horrible. This powder's like flour and I'm going to look all faded out."

He said, "Well, but you know, when you kiss Mr. Baker, you don't want him to look like he got in a jam jar."

Disillusionment set in. So this is what they do, I thought,

they powder down your lipstick and make you wet your lips before you do a kissing scene.

As we got ready to do the scene my knees were actually shaking so much I could barely stand up. Part of my problem, I think, was that I had a big crush on Kenny Baker, a real school girl crush. I thought he was divine, and though I was scared, I was also ecstatic at the thought of being kissed by him.

So I closed my eyes, as the wardrobe lady told me to do. And he kissed me. I shall never forget it. He pressed me to him and I kept thinking about those damn' bust pads but I just kept my eyes closed . . . and closed . . . . and closed, until I couldn't breathe. And I kept wondering why the director didn't call "Cut!" I was still being kissed . . . and kissed . . . and still no cut. Finally, out of sheer lack of breath, I tore myself loose and looked around. There was no one on the set.

All the lights were turned off. Everyone had vanished. What had happened was that all the stage hands, the grips' prop men, cast, crew, everyone including the director had just tiptoed off and left us in total darkness. They had all planned it as a joke. Even Kenny was in on it. He started to giggle and said, "We didn't want you to forget your first kiss," and then ran off the set.

It may have been funny to everyone else but it wasn't to me. I thought it was a cruel joke. I was so embarrassed I could have died.

Kenny Baker had laughed at me.

I didn't speak to that wardrobe lady for a week.

However, it was that picture, *Radio City Revels*, which really set me up on the RKO lot. I was a big hit in it. My salary was raised to $250 a week—not bad for a fourteen-year-old kid in those days.

It was that picture also which put my name up there in lights for the first time and I'll never forget it. It was at the RKO Theatre in downtown Los Angeles. A studio publicist

drove us—Mother and me—down to the theater for some
promotion in connection with the opening of the picture, and
when we got out of the car and looked up, there it was right
in front of us on the big theater marquee, my name in white
shining electric lights. *ANN MILLER!* Of course mine wasn't
the only name. There were all the stars of the picture—*and*
Ann Miller. I had an important role in the picture, a starring role
when I was only fourteen.

I have seen my name up in lights many times since at movie
theaters and on Broadway. I think there is nothing in the world
more thrilling than to see your name up in lights on Broadway,
especially when you're the top star of a long-running show as
I was many years later in *Mame*. But there was something extra
special about seeing my name up in lights the very, very first
time. I remember Mother and I just stood there holding each
other and crying and saying we couldn't believe it. But it
had happened, just as that old gypsy woman had told us it
would. My name up there in lights. I had a little bit of a
feeling that I was dreaming it all and that when I blinked
my eyes it might go away. But it didn't.

Looking back now, I suppose one reason the theater managers
decided to put my name up in lights along with the four male
leads was that tap dancing was all the rage then. Eleanor Powell
and Ginger Rogers and Fred Astaire were all going great guns.
I was newer and younger and a pretty good tapper. Well, for
whatever reasons, there it was, Ann Miller, spelled out in bright
shiny lights on a theater marquee.

And for the first time I even got noticed by that Hollywood
queen of gossip columnists, Louella Parsons.

I was the second lead in her column on February 25, 1938.
Louella wrote:

BREAK FOR ANN MILLER . . .
   Little Ann Miller, who scored such a hit in "Radio City Revels,"
wins out over dozens of candidates for the role of the dance-
daffy ballet-minded daughter in "You Can't Take It With You."

It is going to seem funny to see Ann, who is such a good dancer, playing a girl who can hardly get her feet out of her own way, but it's a splendid opportunity since this is one of the best comedy roles of the play.

The Columbia deal to borrow Ann from RKO for their high priced comedy went through today. As for the roles still uncast in the film—well, Frank Capra is still stalking the dark horses.

Hermes Pan again had been my dance director on *Radio City Revels*, and in doing the picture we had become quite good friends. My mother adored him. He had a great sense of humor and he was a Southerner.

And when he asked to take me to the Academy Awards that year, you can imagine my surprise when Mother agreed to let me go with him—without her tagging along as a chaperone.

Radio City Revels had given me my very first kiss from a boy, and my first glimpse of my name up there in lights. Now it was giving me my first real Hollywood date. Without my mother along.

But I am sure the reason she let me go with Hermes is that she knew we were also going with Mr. and Mrs. Walt Disney. She probably figured we would be adequately chaperoned.

I will never forget that first date as long as I live. I wore my first long evening dress, a yellow taffeta gown that my mother had helped me pick out. And Hermes brought me the most gorgeous gardenia corsage I've ever seen. I had never smelled a gardenia before. In Texas, we have Cape jasmines which are similar but not really the same. To this day I'm still mad about gardenias. My corsage came in a fancy box with a white satin bow. Hermes presented it to me and I was so thrilled . . . but then slowly I began to notice a strange expression on his face.

Finally, in a most uncourtly manner he asked, "Annie, where in hell did you get that make-up? It's terrible."

In those days I wore pancake make-up and I wore it rather

thick in my prodigious efforts to look eighteen. For my first date I guess I went a little overboard on the glamour bit. Pale white face, blue eye shadow, coal black lashes, and dark lipstick. Hermes hated it. He made me go in and wash my face, and I had to do my make-up all over with very little lipstick.

It was an extra treat for me that night to meet Walt Disney and his wife. We all went to the Biltmore Hotel in downtown Los Angeles where the Oscar shows were always held in those days. And this one was especially exciting for me not only because it was my first Oscar show and my first date but because both of the men I was with won Academy Awards.

The Awards were presented that year (1938) on March 10 for pictures made the previous year. The ceremony had been delayed a week due to a storm and flood that had marooned film folk in their mansions from Malibu to Mulholland Drive.

Hermes Pan won an Oscar that night for a number called "Fun House" which he had choreographed for Fred Astaire and Joan Fontaine in the movie, *A Damsel in Distress*. It was really a spectacular number.

Walt Disney won two Oscars that year, one for Best Cartoon of 1937, titled *The Old Mill*, and a special Academy Award for Scientific Production (for a multiplane camera).

This was also the year that the Best Actor and Best Actress winners were Spencer Tracy for *Captains Courageous* and Luise Rainer for *The Good Earth*. *The Life of Emile Zola* was the Best Picture of the Year. Ah, truly Hollywood's Golden Era.

But how exciting for "little Ann Miller" from Texas to be seated between two of the winners and to watch them go on stage and pick up their Oscars!

Through the years Hermes and I have had many a laugh over the "mask" of make-up he made me wash off before he would take me out on that first date. He has always told me he knew I was very young, he guessed somewhere between sixteen and eighteen. "For Pete's sake, with that mask on your

New Faces of 1937, my first picture under contract to RKO.
(*RKO photo*)

Three of the screen's topmost comedians, Jack Oakie, Milton Berle, and Bob Burns were my co-stars in *Radio City Revels*. (RKO, 1937)

Tarnished Angel in 1938, with Sally Eilers and Paul Guilfoyle, was my last picture under my RKO contract because I asked for my release from the studio.

I received my first screen kiss from Kenny Baker in *Radio City Revels* (1937), and it really was my first kiss—ever!

Here I am in my big dance number from Columbia's 1942 production, *Reveille With Beverly*. I loved my "V" for victory costume! (This is the scene in which my costume, hair, and eyelashes were singed by flames. See Chapter 21). (*Columbia photo*)

Right, a photograph I shall always treasure. During the filming of *You Can't Take It With You,* Jimmy Stewart gave me so many candy bars (because he thought I was frightened) that I gained twenty-four pounds! (*Columbia photo*)

I was certainly among the finest stars in the Columbia-Frank Capra production of *You Can't Take It With You.* The 1938 motion picture won two Academy Awards—one for Best Picture of the Year, the other for Best Director. (Left to Right: Mischa Auer, Jean Arthur, Edward Arnold, James Stewart, me, and Mary Forbes.)

face, how could anyone tell who you really were?" It was several years before I screwed up the courage to tell him that on our first date I wasn't quite fifteen yet. I lacked a month and two days.

You would think I might have learned my lesson about wearing heavy make-up, but practically the same thing happened a year or so later when I went to 20th Century-Fox for a screen test for a role in a Sonja Henie film. The role was that of a sophisticated woman, so again I smeared my face with heavy make-up—only to find Hermes Pan on the sound stage. Much to my embarrassment he ordered me in front of everyone to go and wash my face before he would permit me to go in front of the cameras for my test. I didn't get that role. The reason given—I looked too young. I have always jokingly blamed Hermes for causing me to lose that role.

Meanwhile, however, soon after I had finished *Radio City Revels* I started work on *You Can't Take It With You.*

And what a fabulous line-up of stars Frank Capra had "stalked" for this one: Jean Arthur, Lionel Barrymore, James Stewart, Edward Arnold, Mischa Auer . . . and guess whose name was next in the billing. Ann Miller! And then Spring Byington and Donald Meek and the others . . .

Although I was young, I had sense enough to realize what a great opportunity it was for me to work with movie people of such magnitude.

I did pull one boo-boo, though. I knew Frank Capra only by name, not by sight. And since no one bothered to introduce us, my first day on the set I mistook him for an office boy—and I guess treated him like one until someone set me straight. He was good-naturedly letting me get away with it. He was even then on his way to becoming one of Hollywood's all-time great producer-directors.

As Louella Parsons had said, I was only one of many who was tested for the role of Essie Carmichael, the kooky ballerina, but I won the part. Mischa Auer played the role of my Russian ballet dancing teacher, Mr. Kolenkhov, who was always saying, "Confidentially, she stinks." And he was constantly trying to teach me ballet while he was eating ham sandwiches and swinging his arms around, so that the ham and cheese went flying all over the set while he was saying, "*Entrechat, entrechat, entrechat.*"

It was a terribly funny role and a tremendous break for me to get the part.

When I was testing for the role, I was asked if I had ever done any toe work in ballet. Of course I had taken those ballet lessons as a child, but I had never done toe work. I lied again (by now I was accustomed to lying about my age) and said I had done toe work. So they brought me a pair of toe shoes to put on and gave me a wad of white lamb's wool which any ninny knows you're supposed to stick in the hard toe shoes. But I didn't know it. Actually, as I later learned, you're supposed to wrap the lamb's wool around your toes and stuff the rest of it into the shoes to protect your toes while you're standing on pointed toes.

But since I'd never handled toe shoes before, when they gave me this wad of stuff, I thought it was something you put in your hair, like those "rats" as we used to call them, and I tossed it aside. I went out there and did the test standing on my toes, won the part, and then worked throughout that picture without the lamb's wool in my shoes, because nobody told me to stick it in there. Naturally, they assumed I had enough brains to know what to do with it. Some ballerinas prefer to bind their feet first and then stuff the lamb's wool in their shoes to protect their toes, because toe shoes are very hard. It's like dancing on wooden shoes, but on your toes.

I got out there and danced on my toes and did what I was supposed to do, all right. I was supposed to be rotten anyway, in the picture, and I was in such pain that it was easy enough to play the role of a lousy ballet dancer. But what it did to my toes! It almost crippled me. All my toenails were pushed up into my feet, and by the time I finished work my feet were a bloody mess. Every night my mother would make me soak my feet and she would put bandages on them. Then I would go back the next day and do it all over again. I injured my toes so badly in that picture that to this day I have two toenails which won't grow out correctly.

I was bleeding and in great pain most of the time but naturally I wouldn't tell anyone. I remember how Jimmy Stewart sometimes caught me crying. He didn't know why. He thought I was frightened about doing the role and he always gave me a candy bar to cheer me up. He kept his dressing room well stocked with candy bars because he was so painfully thin. And he made me painfully fat with those candy bars. When I started the picture in March 1938, I weighed something like 115 pounds and when I finished I weighed 139. I blew up like a balloon and I still had a lot of baby fat on me. And to this day, when I see Jimmy Stewart I always remind him of the candy bars he gave me and how fat I got doing *You Can't Take It With You*. We always laugh about it.

In spite of the ordeal with my toes, the picture was an important milestone in my career.

First of all, it had its world premiere at that great, glittering "Showplace of the Nation," Radio City Music Hall in New York City's Rockefeller Center. The ads read:

"RADIO CITY MUSIC HALL . . . Presents the World Premiere of one of the most distinguished pictures of recent years . . . Frank Capra's *You Can't Take It With You*."

The four big star names, of course, were Jean Arthur, Lionel Barrymore, James Stewart, and Edward Arnold, and the ads noted "and an unusually strong supporting cast." How thrilling it was to see my name right up there second only to Mischa Auer in the supporting cast, sixth in all the names on the long cast sheet (a total of twenty-two).

But equally thrilling was the really rave review we got from the New York *Times* film critic, Frank S. Nugent, who praised all of us to the skies, including "the ballet-dancing Essie" (that was me, he thought Mischa and I were very funny), and wrote, "It's a grand picture . . . jumps smack into the list of the year's best."

It was, of course, the film version of the Pulitzer Prize-winning play by George S. Kaufman and Moss Hart, and there had been quite a bit of skepticism, as there always is, about grafting a stage play to the cinema—especially this one which was about the slap-happy-go-lucky family of Vanderhofs.

Frank Capra had seen the play in New York and found it so entrancing that he made up his mind that *You Can't Take It With You* had to be his next film. But Broadway producer Sam H. Harris's asking price was staggering: two hundred thousand dollars! Columbia's head man, Harry Cohn, blew a fuse when he heard this but he finally shelled out the two hundred thousand dollars to buy the film rights for Frank Capra.

I was a little young to know about all of this at the time. I only read it recently in Frank Capra's own autobiography, *The Name Above the Title.* I was fascinated to read how Mr. Capra went about casting all of us in our various daffy parts —Lionel Barrymore as Grandpa Vanderhof, Jean Arthur as Alice Sycamore, and . . .

"Then there was Ann Miller. She played Alice's sister Essie, the awkward Pavlova; played her with the legs of Marlene, the innocence of Pippa, and the brain of a butterfly that flitted on its toes.

"And to play the threadbare Russian, Kolenkhov, there could be no one gloomier than the fallen-faced, picture of doom itself —Mischa Auer. His saturnine opinion of Essie's dancing, the Bolshevik Revolution, or of the world in general: 'Confidentially, ett steenks!'"

And I loved reading about the way he auditioned my xylo-phone-playing husband, Dub Taylor, and cast him on the spot in the hilarious role of Ed Carmichael who played the xylophone in a way that would wake up the dead.

Yes, the filming of *You Can't Take It With You* was a memorable experience for all of us—and all the more so because on the night of February 23, 1939, at my second glittering Academy Awards banquet, Frank Capra walked off with two of the top honors for our picture—one for Best Director, the other for Best Picture of the Year (1938).

If I had been thrilled at my first Academy Awards show the year before, you can imagine how I felt now. There are no words to describe it. I can only say that to be in a film which wins an Academy Award as Best Picture of the Year is an experience one can never forget. That was the first and only time I've ever been in a movie which won an Oscar. But the memory of it is enough to last a lifetime.

Mr. Capra, who had already become famous from such films as *It Happened One Night* (which won all five major Oscars), *Mr. Deeds Goes to Town*, and *Lost Horizon*, and who probably holds the longest unbroken string of Motion Picture Academy Awards in theatrical annals, was in his fourth year as president of the Academy and as such was also master of ceremonies at the Academy Awards banquet.

How vividly I still recall this very special occasion, and again it was held in the Biltmore Hotel. As soon as the stirring strains of "The Star-Spangled Banner" died down, Basil Rathbone introduced Mr. Capra, who stepped to the rostrum and looked out over the brilliant assemblage—twelve hundred of Hollywood's finest, all beautifully gowned and carefully groomed.

We all knew that Mr. Capra had worked hard to make this 1939 Awards banquet more glamorous than ever, and he could be proud of achieving his goal. But I don't think any of us, including Mr. Capra, expected an Oscar for *You Can't Take It With You*. Even though his track record was good, we had a lot of competition, for 1938 was another year of fine pictures.

He introduced celebrity after celebrity who held us all in suspense while they opened the envelopes with the well-guarded secret ballots, announced the winners and then presented those shining gold statuettes.

I remember the first celebrity he introduced was Jerome Kern who opened the envelope for Best Song. It was "Thanks for the Memory" (written by Ralph Rainger and Leo Robin). And I remember Bob Hope cracking jokes as he presented the Short-Subject Awards. I'm sure Bob Hope holds the record for longevity as one of the featured attractions on each year's Oscar show.

One surprise that brought down the house that night was child-star Shirley Temple presenting Walt Disney with a Special Award (yes, again!) for his creation of *Snow White and the Seven Dwarfs*. Edgar Bergen and Charlie McCarthy handed Deanna Durbin a special trophy in the interest of Hollywood's "youth movement."

Next, Mr. Capra introduced another veteran director, Fred Niblo, to present the Best Director Award. He opened the envelope and announced: "And the winner is—[long pause] —Frank Capra for *You Can't Take It With You*." There was thunderous applause.

It was Frank Capra's third Oscar for Best Directing. (His others: *Lady for a Day* in 1933, and *It Happened One Night* in 1935.) He was so stunned he could barely mumble his thanks.

Then came the Best Actor Award: Spencer Tracy (again!) for his performance in *Boys Town*, and the Best Actress: Bette Davis for *Jezebel*.

The Best Picture envelope is always saved for the last, the climax. I remember it was Jimmy Roosevelt who opened the envelope and broke the suspense by announcing: "And the best picture of the year is—[pause]—*You Can't Take It With You*."

I couldn't believe it! My head went into a tailspin and when Mr. Capra stepped up to receive his little golden statuette, I got all choked up. Then I started to cry and I just sat there and bawled like a baby. I was so happy. I knew that my own performance, as well as that of all the others, had contributed to making *You Can't Take It With You* the Best Picture of the Year, and knowing that you have been a part of it and helped someone win an Academy Award, the most prestigious of all honors in filmland, well, it is an experience never to be forgotten.

In all my young years, this was my most shining hour and happiest moment on the long-ago Oscar night of February 23, 1939. There would come other glories but never again one like this.

Soon after the sneak previews of *You Can't Take It With You*, in August of 1938, Columbia sent me out on a personal appearance tour with the picture. In Hollywoodese, it's known as a p.a. tour. This was my first.

Adding it all up, that year 1938 seems filled with firsts—my first kiss, my first date, my first Oscar show, my first and only movie that was to win an Oscar, my first p.a. tour, and that first sight of my name up there in lights . . .

I saw it up there again many times on that first p.a. tour, and for the first time in New York City.

In those days it was the custom to have a stage show or vaudeville bill in conjunction with the showing of a new film. They always showed the picture first, then the stage show would come on. And since I was the only member of the cast on a p.a. tour to promote *You Can't Take It With You*, I always had star billing in the stage show—and usually my name was up there in lights on the marquee.

My agent, Abe Lastfogel, who was then head of the William Morris Agency, was a man who believed in stage shows to promote a picture, so he booked me into an awful lot of theaters while I was on tour. Sometimes I played six or eight shows a day, sometimes more, and I hated it. It was extremely hard, tough work, a real grind. But it was memorable in many ways— my first trip to New York where I danced on the stage of the

Paramount Theatre. And I got to meet people like Betty Hutton and Red Skelton and Frank Sinatra. I worked with them at some of the theaters.

They were not the big stars then that they later became. It was Sinatra's early swooning days. He was appearing on the same bill with me at the Paramount Theatre and I saw it all happen —the theater management had paid to have all those swarms of kids come in screaming and yelling and falling in the aisles. That was the beginning of Sinatra and I was there when it all happened in New York. He was just a skinny kid with a big voice. Little did I think then that I would one day be making a picture with him.

Betty Hutton was not well known at that time, though she became a big star later. But she was already a powerhouse on stage and I remember sitting backstage and listening to her sing "Ol' Man Mose," which always brought the house down. I marveled at her endless energy.

It was during this same tour that I first met Red Skelton, who was then a vaudeville performer. It is amusing now to look back and remember the theater marquees that featured ANN MILLER IN PERSON . . . STARRING IN "YOU CAN'T TAKE IT WITH YOU"— with Red Skelton's name billed beneath mine. Red was only one of many acts in the vaudeville show, though already he had audiences laughing so hard they rolled in the aisles. But I was *the* star of the show.

Later I was to meet him again on the RKO lot, in a picture called *Having Wonderful Time*, which starred Red and Ginger Rogers. I had only a small role in that one.

I must say Red had a peculiar off-stage brand of humor, as my mother and I discovered on that p.a. tour. We had been traveling by train. We had never flown before, but for some reason—a tight schedule, I think—we had to take a plane out of Pittsburgh instead of a train. I made the mistake of telling Red and his first wife, Edna, that Mother and I had never flown before and that we were both petrified.

Just before we left for the airport, Red gave us a package and laughed and said, "This is a surprise for you on your first plane trip. But don't open it until you're on the plane." It was large and square and heavy. We had no idea what it could be, but we kept our promise and didn't open it until we were in the air. We could hardly wait to find out what it was. We opened it, and it turned out to be a beautiful leather-bound scrapbook—filled with gory pictures of airplane crashes! He certainly had gone to a great deal of trouble to round up all those pictures and paste them in a scrapbook—obviously an expensive one. If what he wanted was to frighten the devil out of us, mission accomplished. Mother and I just sat there shaking with fear until we got where we were going. I don't even remember where and I don't think anyone can blame me. Red Skelton knew what black comedy was before it even had a name.

Red and I have remained friends, though, through the years. His first wife was a wonderful inspiration to him. She used to write most of his material for him. He wouldn't make a move without her. I was shocked when I read of their divorce. In many ways Red is a strange man, sort of a dual personality type. He always carried trunkloads of things with him—scrapbooks, film, toys. I remember once backstage Edna said, "Come over here, I want to show you something." And she showed me a big trunk packed with electric trains. She said he always took them along on his tours just to amuse himself. He used to collect film too. He had thousands and thousands of reels of film which he carried with him, and cameras to shoot more reels of it. Some of these reels must be real collectors' items because they go way back. I've seen Red drink a bottle of vodka in one sitting, and be as sober as a judge, sharp as a tack and funnier than ever.

He was born in July under the sign of Cancer, and Cancer people are very moody. I guess most comedians are moody, come to think of it. Red Skelton is very, very funny. Sometimes I think he was born funny. But there is a very serious side to Red Skelton, the clown. He is one of the most talented persons I have ever known. He writes poetry and composes beautiful music. And then, of course, he paints clowns. He paints a clown a day—and then files them away, like the letters he writes to his dead son. Red is a strange man.

My own studio, RKO, was very impressed that another studio, Columbia, had borrowed me for *You Can't Take It With You*, a major picture with big-name stars, which became an Academy Award winner to boot. So, when I returned from my p.a. tour, I was considered "hot property" and was immediately put in another major picture, *Room Service*, starring Lucille Ball and the Marx Brothers.

A press clipping from April 15, 1938, reads:

ANN MILLER GETS LEAD . . .
  When Ann Miller completes her role of the nutty sister in "You Can't Take It With You" at Columbia, she will have a nice part waiting for her on her home lot, Radio Pictures. Ann is cast for the leading comedienne role in "Room Service," in which the Marx Brothers will be starred . . . Lucille Ball is to have the other feminine role.

I didn't dance at all in *Room Service*. I played a straight acting part, the ingénue lead opposite a young man named Frank Albertson.

Well, my first day on the set, when I met the three Marx Brothers, was another of those I'll-never-forget occasions. The Marx Brothers had been informed that I was very young and naïve and had stardust in my eyes. My mother brought me to the studio as usual, took me onto the *Room Service* set and deposited me for my day's work. As soon as she had gone, Harpo Marx dashed out of his dressing room and started chasing me around the set.

He was almost completely nude, at least about as nude as you could get in those days. He had on shoes and socks and a high silk top hat and a pair of funny shorts. And he was squeezing a bicycle horn as he chased me around the set. I was screaming and yelling, I thought he'd gone out of his mind, like a wild man. Everyone else thought it was hysterically funny. But I didn't. He scared me to death.

It was supposed to be one of those typically zany Harpo Marx jokes but it was no joke to me. With everyone else laughing wildly, I ran into my dressing room, slammed the door and bolted it, and absolutely refused to come out until they assured me that Harpo Marx had his pants on. I thought he was crazy. I remained frightened of Harpo throughout the filming of that picture. Every day he would come up with new antics—he would make faces and honk his horn at me when I least expected it, and scare me out of my wits. I tried to laugh it off as just a big joke, I'm sure Harpo meant it as such. But just when I was about to feel a little more secure with him, he would come up with new surprises to deliberately frighten me, and there were many times when I would run screaming into my dressing room. I was never so relieved to finish a picture. Groucho and I, however, became good friends and still are today.

This era of my life might be summed up in a copyrighted International News Service story dated March 17, 1938:

ANN MILLER HAS NO INTENTION OF WASTING SALARY

ACTRESS RECALLS LEAN DAYS
AND WILL BUILD UP BANK ACCOUNT.

Ann Miller, 18-year-old beauty from Houston, Texas, whose rise to screen success as a filmland fable, is proving herself a very sensible girl. She's not going to let a lot of money go to her head and make a big splurge.

"Mother and I have planned to own a home, be adequately covered by insurance and have a bank account large enough to carry us for several years if necessary, by 1943," Ann says. "We learned what it means to be without funds during the days I was striving to get a break in pictures. We do not intend to increase our expenses to any appreciable extent during the next five years, but, like any new business, will devote our energies to producing a good product and establishing a substantial reserve. I have seen too many players zoom to the top ranks one minute and slide back to the bottom the next to take any chances."

Ann stormed the gates of Hollywood studios for a year, without success. Then, discouraged, she got a job in a San Francisco night club. There a studio talent scout "discovered" her. In a single year she reached a top spot in R.-K.-O.'s "Radio City Revels" after she had played Ginger Rogers' dancing partner in "Stage Door."

I finished off my early contract years at RKO in a dud—a "B" picture called *Tarnished Angel* with Sally Eilers. She was the star of the picture and she played the part of that great lady preacher, Aimee Semple McPherson. I think it was one of the last movies Sally Eilers ever made, and I really couldn't blame her. We had a scene together in a meeting hall where Sally was preaching to a flock of people. And right behind her was a real live camel. The camel was restless and stomping around and making a lot of noise with his hoofs, and the technicians were having trouble hearing her dialogue.

The sound man far back on the set was yelling, "Louder, louder!" Sally was wearing a long white gown and holding a Bible, and she was preaching, "It is easier for a camel to go through the eye of a needle than for a rich man to enter the Kingdom of Heaven."

I was sitting on a dais in the center of the stage, and the sound man was still yelling, "Louder, please," and the camel was still stomping.

Sally tried it again, louder, and just as she started, "It is easier for a camel . . ." the real-life camel felt the urge and started doing what comes naturally. The sound man screamed, "What's that noise? Is it raining?" It sounded like Niagara Falls. And then suddenly the camel relieved himself of a big flop, flop, splashing everyone within reach. The sound stage was bedlam. Men scurried in with mops and pails. We were all drenched. Sally's gown and shoes were sopped in buckets of camel dung, completely ruined, of course, and she flounced off the set in a fury. That ended that day's shooting. And that picture was my last under my RKO contract, because I asked for my release.

Again I had good reviews. Sample: "Ann Miller sings a song nicely, does a splendid fast tap routine, and comes through well on the dramatics."

But this wasn't enough for me. I left RKO to make my Broadway debut in *George White's Scandals*.

Chapter 6

TOAST OF BROADWAY

It certainly was not my idea to do a Broadway show. The very thought of it scared me silly. I knew I couldn't do it, I would be a flop, and besides I liked Hollywood and I liked doing movies, even though that last one, *Tarnished Angel*, was a bomb. I didn't want to move to New York and I hadn't the remotest desire to work in *George White's Scandals*.

The whole deal was arranged by my agent who talked my mother into it, and it wasn't until much later that I learned the reasons behind it. I was much too young and naïve then to comprehend the kind of hanky-panky that sometimes goes on behind the scenes in Hollywood.

But it seems that M-G-M wasn't too happy about the build-up I was getting at RKO, especially in connection with the musical *Radio City Revels*. M-G-M was spending a fortune on its own whiz tap dancer, Eleanor Powell, for their own big musical productions, and I was regarded as a threat to her. To further compound the problems, Eleanor Powell and I were both represented by the William Morris Agency, a little detail that no one had bothered to tell me when I signed with them. In fact, it was Eleanor Powell who helped to make the Morris Agency so powerful in Hollywood. Needless to say, the crumbs they got from my $250 per week contract with RKO was nothing compared with their take from Eleanor's $150,000 per picture at M-G-M.

So when it came time to renew my contract, I was told that RKO didn't have any more musicals planned for me at the moment and that I would be better off to get my release. The agency said they could put me into *George White's Scandals*, and he told me that a Broadway show would do big things for me.

Although I had not been happy with my last picture, still I had a sense of security with RKO, and I had no wish to give up an established career to start all over again on Broadway.

Nevertheless, my agent convinced my mother and off we went to New York to begin rehearsals.

My mother had more faith in me than I had in myself. On the strength of my contract for *Scandals*, she promised to buy me a fur coat for my sixteenth birthday, one that I could wear for my Broadway opening. And she kept her promise.

I'm sure the William Morris people didn't have too much hope for me on Broadway, but it was one way of getting me out of Hollywood.

Although I didn't realize it, George White was practically washed up and I suppose the Morris Agency felt that if the show was a hit, fine, but if not, that would neatly dispose of Ann Miller. Where could I go from a flop? I would be off the movie screen long enough so that people would forget me, and if the *Scandals* show flopped (as I'll bet they thought it would), then I'd be like the forgotten soldier, buried forever.

Well, it just so happened that *George White's Scandals of 1939* was anything but a flop, and Ann Miller turned out to be, to everyone's surprise, the new smash hit of the show. According to all the critics and columnists, it was Ann Miller who actually helped save the show and kept it going for a year on Broadway and then another year on tour.

I do not remember much of that long hot summer of 1939 in New York except rehearsing, rehearsing, rehearsing, and having costume fittings, and then studying and studying and studying for my school lessons. I was still mailing my homework back to the Hollywood Professional School.

The other big stars of the show were Ella Logan, Willie and Eugene Howard, Ben Blue, The Three Stooges, and the Kim Loo Sisters. And then there were all those beautiful showgirls, the George White trademark. It was a fast sharp revue.

Mr. White tried me out with some dialogue in a couple of skits, but my mother had a fit and made him take me out of them. She said the skits were too vulgar. So I only did two dance numbers but everywhere we played they were singled out as the big hits of the show.

The thirteenth edition of the *Scandals* had its world premiere at the Garden Pier Theatre in Atlantic City. We played there one week only to standing ovations and rave reviews, then moved to the Shubert Theatre in Boston for two weeks.

I had been scared on opening night in both Atlantic City and Boston, but I knew that Broadway was going to be the real test.

It wasn't exactly stage fright, it was just that I was terribly scared I wasn't quite good enough. The theater was a new adventure for me. I never missed a rehearsal of the show, even when I wasn't needed. I even went to all the orchestra rehearsals that were called expressly for the musicians. As a matter of fact, I made it my business to be the first one at the theater before anybody else if only to see the scenery carried in. Every spare moment I had was spent dancing either backstage or in my dressing room.

Finally came that really big opening night that I'll never forget. Monday, August 28, 1939, at the Alvin Theatre in New York. Ann Miller's Broadway debut and I was so frightened that my knees were shaking. Backstage in my dressing room, the wardrobe lady helped me into my costume and I could hear people coming into the theater. I was on the verge of tears and in order to keep myself from crying (I didn't want to smear my make-up) I screwed my earrings on so tight that the intense pain helped me forget my fear. My mother was backstage with me trying to cheer me up. She could never understand why I was always so frightened on opening nights. How well I remember peeking out through the curtains from the wings of the stage and seeing my first Broadway opening night audience—all those women in their fabulous gowns and jewels. How well I remember the overwhelming smell of perfume wafting up from that audience.

In those days New York society was really something fantastic, especially at those big Broadway openings when they all arrived in their chauffeur-driven cars and dressed to the teeth. That was a very exciting era in New York.

George White let me create my own dance routines. One of the numbers which I introduced, and which was to become quite famous, was called "The Mexiconga," and I must say that my Mexiconga costume was really splendid. It was made by Madame Berthe of New York. Its short bodice, in shades of gold, red, and blues, was overlaid with shimmering layers of silver bugle beads, and my ruffled red rhumba skirt was designed to cascade only from my derrière—nothing in front—giving good exposure to my long legs. I wore big wide jeweled cuffs and a huge hat like a Mexican sombrero made of heavy bugle beads. My hair was dyed blue-black and hung almost to my waist. I wore very bright lipstick, a heavy kind of Moorish or Arabic eye make-up, and I wore silver tap shoes.

I'm of Cherokee, French, and Irish descent, and I probably looked all three that night.

My Mexiconga number came about halfway through the first act of the show. First, Ella Logan would come out and sing the song. Then the heavy velvet curtain opened and the spotlights were turned on me as I danced out to the center of the stage. The Kim Loo Sisters, two sets of Chinese "twins" dressed in Mexican outfits were on either side of me, pounding out the rhythm on conga drums. When they beat the drums, I would tap out an answer with my feet and then we would repeat the phrase together.

To every beat of their drums, I gave an answer with my feet, and then the music would start. First the flutes, then the woodwinds, then the rest of the orchestra, and all the time the drums would beat faster and faster, and I had to tap faster and faster to answer them. Then the chorus came out and the number worked up into an exotic, sensuous, whirling dervish finale.

Well, the number had gone over very well in Atlantic City and Boston but I was hardly prepared for what happened at that Broadway opening. It literally stopped the show. I got a standing ovation right there. The audience rose spontaneously and stood clapping and cheering and calling "Bravos! More! More!" I couldn't believe it. Furthermore, I didn't know what to do about it. I didn't have an encore ready because no one had thought it was necessary—least of all me.

I danced into the wings and practically into George White's arms. He was all excited and beaming. "Atta baby, Annie! Just listen to 'em."

"But what'll I do?" I wailed. "I don't have an encore."

The audience was still standing and whistling and cheering. They obviously were not about to let the show go on, so Mr. White said, "Just go out there and do the same number over again." And that's what I did. We simply repeated the entire Mexiconga number from beginning to end. When it was over, we all ran off the stage crying and laughing at the same time because we were so overcome with all the applause and excitement. Mr. White told everyone I was his best dancing discovery since Ann Pennington. She was a big *Scandals* star before my time.

In the second act I danced a number to the song, "Are You

Having Any Fun?" and to a medley of all the songs in the show. For this I had another spectacular Madame Berthe costume, a white beaded and rhinestone leotard, like a bathing suit, with long gloves of the same material up my arms and nothing on my legs.

On my backside I wore a huge black train of ostrich feathers, like a peacock's tail, which I whipped around when I danced. And I had a hat with a marvelous long doodad of ostrich feathers which curled down one side of my shoulder and continued down my back. It was a beautiful, showgirl kind of costume, very Folies-Bergère.

In this number I danced all alone in a spotlight (this was Mr. White's idea), starting out in the middle of the stage against the black velvet curtain—and with my black ostrich feathers, bright red lipstick, chalk white face and blue-black hair, it made quite an impact on the audience. It was a long number and I danced it with lots of whirling and turning and a crash of the typani drums. Again it brought down the house.

When we took our bows at the end of the show there was no doubt about it—that opening night was Ann Miller's night and New York was Ann Miller's town. I just stood there crying.

New York audiences are the greatest in the world. If they love you, they just love you to death and if they hate you, boy, you know it! They're like Texans and Australians. There is no in between.

Oh, what a night for Ann Miller! And for George White as well. From the way he took over paternal custody of me that night, you'd have thought he invented Ann Miller. Well, maybe in a way he did. He took pride in having "discovered" me. Maybe he never really knew that I had been "banished" to Broadway just to get my tippy-tap-toes out of Hollywood where Eleanor Powell was Queen of the Taps. Actually, it was a great compliment to me that anyone thought I was good enough to give *her* any competition.

Anyway, George White paid me the ultimate compliment by

asking me to be his date after our opening that night. He was a producer who always took his star out on opening night, and although Ella Logan was supposed to be the real star of the show —and she was truly marvelous in it—George White took me out after that premiere performance. And my mother, of course.

Mr. White was a rather notorious wolf who had an eye for beautiful long-legged girls. Among the showgirls he had chosen for his *Scandals* that year were Lois Andrews, who later married George Jessel; Frances Neal, who later married Van Heflin; Audrey Young, who married Billy Wilder; and Marie Frye, who married Vic Orsatti and later Harry Karl, and who became known as Marie ("The Body") McDonald.

It was considered a great honor to be selected as George White's date on opening night. Mother was even more excited than I was. In a way she was fulfilling through me her own aborted dreams of being in show business. And she would have been good at it!

I wore my fur coat, an elegant long white fox evening coat, the one Mother had bought for my sixteenth birthday. I wore it over my first really sophisticated long evening dress, and George White took us in grand style to the Stork Club, which Walter Winchell made famous in his column. And there he was in person, the great WW himself, sitting at his very own table and he invited us to sit with him and then he interviewed me!

I also met Sherman Billingsley for the first time that night. He came over to say hello to us, and he sent me four white orchids and some perfume.

Mr. Billingsley had a reputation for keeping his celebrity-lady customers happy by always sending a bottle of perfume and an orchid to their tables. But he sent me four orchids! Mr. Winchell looked impressed, though for all I know, he put him up to it.

One thing I definitely remember about that First Night on Broadway, it was so wonderfully thrilling, exciting, and exhausting and we got back to our hotel so late Mother let me go right straight to bed instead of making me stay up to do my schoolwork. A red letter day in my memory calendar!

But the best was yet to come. I mean, of course, the fantastic reviews in the press.

I awakened the next day to find myself the "Toast of Broadway." And in the following weeks I became the cover girl for all the important newspaper Sunday supplements and magazines.

Here are random excerpts from reviews:

Walter Winchell, New York *Daily Mirror:* ". . . Ann Miller, the tap-dancing show stopper in Scandals. One of the show's top assets."

Ed Sullivan, New York *Daily News:* ". . . On the Alvin stage, she scored solidly and her brunette attractiveness was set off in big-timesy costuming . . . She's a cinch to get another crack at movies and a cinch to make good in her encore effort."

Richard Manson, New York *Post:* "Ann Miller . . . does the stepping in this and stops the show. Mr. White can take a bow for this bundle of rhythm—she has talent, the figure and the assurance for big things."

Robert Coleman, New York *Daily Mirror:* "Ann Miller, the greatest gal tapster to hit Broadway since Eleanor Powell went to Hollywood. Ann is terrific. She's an eye tonic, has loads of style and a personality that whirls with hurricane force across the footlights."

George Ross, New York *World-Telegram:* "Ann Miller of Hollywood, whose trim torso and nimble tap-dancing stopped the show at one point and lifted it at another."

Burns Mantle, New York *Daily News:* "The new faces include those of Ann Miller, a shapely tap dancer with a talent that is exceptional and a pictorial appeal beyond that of many of her tapping sisters."

Lucius Beebe, New York *Herald Tribune:* ". . . Among the most notable attractions . . . Miss Ann Miller, who scattered sex and sequins around the premises in a manner provocative of vast leering and applause . . ."

Damon Runyon, New York *Daily Mirror:* "All the talented and beautiful young ladies are coming from Texas lately. Miss Mary Martin, who is certainly one, if not the other, is from there. So is Miss Ann Miller, who is both. She is a dancer who was unveiled by George White in his new Scandals the other night. She can dance almost any other young lady dancer in the business right out of the theatre."

In a Sunday feature piece on the front page of the entertainment section of the New York *Times* for Sunday, September 3, 1939, again Brooks Atkinson, who was Broadway's most influential critic, wrote ". . . In the case of Ann Miller . . . she is an immensely skillful tap dancer with a mind and legs of her own, and she is very pleasant company whenever she appears . . ."

I was thrilled to be mentioned by another great theater critic, George Jean Nathan, who as might be expected wasn't too keen on the show as a whole but he did say that "Ann Miller does some nifty hoofing . . ." A real compliment from the great Nathan.

Then came the feature stories and photo layouts. I even made the rotogravure section of the New York *Times* in my Mexiconga costume.

Vogue magazine used a full page cover picture of me in color with the Kim Loo Sisters and their drums, with a caption which read in part:

". . . the high point is the delightful Ann Miller, who dances like a tap-dancer's dream, beating out the Mexiconga to the tom-toms of the four Chinese Kim Loo Sisters."

Women's Wear Daily did a feature page of fashion sketches of our costumes from the Mexiconga number, with a photograph of me.

Life magazine did a photo series of my dance with the caption, "A hit in George White's Scandals is Ann Miller, who, with no apparent muscles in her legs, does a slinky version of the Mexiconga."

Look magazine did a big picture layout.

My photo in the *World-Telegram* (September 23, 1939), was accompanied by an interesting caption: "Cafe society is experiencing great difficulty finding this season's Brenda Frazier, but the theatre has already patted on the head its 1939–40 Mary Martin. She's Ann Miller, a 19-year-old stunner from Houston, Texas . . . (She) has black hair, slate blue eyes, twinkling feet and a stage presence that completely charmed Manhattan's critics the night George White's Scandals opened."

The Magazine Section of the New York *Sunday Mirror* had a color cover photo in their Sunday, October 1, issue, with this caption . . . "Ann Miller, youthful principal in George White's Scandals . . . Broadway sensation of the early theatre season . . . Broadway habitue—and especially George White—are delighted with their 1939–40 season toast of the town. Last year it was Mary Martin who got all the raves and then Hollywood called her. This season it's Ann—with the transcontinental journey reversed."

A *Daily Mirror* feature described me as having "tantalizing lips and a face that is brenda-frazier white," and from then on people started calling me "the dancing Brenda Frazier."

She was that very rich and glamorous New York debutante and socialite who had very black hair and very white skin, like mine.

Mother and I lived at the Gorham, a popular hotel with show people. Mary Martin lived in the penthouse right above us for a while before she left for Hollywood. We became good friends. I admired her very much. She had been a big hit in New York in Cole Porter's musical *Leave It to Me*, in which she made famous the song, "My Heart Belongs to Daddy."

Of course, after all those rave reviews came out, Mr. White gave me a better billing in the show, almost equal with Ella Logan's, and she wasn't very happy about it.

It was during this period that I also became friends with Carmen Miranda who was appearing in the Sert Room at the Waldorf-Astoria.

But one of the biggest thrills of my whole life was seeing myself up there in lights dancing on that fabulous big electrical sign in Times Square. Not only my name in lights, but my whole body—me, Ann Miller, up there dancing in bright lights against the New York sky. I think this must have been one of the first of the fast-flashing electrical neon signs in the country. Certainly millions of tourists have stood there in awe gaping at it as the characters come on and off to advertise the newest Broadway show or movie. My name was up there in lights at the Alvin Theatre on West 52nd Street also, but to make it all the way up to that huge bright blinking sign in Times Square is like scaling the Mount Everest of Broadway.

The old gypsy woman's prediction had come true with a Wow!

I was proclaimed an overnight success, the tapster "who saved *George White's Scandals* from oblivion." They called me the "darling of Broadway," the "oomphiest dancer," the "click of the year," a "vision of sex in sequins and sables" and all sorts of other nice things.

But it all came too much and too soon. I was still too young to enjoy the fringe benefits of being such a celebrity.

I had all the rich and glamorous playboys in New York calling me for dates. And where do you think that got me? Sure, I went out with some of them. But my hard-shelled Baptist mother always tagged along. She wasn't about to let me out of her sight. She was determined to keep me as pure as the day I was born and I must say she did a fine job of it.

Oh, yes, we had some great times at those famous show-people hangouts such as the Stork Club and "21" and El Morocco. All the town's most attractive and eligible bachelors were steady habitués of these late-hour night spots, always with an eye out for Broadway's pretty showgirls. They used to sit at a big round table at El Morocco—it was known as the wolves' table—and make bets on who would be the first to take me out—*without* my mother. It became a big joke. But they didn't get very far. My

Above, with Lucille Ball and the Marx Brothers in *Room Service* (RKO, 1938). Groucho, naturally, is the one with the mustache, Chico is in the middle and Harpo is teasing me again with the leg bit. He's the one who chased me all over the set during the filming of the picture. (*RKO photo*)

Here I am with Cobina Wright Jr. at a Career Women's Fashion Show in 1939. At right is Natascha of Paris who designed the gloves. (*UPI photo*)

Mother and I with my very first pair of tap shoes which William Morgan made for me with special taps for the toes and special jingles on the heels. I named them Joe and Moe and I still have and cherish them.

A publicity still from RKO's *Too Many Girls*. Lucille Ball and
Desi Arnaz met during the filming of this picture in 1940. (*RKO photo*)

Publicity shots of my first "real" home on Laurel Drive. I loved this house. (*RKO photos*)

mother absolutely would not let me go out with any of them alone.

I had never been permitted to have dates, like other girls. At an age when I should have been going out with boys to football games and high school proms, I was being teethed on champagne and caviar and white orchids and pursued by older men.

Some were willing to take my mother along on our dates, and I suppose I should have been flattered by that—to have men interested enough to put up with a mama-hawk chaperone.

But sometimes I wished I could have a normal date with someone my own age—without my mother tagging along.

I received many expensive gifts from rich men. My mother made me send them all back. I remember one wealthy playboy who came to see me every night for a whole year. He always sat in the same seat right in front. Every night he sent flowers to my dressing room. Then he began sending other things—like diamond bracelets. I received some really fabulous pieces of jewelry from one rich man-about-town who was mad for me. He always tucked the jewelry into the long-stemmed roses which he sent backstage to my dressing room. Mother explained to me that it isn't right to accept jewelry or other expensive gifts from a man unless you're in love with him and expect to marry him. So one by one and piece by piece all my lovely gifts were always sent back to the senders. And so that was the end of that.

Sometimes now I think I was a ninny not to hide some of that loot from my mother and keep it.

In the big bulging scrapbook of my clippings from this era of my life is a story written by Kyle Crichton of the old *Collier's* magazine. There is a big color photo of me dancing, and it is a very good story about me and my background and how I started in Hollywood and came to Broadway. Of course Mr. Crichton did not know all the true facts but he must have been a very astute man. For toward the end of the rather lengthy feature piece he wrote:

"At the moment she is the toast of Broadway, with wealthy blades sending in flowers, mash notes and invitations to midnight suppers. It is somewhat embarrassing because La Miller is almost the most naive lass ever to appear on the native stage. Her mother says she is nineteen but reports from Houston say that she was born in St. Joseph's Infirmary in that city on April 12, 1923. No matter what the official date may be, the girl is a kid. It is a baffling matter. On the stage she has all the allure of Gaby Deslys, and s.a. radiating from all directions. At home she is the long-legged tomboy who lives down the street. She has never had a date with a boy alone, doesn't smoke or drink and always says her prayers before going to bed. She has a feeling that nothing she does is any good and during the road tour of Scandals it required the combined efforts of her mother, George White and assorted press agents to keep her bolstered up. When anybody says her dancing is swell, she peers up eagerly and says: 'You really mean it?'

". . . Her hair is jet black and she looks sexy and her tap routine is as miraculous as anything now extant . . .

"If the Houston statistics are correct, she is only sixteen years old. If her mother's story is right, she is nineteen. In any event she is a kid.

"She doesn't give that impression in the Scandals but she will most certainly prove that to the eager gentlemen who are wasting their time on the theory that she is Woman Incarnate. They might better be sending dolls."

The critics were right. After I was proclaimed a smash hit on Broadway, Hollywood began trying to get me back. The night after I opened—as soon as the reviews came out—I had four offers from Hollywood producers.

In my scrapbook of clippings there is a feature story about me in the New York *Journal American* of September 30, 1939: "Broadway's Magic Wand Touches Ann Miller . . ." and a picture of me resting between taps and saying, "This all seems like a dream."

Beside the story and picture is my own pen-and-ink notation, "As I sit in my apartment looking out over New York, I think how wonderful to have such good fortune, to be a hit in a show. Maybe someday I'll be in a book show and sing and act too. But Hollywood *is* tempting . . ."

Exactly thirty years later in 1969, I was to have my own book show on Broadway, taking over the lead role in *Mame*, and again to rave reviews. But that was far in the future . . .

George White's Scandals played a year in New York, and then we took the show on the road.

One of the most embarrassing moments of my life happened on our opening night in San Francisco. It was a big thrill for me to be back in the city where I was originally discovered, and especially to come back in a blaze of glory as the new-found "Toast of Broadway." My San Francisco opening should have been a big smash for me. And that's exactly what it was. A big smash, literally.

My second act in the show always followed The Three Stooges in a pie throwing skit with Ben Blue. Real pies—blueberry, custard, and lemon—were used in the skit. The Three Stooges threw the pies and slapped each other in the face with them. But there was always a big rubber mat put down on the floor to catch the pies. Well, would you believe on our opening night in San Francisco the stage manager forgot to put the rubber mat down to catch the pies, which of course I didn't know.

It all happened so fast. One minute I was standing there in my fabulous costume of black ostrich feathers . . . I struck my pose as the curtain opened and was caught in the spotlight in in this pose . . . I tippy-tapped forward in a very dramatic turn and the next thing I knew I was sliding across the stage and heading straight for the orchestra pit.

I made a crash landing on my ostrich feathers, and just in the nick of time. There was a big crunch as the feathers broke and a big splash as I kicked blueberry pie all over the conductor's white shirt and custard pies down the tuba. The whole orchestra was splattered with pie. And so was I.

I got up and shook my tail feathers and danced into the wings. The audience, fortunately, thought it was hysterically funny and clapped long and loud. Someone announced there would be a short wait for my number. Then the lights were blacked out, and some prop men came out with mops and buckets to clean up the mess. And what a mess!

Backstage everyone was trying to console me and clean me up for my number. My costume was ruined and I later ordered a new one from Madame Berthe. But that night I had to dance in the same costume. The wardrobe people washed off the feathers, cut off those that were broken, and mopped me up so that I was at least presentable. The poor musicians in the orchestra were stuck with pie all over their white shirts. As soon as the stage was ready, I went out there and did my number. And to great applause. But that's one night when I felt I had really earned it the hard way.

After touring a year with the *Scandals,* I came back to Hollywood and went immediately into another picture for RKO—but this time for $3,000 a week instead of $250.

That's how being the Toast of Broadway can boost your career in Hollywood.

My new RKO picture was *Too Many Girls* with Lucille Ball and Desi Arnaz. It was during the shooting of this movie that Lucille and Des met for the first time. The producer of the picture was George Abbott. I had met him in New York and had gone out with him, chaperoned by my mother, of course. He was much older than I but Mother liked him.

He had urged me to stay in New York and pursue my career on Broadway. Thirty years later when he came to see me in

Mame, he still remembered his advice to me when he saw me in *Scandals*.

"Annie, you damn little fool," he said, "if you'd only listened to me and stayed on Broadway and starred in one show all your own, you could have written your own ticket in Hollywood. You would have been a big, big star. But you and your mother wouldn't listen to me."

Who knows whether he was right? But at the time I was doing *Scandals*, I was still just a mixed-up kid doing my schoolwork by day and living in a grown-up's glamour world at night. And after a year on Broadway and a year on the road, I was very homesick for California, which I always considered my real home after Mother and I moved there.

Mother liked George Abbott so much that she let me go out on dates with him in Hollywood, although we were never out alone together. We were always with Lucille and Desi. The four of us became good friends. Both George and Desi loved to dance and they were marvelous dancers. They're the men who really taught me how to rhumba. The rhumba was the big craze at the time and the four of us loved going to a place called the Zarape on Sunset Boulevard, which featured some fantastic Cuban bands. Cubans from all over always came to the Zarape to rhumba. I couldn't have had two better rhumba teachers than Desi Arnaz and George Abbott.

After *Too Many Girls*, I did two pictures for Republic. The first was *Hit Parade of 1941* with Frances Langford and Kenny Baker, the one who had given me my first kiss in *Radio City Revels*.

The next was another million-dollar musical called *Melody Ranch* with Gene Autry. It was the first musical he had ever made and he especially asked for me as his leading lady. I received my second screen kiss in this one. Oddly enough, Gene told me I was the first girl he had ever kissed on the screen.

Let's just say these pictures weren't exactly smash hits. Then came another little musical for Columbia called *Time Out for Rhythm* that was to change the course of my career—and my life. I had the lead in it. Rudy Vallee was in it, too, but he didn't have much to do. The film critics didn't think much of it. But again, that eminent critic for the New York *Times*, Bosley Crowther singled me out for some kind words:

> Midsummer is no time to expect a knockout musical picture, we know. But on the basis of the title alone, one might have antici-pated more from Columbia's "Time Out for Rhythm" than what one gets . . .
>
> But the truth of the matter is that this slight picture, which opened yesterday at the Rialto, is a hopelessly heavy and labored attempt to entertain humorously; and, except for the lovely and lively Miss Miller, who simply won't be suppressed, it has the distinction of being one of the dullest diversions in months . . . *Miss Miller, when she dances, does so charmingly and with ease.* [Italics mine.]

It was this picture that ushered into my life in fast and frantic succession two of the most powerful motion picture tycoons in the history of the industry, Harry Cohn, the formidable big boss of Columbia Studios, and Louis B. Mayer, head of the huge Metro-Goldwyn-Mayer empire which he ruled over in lordly fashion. He was known as the Czar of Hollywood.

And if it hadn't been for my mother I could have been his czarina.

That first picture for Columbia, *Time Out for Rhythm*, launched a time-out-for-romance in my personal life. It signaled the end of an era for me and the beginning of another, a graduation from childhood into adulthood, if we can ever call ourselves adults. I guess I never have been. But I was finally eighteen! And I had finallly finished my schoolwork! At last! Praise be!

Time Out for Rhythm had its New York premiere in the summer of 1941. I had been cast as the lead in this musical in a one-picture deal for Columbia. By now I had changed agents. My new agents were Frank and Vic Orsatti. The Orsatti Brothers (there were many of them) were very big on the Hollywood scene, especially at M-G-M. They bought out my contract from the Morris office.

I'll never know whether Harry Cohn was more impressed with me or with Bosley Crowther's review of me as the only un-dull thing in the picture. That review certainly must have shaken him.

I had never met Mr. Cohn during shooting of the film. But soon after it was released I got a call from Vic Orsatti with the happy news that Columbia's "King" Cohn wanted to see me. Meet me. Personally. He was so pleased with me in *Time Out for Rhythm* that he wanted to turn my one-picture deal into a seven-year contract.

I could hardly wait to meet the great "King" Cohn. I was about to be launched into those "Fabulous Forties," the era which columnist Earl Wilson later described (*The Show Business Nobody Knows*) as "the King Henry VIII years of Louis B. Mayer, Harry Cohn and Darryl F. Zanuck." Those were the Golden Years of Hollywood, when the empire building dynasty was at its height, an era of star-studded glory that has long since vanished from the American scene. And what a pity!

Chapter 7

QUEEN OF THE BEES

I must say that Harry Cohn was a rather awesome sight to behold. Or at least this was my first impression of him when Vic Orsatti took me in to sign my contract.

There he was sitting behind his big desk. He looked like a large grizzly bear. And when he stood and shook hands with me, I thought he was going to break my arm, he was so big.

He was very tall, with broad shoulders, and a roar like a bear. He was a rough, tough, and gruff man and he ran his studio with an iron hand. But he had a kind, decent side to him. He was always very polite and kind to my mother and me. I'm sure he had girls, all kinds of them. But he never played the wolf-role with me and I never had any run-ins with him—until later when he wanted to sell my contract to Louis B. Mayer . . .

Harry Cohn was known as one of the most hated men in

Hollywood. He kept a riding crop on his desk which he was apt to pick up and crack at anyone who got out of line. But I always felt that his bark was much worse than his bite.

He put me in a little nothing-picture called *Go West, Young Lady*, with Penny Singleton, Glenn Ford, and Charlie Ruggles. Again I was singled out by critics: ". . . The brightest item by far is Ann Miller, the hectic little lady from Texas who trips rhythmically . . ."

And thus began my reign at Columbia as Queen of the Bees, as I became known, for turning out quickie B pictures during those early years of World War II.

Among my most notable ones was a happy-hearted little film called *Reveille with Beverly*, which really cleaned up at the box office, racking in millions more than the $400,000 which Columbia spent to make it. It was the story of a female disc jockey who played records and talked to the boys in the armed services with messages from home. The movie was a smash hit among the armed forces. And not only because of Ann Miller. It featured some of the biggest bands in a big-band era—Bob Crosby, Duke Ellington, Count Basie, Freddie Slack. And it also featured a new young singer in his very first motion picture, Frank Sinatra. I'll never forget it. A record would start to spin, then the cameras would pan into the record while the voice came on, and then to Frank's face with a big band backing him. Even way back then he was great, his voice sent tingles up your spine. And to think—the name Ann Miller (as well as a few others) topped him in the billing. How times do change!

Soon after Harry Cohn came into my life, with that seven-year contract and a hit picture or two, I bought our first home for my mother and me. It was gorgeous! I suppose any home at this stage of my life would have seemed gorgeous to me, but this one truly was. It was a Frank Lloyd Wright house, built on four levels, high in the Hollywood Hills overlooking the lights of the city. On a clear day you could see Catalina and the snowcapped peaks of Mr. Baldy.

We didn't have smog in those days.

It was a typical Aries home . . . you could go from heaven to hell in four seconds! The top floor was one large room where the former owner had kept a huge organ, and from the windows you could see for hundreds of miles in all directions. On the next level down was our "receiving" hall, our bedrooms, and the dining room which looked out on our Japanese garden. On the level below that was our sunken living room, with a baby grand piano and two enormous bay windows.

I furnished the house with all custom-made furniture and antiques.

Mother let me spoil myself a bit when I did my bedroom. It was done all in white and deep pink—white satin curtains, throw pillows of red American rose. The walls were a faint shade of strawberry pink. I had a large dressing room with white rugs, a white bedspread trimmed in deep rose satin and mirrored walls and a dressing table in white satin.

My dear friend Linda Darnell loved that room. She was always saying she wished her mother would let her have one like it.

And there was the playroom on the bottom level. We called it Miller's High Life Room and it was really wild. Jungle scenes on the wall, lions and tigers fighting, monkeys hanging from trees, elephants in the forest . . . We installed a couple of fake palm trees, a big fireplace, and a ceiling with little lights that went on and off. And when people came down the stairs, the first thing they saw was the figure of a tall witch doctor, wearing a black high top silk hat, a grass skirt and bangles, and holding a bottle of beer.

Miller High Life, of course.

My bar was a thatched hut with a fake skull hanging over it. And I had a big banner stretched across the top of the doorway, saying MILLER'S HIGH LIFE ROOM.

I didn't drink (my mother saw to that) but that room—in that house—was a wonder place for parties.

Marlon Brando later bought the house, after I started on my marrying sprees and moved out.

But at this stage of my career at Columbia everything looked rosy, for a change. Mother and I were at last living like human beings, eating three regular meals a day. We had bought a car. I remember how thrilled I was that I could buy my mother a brand new car. And now she could afford to go to the beauty salon to have her hair set and her nails done, instead of doing them at home.

Those "King" Cohn years were very happy ones for me. Johnnie Lucille Collier seemed long ago and far away. The Ann Miller image of movieland was being born, the public image that has stuck with me most of my life. Ann Miller, the dancer. Ann Miller, Hollywood party girl. Ann Miller and Men. Ah, men, men, men. I suppose Ann Miller's name has been linked with more high-flying, free-spending party playboys and millionaires than anyone else in Hollywood with the possible exception of Zsa Zsa Gabor. I do not mean this to be boasting. I think it happens to be true. Zsa Zsa has remained my good friend in spite of the fact that I once dated all over the world with one of her ex-husbands, Conrad Hilton. But that one was purely platonic.

Zsa Zsa has always been generous with her former husbands. She even encouraged one of them, the late George Sanders, to marry her sister, Magda, but that didn't last long.

Connie Hilton was one of the three older men in my life. The other two were Louis B. Mayer and Arthur Cameron. I suppose a psychiatrist would say I was attracted to all of them because I had a father complex.

At the time, though, I felt I was attracted to them because they all loved to dance and they were all marvelous dancers.

I was mad for dancing, not only on screen but off. And after I reached the age of eighteen, my mama-hawk finally decided to let me go out alone with a handful of men who met with her approval. I think she was beginning to worry a little about being too overly protective, so she would sometimes let me go out with a man on an early dinner-and-dancing date. But I always had to be home by twelve, just like Cinderella. And if my date didn't get me back in time, I was not allowed to go out with him again.

Looking back now, I feel sure that part of my problems with men stemmed from the fact that I had to grow up too fast and assume the responsibilities of an adult, and I had simply skipped the normal boy-girl dating relationship that most youngsters experience while they are in school. When I did finally start going out with men, they were not men my own age, they were all older. And because of the kind of business I was in, most of the men I met were very rich or very social, or very influential. Many were involved in some phase of the motion picture business.

Though I was of legal age now, and had been our breadwinner for a few years, I think I was probably too immature to cope with men, at least the kind of men I was meeting. I often wonder what turn my life might have taken if I could have dated just ordinary boys my own age when I was a teen-ager and in my early twenties—instead of all those not-so-ordinary men of the glamour world I was living in.

One of my most frequent escorts was my agent, Vic Orsatti, but there was nothing romantic between us. It is the custom for Hollywood agents to be seen with their clients, to escort them to parties and see that they make the rounds of all the "in" places. Vic was madly in love with Linda Darnell at the time, and we often double-dated.

Another of my escorts was Warren Cowan who was to become one of Hollywood's top press agents. He later married the beautiful Barbara Rush. They are now divorced.

I went out a great deal with wealthy, society playboy types such as Al Bloomingdale, of the Bloomingdale department store family, and Jerry Orbach, of the Orbach's department stores, but my most serious suitor in my early dating years was shoe tycoon, Harry Karl, the man who married Debbie Reynolds after that debacle with Eddie Fisher.

Many of the men I went out with lavished expensive gifts on me, but my mother still always made me give them back. Mother liked Harry Karl, though. She let me keep a watch he gave me for my birthday and a small ring. He was a kind man.

I worked very hard and long hours at the studio and during the filming of a picture I never went out in the evening. But between pictures, or when I had a few days off, I loved to go out dancing. This was such a glamorous era in Hollywood and though I had been on the scene a long time, it was almost as if I was starting all over again and tasting for the first time the *real* Hollywood that I had read about. Places like the Mocambo and Ciro's were always filled with the really big stars of that era—Lana Turner, Ava Gardner, Ginger Rogers, Hedy Lamarr, and Joan Bennett—who parted her hair in the middle at that time because she was trying to look like Hedy.

Hollywood was gay, glittering, and exciting. Everyone went out on the town—dinner at LaRue's or Romanoff's or Victor Hugo's or Chez Roland at the Beach . . . There were great restaurants in those days.

And then to the Mocambo or Ciro's to dance, dance, dance. I never got my fill of dancing. "I Could Have Danced All Night" might have been written for me.

And how I loved to dress up! When I was filming a picture, I worked so hard in those bleak studio rehearsal halls and I was always dressed in tennis shoes and sweaty leotards. All during the long hours and weeks of rehearsing, I lived for those days off when I could get dressed up in something pretty and go out dancing. It gave me real physical pleasure to wear glamorous and feminine clothes.

And I went through certain crazes and I started collecting

things—hats, earrings, perfumes. I love anything feminine and to this day when a woman walks into a room I can always tell her the name of the perfume she is wearing and the house that makes it. I had a wild collection of earrings.

And hats! Every time I had a date I would go out and buy a new hat and a different kind of perfume. I literally had a different hat for every date. Mink hats, flowered hats, chiffon hats—all kinds. You name it, I had it. The Mocambo gave a prize every night to the lady with the most glamorous hat. Linda Darnell and I came home with most of the prizes. They also had Charleston contests and the winner was given a little silver champagne bucket. One night I remember Ginger Rogers and I tied as winners and we got a great ovation. Can you imagine both of us up there on that dance floor doing the Charleston? It brought down the house. Ginger was discovered in Texas doing the Charleston.

Yes, those were the Fabulous Forties and I was there, lapping it up like a kid at Santa Claus time.

I'll never forget that big cage full of exotic parrots that hung up above the swirling dance floor of the Mocambo, which was run by Hollywood's then most popular supper-club hosts, Mary and Charlie Morrison. It broke my heart when the Mocambo was torn down. That was the end of an era.

Another popular place to see and to be seen was Ciro's. I happened to be there one night when Marlene Dietrich came in, dressed in a fantastic beaded gown and a floor length white fox coat. There were spotlights at the entrance and three or four steps leading down into the room, and Marlene stopped for just a moment at the top and struck a glamorous pose. Naturally, all heads turned to look at her but as she started down, her foot caught in the hem of the dress and she fell flat on her glamorous face. It was quite an unglamorous entrance. But very funny. To me.

Maria Montez became a star by being seen at Ciro's. She had a little trick she'd pull to make sure she was seen. She always

sat at a table as far away as she could find one from the
ladies' and gents' washrooms. Then she would make five or six
trips a night clear across the room to go to the john, and
always flouncing herself sexily as she went by all the tables,
intending for every male in the room to notice her. Which
they did. Some of those males were important producers and
directors. Miss Montez also sometimes bumped into more males
emerging from the men's room. She always said she was going
to be a star some day and word got around that she finally
made it by going to the john at Ciro's. I'll bet a lot of
people just thought she had bladder trouble.

I also happened to be at Ciro's the night of that famous—or
infamous—"incident," when a very popular and beautiful dark-
haired Big Star actually made love to a well-known director
behind the bar. I think if my mother had known about it,
she would never have let me go there again. By the next
morning everybody else in town knew about it and by now
it has become part of the scandalous Hollywood folklore.

I made one picture after another at Columbia and believe me
it wasn't easy. Contrary to popular opinion the movie business
isn't all glamour. I had to get up at dawn to be at the studio
and in make-up by six o'clock. Mother always drove me to
work and came after me when I finished. Many times, after
working in front of the cameras all day, I would go to the
rehearsal hall and work until ten or eleven at night, preparing
and rehearsing my numbers for the next day's shooting. Then
to bed dead tired and up again for the next day's grind.

All my pictures for Columbia, I am the first to admit, were
only B pictures. That's why I was known as Queen of the
Bees. I was no big star but the critics invariably singled me out
for quite flattering comments on my singing and dancing and
my legs, and sometimes my flair for comedy. I didn't mind
doing the B pictures (the money was good) though I hoped

that someday Harry Cohn would think I was good enough to start putting me in A pictures.

There's one thing for sure, he couldn't have been too unhappy with me because all my pictures made money at the box office, and that's what counts with the producers. My little old B pictures only cost $300,000 to $400,000 to make—but they made millions for Columbia.

During my reign as Queen of the Bees, the reigning sex goddess at Columbia was Rita Hayworth. Her pictures made a fortune for Harry Cohn. There was a while when Mr. Cohn used me as a threat to Rita, because she was always going off and marrying various people like Orson Welles and Aly Khan, and leaving her career temporarily. This made Mr. Cohn very nervous, as he had a great deal of money invested in Rita.

So, when he wanted her back for a certain picture, he would tell her that unless she reported on such and such a day, he would put another star in the movie—like Ann Miller or Janet Blair. That always brought her back.

I had first met Rita at the Fanchon & Marco Dancing School when she was Rita Casino and doing a dancing act with her father. At twelve years old she was as tall as I was, quite well developed, and dancing professionally. Her start in films paralleled mine. In fact, we had actually signed our contracts in films the same day, I at RKO, she at Fox.

I have mentioned Linda Darnell, who became and remained one of my closest friends until her tragic death in Chicago in 1965.

Linda was under contract at 20th Century-Fox while I was at Columbia. We met for the first time on Catalina Island, where our respective studios had sent us to represent them at a big benefit. Comparing notes, Linda and I found that we had quite a lot in common and we hit it off from the start. We were both from Texas and both had started our careers when we were very young. And yes, Linda had also lied about her age.

Linda lived with her mother, too, and the two of them often

came to my home, and while the two mama-hens clucked, we would gossip about our two studios and all the goings-on there. We found that we had something else in common. While Harry Cohn was using me as a threat to Rita Hayworth, Darryl Zanuck was using Linda to keep Loretta Young in line. He was also dating Bella Darvi and Gene Tierney while she was doing *Razor's Edge* at Fox.

Ah, girl talk. Linda and I became fast buddies and then at another big benefit I met M-G-M's Kathryn Grayson, and we became a close threesome.

Columbia was shooting *Cover Girl* with Rita Hayworth and Harry Cohn imported some beautiful models from New York to be in the picture with her. He rented a big house for them in Beverly Hills and put Anita Colby in charge. Those models were kept in that house like hens in a hen house, with Anita keeping a sharp eye on them and Mr. Cohn's guard at the door. The girls, of course, were very unhappy at this arrangement because they wanted to go out at night with their boy friends. Mr. Cohn wanted them to look fresh and beautiful when they reported for work in the morning. I must say Mr. Cohn was a tough taskmaster when it came to keeping his cover girls in line.

I had nothing to do with *Cover Girl* but during shooting of the picture, I was chosen as the studio's representative at a big benefit in Boston for the Russian War Relief. And one of the imported models for *Cover Girl*, beautiful Jinx Falkenburg, was chosen to go with me. We had a glorious time. And it was at this benefit that I first heard Kathryn Grayson sing. I'll never forget hearing her hit that high note when she sang "The Star-Spangled Banner." I thought it was the most fantastic thing I'd ever heard, and when I told her so later, it was the beginning of a close friendship that has lasted to this day.

Chapter 8

ANNIE CZARINA

I had heard terrible things about Louis B. Mayer. He was known as the mean old Czar of Hollywood.

I never saw that side of Louis B. Mayer. And I'm glad I didn't. I knew him only as a very kind man with a soft heart, a man who loved beauty and goodness, a man who respected respectability. If he were alive today I'm sure he would go out and shoot the movie producers who are responsible for the kind of filth they're turning out now.

Louis B. Mayer was a Russian Jew who rose from a rag-picker and junk-dealer to head of the largest movie studio in Hollywood, Metro-Goldwyn-Mayer, and he reigned over the most glittering stable of stars in the history of the film industry. From Judy Garland to Joan Crawford and all the in betweens.

I first met Mr. Mayer in 1944 while he was on the rebound from a broken romance with singer Ginny Simms.

We were introduced through my agents, the Orsattis.

Frank Orsatti was one of Mr. Mayer's close companions.

He was terribly concerned at Mr. Mayer's state of mind after Ginny Simms turned him down to marry someone else. According to all the reports at the time, Mr. Mayer was so brokenhearted that he wept for days. He had pulled the same Camille act when another love-of-his-life, Jean Howard, ditched him to marry that well-known agent, Charlie Feldman.

This "mean old Czar" of Hollywood was a sentimentalist who cried easily, as everyone who knew him soon learned.

I have no idea how many broken romances Mr. Mayer had been involved in when I met him. I was like twenty, going on twenty-one, but still living in the glass bubble which my hard-shelled Baptist mother had kept me incubated in, and so I probably had the emotional maturity of a fourteen-year-old.

As a result I was to experience my first "school girl crush" on Louis B. Mayer, and he was old enough to be my father. At least. He was in fact my father surrogate, as they call it.

Mr. Mayer loved to dance, and that's how I came into the picture, after Ginny. He was in a state of depression and Vic Orsatti told his brother Frank, "Annie Miller is just the girl to bring him out of this. She's always so gay and happyhearted and she loves to dance. She's a good girl, too, a real mother's girl, and you know how L.B. loves mothers."

So the Orsattis gave a lovely dinner party at Frank's fabulous home in Bel Air to introduce my mother and me to Louis B. Mayer.

I'll never forget it.

Among other things Frank Orsatti was known for his wild parties and his orchids. He raised orchids, and I remember when we were ushered into his hillside mansion I was dazzled by the sight of orchids, orchids everywhere.

This wasn't one of Frank's wild parties. After all, my mother was there. And L.B. hated wild parties. He was a very proper man.

At the time I didn't know that Mr. Mayer had this fetish about mothers, but I guess everyone else knew it. He had worshiped his mother when she was alive and he adored my mother from the moment he met her. I am sure that is one reason he was attracted to me. I was truly a mother's girl, if ever there was one. He may have had his flings with wild women but basically Louis B. Mayer respected a girl who was a lady, who was morally a "nice" girl, a "good" girl—and especially one who could remain so in the sometimes morally corrupt community of movie stars that he reigned over. Mr. Mayer, I was to learn, had problems aplenty with his great stable of stars. No wonder they drove him to tears. Lana Turner and Ava Gardner were two of his prize problem stars. He was always getting them out of scraps of one kind or another.

My mother and I were thrilled and awed to meet this great man who was head of the biggest movie studio and film colony in the world, the man who was known as the tyrannical Czar of Hollywood.

I remember listening to him talk at the dinner table that night and thinking how brilliant and brainy he was, talking "trade-talk" that was incomprehensible to me but instinctively I knew it was important.

After dinner, as we were milling about the living room, Mr. Mayer came over to me and said, "I have enjoyed your dancing on the screen so much, Miss Miller. Perhaps you would give me the pleasure of permitting me to take you out to dinner—and dancing?"

For once I was at a loss for words. The big M-G-M mogul asking a Columbia contract player for a date?

Number one, of course, I knew my mother wouldn't let me go out with a man that old. He was in his late fifties, around fifty-nine, I would say, though I don't think anyone ever knew his exact age, but he should have been asking my mother out instead of me.

I remember looking pleadingly at my agent Vic Orsatti who was standing beside me, and as though reading my thoughts he said, "It's all right, Annie. You can bring your mother. Mr. Mayer loves mothers."

And Mr. Mayer added gallantly, "Of course I meant your mother would come with us. She is a very beautiful and charming woman."

With that he crossed the room and invited my mother to go dining and dancing with us.

That's how it all started.

My mother always went along on my dates with Louis B. Mayer because he always invited her. She was a very beautiful lady and she was great fun even if she didn't know how to dance. He enjoyed just sitting and talking to her. Even if she had known how to dance, she would have been petrified to dance with the great Louis B. Mayer. But I wasn't. I wore out more nice shoes dancing with him than anyone else. He was a superb dancer. He had feet of gold and he loved to fly around the dance floor. And what's more, he never stepped on my feet.

I'll never forget dancing with that Argentine dictator, Juan Perón, one time when I was on a junket down in South America. He was quite smitten with me and when we danced the tango, he held me so close I couldn't breathe and stomped all over my poor feet until I felt like a cripple.

It was a big thrill for me to be courted by a man of such eminence as Louis B. Mayer. He was not a handsome man but he was brilliant and he had compassion and he was kind. He was virile and strong, with a big neck, broad shoulders, and the muscular build of a man half his age. I must say he looked and acted much younger than he actually was. He was born on July 4, a typical Cancer, with the personality of a bull. He had energy, he was vital, and he had a commanding presence. When he walked into a room, you knew it. Every head turned to attention. His personality was so strong that it took over the room. He didn't need to be tall or beautiful of face. He walked with a lofty and regal air. He had great personal magnetism and charm.

I found him physically attractive because of his masculine
vitality combined with his gentleness of manner. I suppose he
wasn't always so gentle in his business affairs. I had heard that
he could be very tough and that he liked to play God. But I
never knew that side of him. In my presence and in the presence
of others we went out with, he was always a perfect gentleman, always impeccably groomed and as impeccable in his manner and behavior. I am sure he had a genuine love of beauty
and goodness or he could not have turned out the kind of motion
pictures that he did, many of which became classics.

In my eyes then and upon reflection now he seemed to be a
very sensitive man who was sometimes hurt by the ugly ways
of life, especially of the business he was in. He didn't like ugly
language. I never heard him use curse words or obscene language.
I never heard him tell dirty jokes or off-color stories.

I never knew him to be anything but utterly gracious, charming, attentive, and solicitous of the comforts of others around
him.

I especially noticed how gentle he always was with women—
with my mother and me and the others we frequently met when
with him.

In a room, in a large gathering, his power and forcefulness
could be felt immediately, but on a more personal level there
was a softness about him that I found rather appealing.

He had great respect and tenderness for the feminine sex.
Perhaps it was his heritage and background that developed in
him such strong feelings on the sanctity of motherhood and
home. He could get very emotional about it, even melodramatic.

He was truly a sentimentalist, a romanticist, an idealist.

Well, so was I. Change that. Make it—so am I. Incredible as
it may seem, after all these years I am still waiting for my Prince
Charming to come riding along on a white horse and swoop me
up and off to some fantasyland. And I don't mean Disney World.
If I'm still like this now, you can picture how I must have been
when L. B. Mayer entered my life on the rebound from Ginny.

Not that I considered him my Prince Charming. He was a little older than I imagined any Prince Charming ought to be. But he would do until one came along.

That eminent critic again, Bosley Crowther, who always seemed to have a kind word to say for me, duly took note of our courtship in a flattering way in his book, *Hollywood Rajah . . . The Life and Times of Louis B. Mayer* (Holt, 1960).

". . . the peak of personal triumph and glory for Louie Mayer was reached and maintained in the decade after 1938. For it was in those ten years that he was able to exercise and enjoy the authority, wealth, and personal freedom that he had battled all his life to attain . . . Now he was on top, unchallenged, a Hollywood rajah in every respect . . .

"In the next few years he showed amazing physical vitality and was unrestrained in courting several prominent actresses. Ann Miller, a long-legged dancer at Metro-Goldwyn-Mayer [*wrong, I wasn't at M-G-M yet*], was a frequent decorative companion in his regular night-club hops. It was evident that he chose tall, graceful, lovely and distinctly non-Semitic types to be his partners in public. He was sensitive about his own Semitic looks."

For whatever reasons Louis B. Mayer chose me it was all right with me. I had the time of my young life helping him recuperate from his brokenhearted romance. My little flirtation with L.B., as I called him—*never* Louie—happened along just about in the middle of his "peak of personal triumph and glory," as Mr. Crowther called it.

His idea of relaxation was to gather up some good friends and their dates—often his brother Jerry and the Orsattis—and my mother and me, and go to the Mocambo for dinner and dancing.

Then there were those fabulous and famous Sunday-night dinner parties that he gave at his home, a palatial mansion at 910 Benedict Canyon Drive in Beverly Hills, and his whole stable of stars would be there—Spencer Tracy, Clark Gable, Greer Garson, Ava Gardner, Lana Turner, Hedy Lamarr, Esther Williams, and on and on. During our little whirlwind courtship, my mother and I were always included in those happyhearted evenings.

Mr. Mayer's Benedict Canyon home had a very long dining room with two separate tables that would seat sixteen persons each. He would put these two tables together to make a long banquet table, and he would preside over his buffet feast in high style, like a potentate.

Then when it was over he would gather up his little family of stars—he *always* looked on them as his family—and my mother and me, and off we would go to the Mocambo to dance the evening away. I must say Mr. Mayer and I were very often the most attention-getting couple on the Mocambo dance floor. And I loved it! (Confidentially, I think he did, too.)

We didn't go dancing *every* night. Sometimes after dinner Mr. Mayer would shepherd us all into his big projection room to see a new movie that had not been released yet. Or maybe he would show us screen tests of people he was considering for an M-G-M contract.

Little did I know then that I would one day be mistress of this very same house at 910 Benedict Canyon Drive. The palatial mansion in Beverly Hills was to be my home during a short frantic period of my life when I was married to Arthur Cameron.

The house was, in fact, quite a famous one, as Hollywood houses go. It had once been the original Marion Davies dressing room on the M-G-M lot, the one Mr. Mayer had built for this star-lady and her publisher-consort, William Randolph Hearst. It had been used to entertain numerous nabobs and visiting dignitaries at M-G-M, and then when the Hearst-Davies-Mayer alliance broke up, it was dismantled and moved in three sections first to the Warners lot and then to Mr. Mayer's five-and-a-half acres on Benedict Canyon Drive.

He built onto it, of course, and it became known as one of the fabulous Hearst estates. Marion Davies and Hearst had lived there for a while, and I do believe the house was haunted by

Walter Winchell interviewed me on his coast-to-coast radio show on a Sunday evening in 1937. Mr. Winchell was the one who nicknamed me Annie "Legs" Miller—the lucky "legs" tag has stuck with me throughout my career. (*RKO photo*)

Walt Disney was a friend, and a very dear man. On the left is André Kostelanetz and we were all having a Coke together in 1938. (*Photo by Christy Shepherd Studio*)

I celebrated a double birthday party with Jane Withers in 1943. I was twenty and she was seventeen. With us are Linda Darnell and Mrs. Withers. Fate is strange—I later married Jane's ex-husband, Bill Moss.

A Columbia Pictures publicity photo titled "Greetings to 1946."

My baby shower in October 1946, when I was married to my first husband, Reese Milner. Linda Darnell was a blond then because she was making *Forever Amber* at 20th Century-Fox. That's Marjorie Reynolds on the right. They were also bridesmaids at my first wedding. (*Columbia photo*)

their spirits forever after. I know I certainly wasn't very happy
when I lived there later as Arthur Cameron's wife, and my friend
Kathryn Grayson always said the house gave her the creeps.

But Louis B. Mayer lived in it and ruled it like a king. And
I loved the house on Benedict Canyon when Mr. Mayer had it.
Many times after everyone else had left Mother and I would
stay with him and talk far into the night . . . And many times
at all hours the telephone would ring and it would be one of
those big Hollywood star-ladies wanting to come over and hold
L.B.'s hand—meaning spend the night—in return for a certain
part in a certain film. I could hear his part of the conversation,
of course, and sometimes he would wink at Mother and me, and
the lady at the other end of the line had no idea we were there.

It took me awhile to catch on that they weren't calling just to
say hello.

I remember one night especially when Mother and I stayed
with Mr. Mayer after the others left, discussing a big musical he
planned to make. He was considering borrowing me from Columbia for a role in it but nothing ever came of that. He was in the
midst of casting the lead roles in a dramatic film, and had nar-
rowed his choice of female leads down to two prominent actresses.

We were sitting there chatting when the telephone rang. It
was one of the two stars he was considering and she was inviting
herself over to spend the night. Within twenty minutes the
other leading contender for the role called with the same prop-
osition.

I believe this was the first time I was ever aware that Hollywood stars or starlets so willingly, even eagerly, went to bed
with movie producers to get roles in their movies.

I remember Louis B. Mayer saying to me on this particular
occasion, "You see, Ann, this is why I like you. You would
never do anything like that. This is the ugly side of Hollywood."

Don't get me wrong. I'm not all that naïve. I'm sure Mr.
Mayer had many of his star-lady friends over to spend the night

with him or vice versa. He may have enjoyed them but he did not respect them.

He often came to our home for dinner. His chauffeur would drive him over and then stand at attention outside the house until he was ready to leave. We had a full-time Texas cook then and L.B. loved her roast beef, her spinach soufflés and her chocolate soufflés. He always brought his favorite whiskey with him. Rock and Rye. He often told me that he loved coming to my home because he loved music—and I always had records playing.

We could hear the records in the dining room while we were having dinner. It was quiet at my house for L.B., away from the phones, the studio and all his troubles . . . and he would sit and talk to Mother and me for hours.

And sometimes after dinner he would take me walking up and down the streets of Beverly Hills—*alone!* It wasn't often my mama-hawk ever let us out of her sight . . . only for a few minutes at the door when we came home from the Mocambo and on those occasional moonlight strolls down the palm-lined streets of Beverly Hills.

Surprisingly, my mother had let me keep the gifts L. B. Mayer gave me—a topaz ring for Christmas, a diamond and ruby bracelet watch for my twenty-second birthday.

But when he proposed marriage to me, all hell broke loose. Absolutely no way, said my mother. Czar or no Czar.

I remember my agent, Vic Orsatti, arguing with my mother, "Mrs. Miller, think of the advantages. This man owns the town. He's the Czar of Hollywood."

And my mother would say, "So you want Annie to be the Czarina? Heavens no, he's much too old for her."

Vic would say, "It's better to be an old man's darling than a young man's slave." How truly prophetic.

My mother was fond of L. B. Mayer but she simply thought he was too old for me and she couldn't be budged from her position. I sometimes wonder what would have happened if I had married Mr. Mayer. I'm sure my mother also has often wondered whether she did the right thing in discouraging our friendship . . .

I think one reason Mr. Mayer fancied himself in love with me was that he was lonely. He was constantly surrounded by important people—big-name stars, celebrities, and prominent persons outside the film industry, such as William Randolph Hearst and Francis Cardinal Spellman of New York. But deep inside he was a very lonely man, who wanted badly to have something he could call his own, someone who wouldn't run out and cheat on him, someone he could trust.

Another reason Louis B. Mayer was attracted to me, I think, was that he knew or sensed that I was as virginal as the day I was born.

How could I have been otherwise?

In some ways L. B. Mayer was very much like my mother with his own two daughters, Edith and Irene. He had been a very strict parent while his daughters were growing up, forbidding them to have dates until they were virtually grown, and then diligently screening their escorts and demanding of them that they bring his daughters home by midnight. He and my mother would have made a great pair!

And in one way he was like my father. He wanted a son, poor man, and all he got was girls.

I'm sure one of the reasons my mother even let me go out with a man so much older was that she was very much aware of Mr. Mayer's father-image fulfillment for me. But she kept her sharp hawk's eye ever alert to detect the slightest transgression on his part.

He pleaded with her to let me marry him. She continued to adamantly refuse.

He also wanted to buy out my contract from Harry Cohn. And Mr. Cohn refused.

I was not in love with Louis B. Mayer. I was just so in awe of him and flattered that he liked me enough to want to marry me. And I think I might have gone ahead and married him even against my mother's wishes if I had not suddenly found myself in the middle of a little plot that was thickening in a way I did not like at all.

Gradually I sensed that I was being pushed into marriage with L. B. Mayer by people other than Mr. Mayer himself and for the most appalling reasons.

While the Orsattis were urging my mother to let me marry him, Harry Cohn was also encouraging me in his own fatherly way—and discreetly—to marry Mr. Mayer. Why would he want me to marry the head of a rival studio?

Then one day Harry Cohn called me in and said he was going to star me in a lavish big musical called *The Petty Girl*. It was to be my first A picture, and a big break for me. Mr. Cohn had bought the picture especially for me. The Petty Girls were all the rage at the time. They were those long-legged beauties drawn by George Petty and featured in *Esquire* magazine. Since I was known primarily for my legs, Mr. Cohn said he thought I would be perfect for the lead.

Of course this would have been a tremendous coup for me and I was walking around on Cloud Nine until the rumors finally caught up with me and everything started to add up.

On the surface it all seemed *kosher* but the wheels had started turning in Harry Cohn's head. He had used me as a sometime threat against Rita Hayworth. Now he was hatching up another plot to use me as a bargaining tool with Louis B. Mayer. Mr. Cohn always kept a close eye on the personal activities of his contract players, and as soon as he knew that Mr. Mayer's ardor for me had deepened to the point of a marriage proposal, he went into action.

Mr. Mayer had already once offered to buy out my contract from Columbia and Cohn had refused—but only because he saw a better opportunity.

Up to this time I had been only in B pictures. By starring me in an A picture, especially one as expensive and important as *The Petty Girl*, my contract asking price would go up. Like maybe to $250,000 or $300,000. Those were the figures being bandied about. Louis B. Mayer could afford it. And there was no doubt that he wanted Ann Miller—both as a young bride and as a dancing addition to his own M-G-M stable of stars.

So my jump from Queen of the Bees to a big musical A picture was going to be Harry Cohn's *pièce de résistance* in selling me like a race horse to Louis B. Mayer and Metro-Goldwyn-Mayer.

And my agents, the Orsattis, were undoubtedly rubbing their hands with glee at the thought of all that money they would make on the deal when L. B. Mayer bought my contract, which they were sure he would.

All of this, of course, was going on behind my back. When I found out about it I was furious. I felt like a lamb being fattened up for the slaughterhouse. So, as they say in Texas, I jumped the corral and blew the whole scene—the M-G-M contract, Columbia contract, L. B. Mayer, everything. I blew it all. And look where it got me. Nowhere.

Chapter 9

FORGIVE ME, L.B.

Louis B. Mayer was a great influence in my life and I'm proud of it. He was known as the most powerful of Hollywood's famed tycoons. He was a self-made man and his was a fantastic success story. He rose from a ragpicker to become the highest salaried man in the United States. And he was at the peak of his success when he asked me to be his wife.

Despite the difference in our ages—nearly forty years—I think I could have been happy with him. Certainly our May–September relationship was a happy one.

True, he had an immensely complex personality. It was said that he was subject to melodramatic "seizures" and fainting and crying spells to get his way and that he was ruthless in his business dealings. But I never saw that side of him.

He was one of the greatest gentlemen I've ever met in show business.

He was my idol, both personally and professionally. Throughout our courtship I remained in awe of him as a film producer.

After all, he was the head of the biggest, most glittering film factory of them all—Metro-Goldwyn-Mayer. He was the top man in the Golden Age of motion pictures, turning out great films from *Ben Hur* and *The Big Parade* to *The Good Earth* and *Battleground*, and commanding armies of producers, directors, and stars—many of the screen's most famous and idolized personalities.

It was Louis B. Mayer (with Irving Thalberg) who started the fabulous star system, who discovered and/or molded the careers of such all-time screen greats as Greta Garbo, Greer Garson, Judy Garland, and Clark Gable; who gave us those marvelous musicals of the '30s and '40s and the popular Andy Hardy pictures with Mickey Rooney.

Judy and Mickey in their youth were definitely reflective of the taste and sentiment of Louis B. Mayer. No other studio had such a galaxy of child stars and teen-agers as M-G-M, and many prominent young actresses were graduates of the Andy Hardy movies—including Lana Turner, Kathryn Grayson, Esther Williams, and Donna Reed. Jane Powell was a top teen-age singing star at M-G-M for several years. And then there were Freddie Bartholomew and Jackie Cooper and a little girl named Elizabeth and a dog named Lassie.

All of these were a part of Louis B. Mayer's film family. He took a personal interest in them and in shaping their careers.

From Louis B. Mayer came films of great beauty and music, films that had heart and soul and love and perhaps a little bit of a message—films such as *Captains Courageous, Boys Town, Mrs. Miniver, The Wizard of Oz*, and *Meet Me in St. Louis, Easter Parade*, and all those Eleanor Powell *Broadway Melody* films, and Myrna Loy and William Powell in the Thin Man series.

It was Louis B. Mayer who had the courage to sign Katharine Hepburn for *The Philadelphia Story* after a prominent New York exhibitor called her "boxoffice poison." Her next M-G-M picture was a comedy, *Woman of the Year*, in which she was teamed with Spencer Tracy—and that was the beginning of all the great Tracy and Hepburn films.

He had an elusive, intangible ability to recognize star qualities and the ability to develop them. No matter what else has been said or written about Louis B. Mayer, I still say that a man who can assemble such great talent and turn out the kind of motion pictures he did was basically a man who had love in his heart. And when he died in 1957, the film industry as I knew it died with him.

As a young contract player in B pictures at Columbia, I would have given literally anything—well, almost—to join L. B. Mayer's family of stars at M-G-M.

But I could not do it the way Harry Cohn was trying to manipulate it.

Everyone in town knew that I was going out with L. B. Mayer. And I knew that if Mr. Cohn sold my contract to Mr. Mayer, no one would ever believe that I had any talent. They would say I became a star because of Mr. Mayer's romantic interest in me, or because I was going to bed with him—like some of the others I knew about. The fact that I wasn't didn't change my way of thinking.

You see, there was a difference between me and those big-name stars. I hadn't made it there yet. I was still only in B pictures. At first I was ecstatic when Harry Cohn told me he was going to star me in *The Petty Girl*. But when I learned about the whole plot behind it, I was shattered.

I wanted to become a big star on my own talent, not with a FOR SALE sign on my legs or on a producer's casting couch.

I'm sure that if Harry Cohn's scheme had worked or if I had married L. B. Mayer and let him take over my career he could have made me a big star, as he had others.

In retrospect, I guess maybe I should add that to the list of the lulu mistakes I've made.

But at the time, I was virginal, ambitious, and naïve. I felt that

Harry Cohn was pushing me into a trap and this was the beginning of the end of my romance with L. B. Mayer.

I couldn't bring myself to tell him of Mr. Cohn's bargaining plot with me. I knew that there was great competition between the two studios, and between Harry Cohn and Louis B. Mayer. Columbia was a small but mighty studio, though Mr. Cohn of course was not quite as powerful as L. B. Mayer, and I am sure he was envious of Mr. Mayer's social position as well as his kingpin niche in the industry. But they were on friendly terms, and they were always very respectful of each other.

Mr. Mayer thought it was wonderful that Mr. Cohn was going to finally star me in an A picture, *The Petty Girl*. I'm sure he would have been very hurt if he had known the plot behind it. L.B. himself was still patiently trying to persuade my mother to let me marry him and he refused to give up hope that she would one day change her mind. He was willing to wait.

So respectful was he of my mother that I doubt whether he really would have married me against her wishes.

But with our courtship now complicated by Harry Cohn's career-manipulating—what a feather it would have been in Cohn's cap for him to have one of his own contract players married to Louis B. Mayer—I began casting my eye for romance in other directions.

I had never dated L. B. Mayer exclusively. I always went out with other men of whom Mother approved. But now I began going more and more with the others, and less with L.B.

I'm sure he was hurt a little by this change in our relationship. At the same time it was characteristic of him to chide me gently . . . "Go ahead and have your fun, child." (He always called me either child or Annie.) "But you'll come back to me. I'll wait."

With me he never threw any of those tantrums for which he was famous—except once. At the end. And I'll come to that later.

He continued to ask Mother and me to those Sunday-night buffets with the stars at his house. And sometimes we went.

And sometimes, too, we would go with him to the races or to

his Perris Valley horse ranch near Palm Springs where he kept and bred horses. Mr. Mayer's passion for horses was well known and he went at horse racing and breeding the way he went at everything else, with energy and enthusiasm and a strong determination to succeed. As a result he became one of the leading thoroughbred owners in the United States. His five-hundred-acre horse farm was generally regarded as the finest horse farm on the West Coast, and his record as a breeder of fine race horses was almost as great as his record in film-making. He made a phenomenal success in a business that is even more difficult and unpredictable than that of films.

He loved horses, and he loved going to the races, particularly when one of his many horses was running. He never bet more than $2 per race, but he was constantly up on his feet—to place his bets, to go and look at his horses and at their competition.

He had started accumulating race horses in 1938. He said he intended to build his stable as he did his studio on "personalities."

Personally, I think it's ridiculous to blame the downfall of Metro-Goldwyn-Mayer on Mr. Mayer's love for horses. But he did spend a lot of time at this "sport of kings."

Many times he would gather up several of his biggest stars and their husbands, wives, or sweethearts and take them by limousine out to his horse ranch for Sunday lunch and to see his stable of horses. Mother and I were frequently invited on these outings.

One of my happiest memories of the L. B. Mayer era of my life was the time he invited us to his ranch to watch the birth of a little foal. It was a most moving experience and the only time I ever actually saw Louis B. Mayer weep. I didn't know until that day that this big mother complex of his extended even to horses. Mr. Mayer would not leave the mother horse's side even for one minute. He just sat there with tears streaming down his face as we watched the mare giving birth to her colt, then the bag of water breaking, and the little horse staggering to its feet while the mother horse nuzzled the baby with her nose to help it up.

I had never witnessed anything giving birth and I found it a beautiful experience. And watching a strong, dynamic man like Louis B. Mayer actually cry with emotion provided me with another insight into the finer side of this so-called Czar of Hollywood. Others might laugh at him. I did not. I loved him for it. And so did my mother. But not enough to change her mind about his proposal of marriage.

L.B.'s brother Jerry and his wife were with us that day. So were Greer Garson and Clark Gable.

Mr. Mayer had a habit of asking his favorite stars and friends to name his horses for him. After we watched the colt being born, he picked out a beautiful chestnut filly with a red mane and asked red-haired Greer Garson to name it. Greer named the horse Busher and it turned out to be one of the greatest horses in the Mayer stable.

Busher started going to the races in 1945 and won more than $300,000, which I understand made her the greatest money-winning filly of all time. She was chosen the horse of the year, the second filly ever to win that honor. How proud and happy Greer Garson was every time Busher won.

For me, Mr. Mayer picked a gorgeous black-maned filly to match my brunette hair and asked me to choose a name for her. I named her Eiffel Tower (because I had a yen to go to Paris) and she too became one of his best race horses, and also had many children for Mr. Mayer.

It was a real thrill for us to meet that famous stallion, Beau Pere, which L.B. had purchased from a stud farm in Australia for the staggering sum of $100,000, and the mare named Alibhai, which he bought from the stable of Aga Khan. The progeny of these two great horses in the Mayer stable won eighty-five races and earned some $835,000 prize money in one year alone (1947). By then my L. B. Mayer era had ended. But I shall never forget that day he took me to see Beau Pere and he said, "Annie, that horse will make many, many babies for me. He should be named Clark Gable because he is a king among stallions."

In all my naïveté I asked him, "Is that why they call Mr. Gable the King of Hollywood?"

And he said, "Of course, my child."

In the fall of 1944 Mr. Mayer suffered a painful accident at his Perris Valley farm. He was spending a weekend there with a group of convivial friends, which included Jessie Marmorston, his personal physician who was very close to him, and Mother and me.

On Sunday morning he invited everybody to come out to the training track to watch him ride one of the thoroughbreds that had a reputation for being a brute. The horse became skittish, reared, and hurled Mr. Mayer to the ground.

He wound up at the Cedars of Lebanon Hospital in Hollywood where X rays showed that he had a fractured pelvis. Then he developed pneumonia. But the miracle happened and he came out of it.

I went to see him almost every day while he was in the hospital.

I spent many happy times with Mr. Mayer at Santa Anita and Hollywood Park, and though our romantic interlude had long since ended when he put his great horses on the auction block early in 1947, I attended the sale of Louis B. Mayer's famous racing stable and it was one of the saddest experiences of my life. I can't even remember which of my current beaus took me, but I went. And I wept.

In the period when I was trying deliberately to see less of L. B. Mayer and more of other prospective suitors, I met Reese Milner. He was thirty-one, blond, and he was virile and handsome, with big broad shoulders, a bull neck and thin hips, cherubic cheeks and blue eyes. Here finally was my Prince-Charming-on-a-White-Horse. I met him through friends at the Mocambo. He too was a marvelous dancer.

I started dating Reese. Mother approved of him because he always brought me home by twelve. I really didn't know much about him. I just knew there was a kind of magnetism, a chemical attraction between us, and I thought it was love. I *wanted* it to be love. I knew that whatever it was with L. B. Mayer and me simply could not work out.

Three months after I met Reese Milner he asked me to marry him.

"You'll never have to work again," he told me. "You've worked hard all your life and I want to make all this up to you."

I also had been seeing more and more of Harry Karl, the shoe magnate, and he too had proposed marriage.

There I was, with two new proposals of marriage to choose from and all set to star in my first A picture, *The Petty Girl*. But instead of being thrilled about it all I was worried, nervous and terribly upset over Harry Cohn's plans to sell me like a race horse to Louis B. Mayer. It was all simply too much for me to cope with.

So I decided just to solve my problems by marrying Reese Milner. *Solve* them!

I never will forget when I walked into Harry Cohn's office and announced to him that I was going to leave my career and marry Reese Milner. His jaw dropped a mile and he said, "What did you say?"

I repeated that I was going to marry this young man whom I had just met and all I knew about him was that I loved him.

Mr. Cohn did a double take and then told me, "You can't marry that man." He regaled me with stories of Reese Milner's escapades with women, none of which I believed. I walked out of Mr. Cohn's office and I no sooner got home than my agents called. They were practically hysterical. They virtually forbade me to marry Reese Milner.

I told them I thought they were crazy and that I didn't believe one word of Cohn's stories.

But I did have an uneasy feeling, and when Reese came to my house that night to take me to dinner, I told him that we had to sit down and have a serious discussion about a few things. One

by one I asked him about each of the incidents that Mr. Cohn
had related to me. He denied them all, of course.

I breathed a secret sigh of relief. I really wanted to believe
in him.

Then suddenly—I'll never forget it—Reese turned on me like
a raving maniac, shouting, "It's all because of that fat old Jew,
Louis B. Mayer. He's behind all this. How can you be in love
with a man like that?"

I was stunned.

I ran upstairs sobbing so hard that I couldn't even tell Mother
what had happened. She assumed it was just a lover's quarrel. I
think Mother was actually anxious for me to marry him—so I
wouldn't marry L. B. Mayer.

I was still in a state of shock and weeping upstairs in my bedroom when the doorbell rang an hour later. I went downstairs
and called out through the door, "Who is it?"

A voice said, "Telegram."

I opened the door. There stood Reese, furious. He brushed by
me and into the house, saying that if I didn't marry him, he
didn't want to live. He apologized for his behavior and admitted
that he was insanely jealous of L. B. Mayer—but it was only
because he loved me so much.

Well, with a sob story like that, what could I do? I finally said
yes.

I ran upstairs to tell Mother about my decision. She was elated.
Then we all went out to dinner together to celebrate our engagement.

These events took place only a few days before Christmas . . .
And I had a few other decisions to make. My marriage proposal
from Harry Karl, for one thing. I had not yet given him an
answer. I knew I wasn't in love with him. But Harry was kind
and patient—and extremely generous. In expectations of marrying
me he had sent me a silver fox coat and a diamond and ruby
bracelet for Christmas—which my mother consented to let me

keep during the holidays while I made up my mind about his proposal.

But as soon as I had decided to marry Reese, I called Harry Karl and told him to come and get his gifts because I couldn't accept them. I also told him why.

In two minutes flat, his chauffeur was at the door to pick up the coat and bracelet.

Harry also had given me a beautiful clip and pair of earrings that Mother had permitted me to keep. Now that I was going to marry Reese, I asked him whether I should give those back also. "Hell, no," he said, "I'll buy you a ring to match."

And he did.

Whoever would have thought that Orphan Annie would wind up with a set of matched jewelry given to me by two multi-millionaires who asked me to marry them at the same time—with a third one waiting patiently for me to outgrow my childish romantic flings and marry him?

How was I going to break the news to Louis B. Mayer? But it had to be done. And I knew I had to tell him myself rather than have him hear it from someone else. He knew, of course, that I had been going out with Reese, as he knew I was going with others. But I'm sure he never believed I was serious enough for marriage with any of my beaus.

I couldn't bring myself to tell him face to face, so I telephoned him at home. I told him that I had some news for him and I asked him to take it calmly. I tried to explain it as gently as possible that I was in love with someone else and that I was going to be married.

There was a long pause over the phone, and then I heard this terrible sobbing, choking. I begged him to stop, I pleaded with him, but the sobbing continued until finally without ever having said a word to me he just hung up the phone.

So this was the kind of "seizure" or "sobbing spell" I had heard about that he used to get what he wanted. But this time he carried it rather far.

For a short while later that evening the doorbell rang and it was Mr. Mayer's chauffeur, Frank, terribly upset and saying, "Please, Miss Ann, you've got to come with me right away. Please hurry. He's trying to kill himself. He keeps calling for you, Miss Ann. This time it's for real, he's dying . . . Please hurry, Miss Ann . . ."

Mr. Mayer had taken a whole bottle of sleeping pills. The doctors were there now trying to pump out his stomach . . . and the ambulance was waiting to take him to the hospital . . . But he kept calling for me, Frank said.

During the ride back with Frank I was close to hysterics. I thought, dear God, why did this have to happen to me? Have I hurt this man so much? How could he be so in love with me when I had never really spent a whole evening alone with him? Was it only histrionics to win me over because of his pride? After all, I was the third girl in a row—Jean Howard and Ginny Simms before me—to go through a big romance with him and then turn him down to marry someone else. And I guess a man's pride can take only so much.

I arrived at the house as they were about to take him to the hospital.

Of course they did pump out his stomach and of course he did recover.

I was advised not to visit him in the hospital because of the publicity it would create but I later telephoned him and begged him please to forgive me for marrying Reese, and I hoped we could still be friends.

He said, "I'll aways be your friend, Annie, if you need me. But I can never feel the same toward you again. I thought you were different."

I tried to point out that marriage for us wouldn't have worked because there was too much difference in our ages, and that Mother and I both thought it best for me to marry a younger man.

He answered me solemnly and I'll never forget his words,

"That boy will hurt you, my child. He's not right for you. Harry has told me all about him. You'll be crawling back home to all of us on your knees before long, mark my word. You may think I'm too old for you but I can give you the kind of life you need and the protection. You'd be far better off with me, Ann."

For a minute I almost wavered. I loved this man very much. But I loved him more like a father. And it's not right to marry a man you love like a father. I was young. I wanted my Prince Charming on a white horse.

I quietly told Mr. Mayer I had made up my mind and said goodbye.

Then I went out to Columbia and into Harry Cohn's office and I told him the same thing.

I'll never forget his words, either.

"You're going to live to regret your decision," he said coldly. That was all.

It was like both men pronouncing a curse on me. My karma again—for all those evil things I had done to men in one of my previous incarnations, when I was a lady Pharaoh.

Chapter 10

PRINCE CHARMING
FALLS OFF HIS HORSE

I never gave it much thought before, but looking back on my track record in the romance department I guess I'd have to say that I had an affinity for men who had an affinity for flamboyance and the melodramatic.

Most of the men in my life—from Connie Hilton to the Maharajah of Cooch Behar—were rich, dynamic, quixotic, and colorful, and none more so than my first husband, Reese Milner.

We finally got our marriage license on Valentine's Day and were married two days later, February 16, 1946, in Montecito, California.

By November of that same year it was all over. It lasted all of nine months, just long enough to have a baby—who died soon after birth.

And in between was a nightmare.

It had been one of those on-again, off-again engagements. Reese had promised his family that he would never marry an actress, so he demanded that I give up my career. I didn't want to give it up so I broke our engagement. But we finally made a compromise.

I was in the middle of making a picture, *The Thrill of Brazil*, which I knew I had to finish. I couldn't just up and walk out on it. If he would let me finish this one, then I told him I would give up my career—including my forthcoming *Petty Girl*—and walk out on my $2,000-per-week contract with Columbia.

Harry Cohn had other ideas. He was willing to let me take two weeks off for a honeymoon in Mexico and shoot around me in *Thrill of Brazil* while I was gone. But he had an investment in dancing Ann Miller, not Mrs. Reese Milner, and I had a contract to fulfill. He raved and ranted and finally wound up suing Reese for $150,000 for making me break my contract. The case was resolved out of court.

But Harry Cohn was furious with me for not doing *Petty Girl*. Furthermore, he demanded that when my marriage broke up—which he was certain it would—I would have to return to the studio and finish out my contract obligation.

We had a lovely wedding and a beautiful reception. Linda Darnell and Marjorie Reynolds were my bridesmaids. Marjorie was Bing Crosby's co-star in *Blue Skies*. It was she who tried to explain some of the facts of life to me when she learned that my mother had not. My mom had succeeded in keeping me pure and virginal, all right. And ignorant as well—about such intimate things as how not to get pregnant. So within a couple of weeks I was. Personally, I thought it was marvelous until I began to realize that there was something quite wrong with my husband.

Actually I didn't know that Reese was wealthy until after I married him. He had told me that his family was in the scrap-iron business and I didn't know what that meant. I wasn't even sure he made money enough for us to live on. He had always made me feel that he was practically without funds,

barely making ends meet. But I had been making good money
at Columbia—in the neighborhood of $100,000 a year—and I
had saved a little and was willing to use it to help support
us if necessary. Obviously I didn't marry him for his money.

It wasn't until after our wedding ceremony that he told me
about his family. "I am Reese *Llewellyn* Milner," he said, with
emphasis on the Llewellyn, "and my family made all the Llewellyn elevators." As it turned out, he was from a Blue-Blood
Social Register family, and rich scion of the Llewellyn Iron
Works company. Scrap iron yet! Every time you walk into an
elevator, it's Lewellyn, right? And Reese Llewellyn Milner was
heir to the family fortune.

He said he had not told me of his wealth because he didn't
want to take a chance on my marrying him for his money.
"But I'm worth at least seven and a half million," he informed
me, "and now that I have you, I'm going to take you out of
all this picture business. You're now under my protection.
You'll never have to dance again as long as you live."

I wasn't sure I appreciated this last bit because I loved dancing.
But I had married him. The deed was done. And I did experience a rather exhilarating and grateful feeling of joy that
the man I had married was surprisingly affluent enough to take
care of my mother and me at least as well as I had been
doing.

Affluent! I had never seen such a lavish outlay of wealth
except in Louis B. Mayer's empire. Reese had a beautiful ranch
near Ojai, which was one of the biggest in California, ranking
next to San Simeon, I was told. And the home he bought for
us on Delfern Drive in Holmby Hills wasn't exactly a little
old cottage. It was a $250,000 mansion. He poured another
$200,000 into the furnishings. He ordered every piece of furni-
ture especially hand-carved. We could seat twenty-four at our
dinner table. We had gorgeous chandeliers and marble floors. And
we had four gardeners, a chauffeur, an upstairs maid, and a
couple who served as cook and butler.

Materially, I had everything a poor little rich girl (trying to play Society Matron) could want—an elegant home, beautiful clothes, furs, and jewelry . . . And my husband also let me spend as much as I wanted to decorate a fabulous nursery for my coming baby. There were times when I was sure he really wanted our baby and I was deliriously happy. It was like living in a dream castle.

But between deliriums, I was to become acquainted with the other side of Reese Milner, the one I had been warned about. He was like a Jekyll and Hyde.

We hadn't been married even two weeks when I began to see that Reese Milner's personality would change radically when he was drinking.

I was horrified, heartsick, frightened—and trapped. I was afraid to tell my mother that my life was in danger. I hadn't even told her that I was pregnant. All I could do was pray that everything would be all right, that perhaps our baby would help Reese stay in control of himself.

Pregnant or not, I still had a commitment to Harry Cohn to finish that movie, *Thrill of Brazil*.

I had quite a few scenes to do with Evelyn Keyes and Keenan Wynn, but the most difficult one for me to do was the big finale number. For this, I had to climb way up high on a big platform to dance. Ordinarily this wouldn't have bothered me but because of my pregnancy I was frightened that I would get dizzy and fall. I was so nervous about it that we had to do the scene over and over. We continued shooting beyond six o'clock—the time I usually left to go home. I finally got the number right and was about ready to leave when Reese burst onto the set. He grabbed me by the arm, jerked me into the car and shouted at me all the way home that "those Hollywood people" were breaking up our marriage. He said he was absolutely going to forbid me from going to the studio any more. He had forgotten our compromise and his promise to let me finish *Thrill of Brazil*. I pleaded with him, in tears, explaining that

I had only two more scenes to shoot and then it would be over. But he wouldn't listen.

When we arrived home, he literally threw me inside and then began hitting me. It was the first time I had ever been physically beaten by a man, but it was not to be the last. It is an utterly dehumanizing and horrifying experience. I ran into my bedroom, then into the bathroom trying to protect myself. But he kept hitting me like a punching bag, knocking me to the floor.

I knew then what everyone had been trying to tell me.

It was two weeks before I could report for work. My nose was still swollen, my eye was cut, and I was all black and blue. I looked awful. And even when I did return to work, the make-up people had to cover me with extra thick make-up to hide all the welts and bruises.

I must say that during this ordeal my admiration and respect for Harry Cohn took a turn for the better. He had every right to be angry with me. I had displeased him first of all by not marrying Mr. Mayer and not doing *The Petty Girl*, and I had disregarded his warnings and married Reese Milner. Now, here I was holding up production for two weeks on *Thrill of Brazil*, requiring extra make-up, and vomiting between takes. But not once did Mr. Cohn say, "I told you so," or berate me. Not a word of reprimand. I'm sure he felt sorry for me, though he would have been quite justified cutting my role out of the picture. He probably would have done so if the picture had not been almost finished.

Thrill of Brazil was to be my last picture for Columbia. But Harry Cohn, bless him, was a gentleman to the end.

By now I realized that my marriage was a grave mistake. But I was too proud to tell anyone. I was pregnant. I was scared. And I was trapped, like a rat.

I tried to excuse Reese by reminding myself that he was not to be blamed for his behavior.

But this didn't make it any easier to live with him.

He was jealous of all film people and rude to my friends. He never let me invite any of my Hollywood friends to our dinner parties. They were always his friends. He never trusted me and when I went to lunch at a restaurant with a girl friend, he would either call me there and have me paged or come in unexpectedly to check on us and see if there were men with us. And he was constantly accusing me of affairs with both Mr. Mayer and Mr. Cohn.

The fights got worse but I stayed with Reese because he was the father of my child and I didn't think it was right to bring a child into the world without a father. I would have done anything to make our marriage work for the sake of our child. But my heart was slowly being broken and I knew this was the beginning of the end. The end, in fact, came when I was nine months pregnant. We were spending a few days at Rancho La Vista, Reese's ranch near Ojai. Reese and I had a row and I don't remember clearly all the details of the fight but I do remember slipping and falling, falling, falling down a long flight of stairs, landing on my back and screaming in pain.

The couple who worked for us at the ranch came running and somehow got me into the back seat of our station wagon and rushed me to Good Samaritan Hospital in Los Angeles. I don't remember much of that ride except the pain. I remember screaming and then blacking out and then screaming again, all the way to the hospital. I was sure I had broken my back. And then the labor pains started. I don't even remember whether Reese was with me in the car, nor who was driving.

All I know is that we arrived at the hospital in time for me to give birth to a baby girl.

My baby died three hours later.

When they broke the news to me, I became hysterical. I was put under sedation and lapsed into a semi-comatose state. I don't remember how many hours or days I remained this way. I don't remember seeing Mother or Reese or anyone with me except nurses and doctors.

Again Reese went through the let's-forgive-and-forget routine. Again I told him I loved him. I suppose in my own way I always will. Because he was the first.

But when I lost my baby, I knew it was all over with him. I could never live with him again. All I wanted now was my freedom and a chance to regain my health. My back was not broken. But it had been badly injured in that fall.

The doctors told me that I would never dance again. And that I could have no more babies.

I filed for divorce from my hospital bed.

I never went back to our magnificent mansion in the Hills of Holmby. I never saw my baby's beautiful nursery again.

Hedda Hopper interviewed me at the 1947 Look Awards Broadcast. I had just completed Columbia's musical, *Thrill of Brazil*.

Junket time—I'm off again on one of my many tours for M-G-M. (Left to right: Anita Ekberg, Lana Turner, Joanne Dru, me, Hedda Hopper, and Alexis Smith). (*Photo by Panagra*)

At the party Arthur Cameron and I hosted for Maurice Chevalier to celebrate his 66th anniversary in show business (October 16, 1965), Mr. Chevalier paid me a great compliment when he told me that I had legs just like Mistinguett's.

With my very dear friend, Hermes Pan, in 1960.

(*M-G-M photo*)

One of my former beaus, Maharajah of Cooch Bahar, and I visited Clark Gable on the set in 1952.

Chapter 11

THE GOLDEN YEARS

When I was dismissed from the hospital, I went to my mother's house, and for many weeks I lay in a hospital traction bed, loaded down with weights of all shapes and sizes. As a result of the fall, I had some pinched nerves between the discs of my spine and each night mother had to put me into a harness, each of my feet with an eight-pound weight on it, to keep the discs separated so they would mend properly.

Harry Cohn had said that when my marriage broke up I would have to return to the studio and finish out my contract. Instead, he let my contract lapse and I was out of a job. I really couldn't blame him. I had made my own bed, let me lie in it. I was literally spending a great deal of my time in that hospital traction bed, which we had installed at home, lying immobile in all those traction ropes and weights, and praying like mad that my back would heal and be strong enough so that I could dance again.

I refused to accept the doctor's word that I could not go

back to dancing. I did everything my doctors told me to do to speed my recovery. And Mother was a marvelous nurse. She encouraged me to stay in bed for hours even when I didn't feel like it, always reminding me that this is what would make me strong enough to dance again. She waited on me hand and foot, attended to my every comfort, pampered me like a baby, did everything possible to keep my spirits up.

The doctors were amazed at my progress.

When I was able to be up and around, I had to wear a steel brace. It was uncomfortable but I lived through it.

What really hurt most during this painful period was that neither Louis B. Mayer nor Reese Milner sent a note of sympathy or offered a helping hand.

At least Harry Cohn was kind enough to send me his attorney, Jerry Geisler. He helped me file my divorce suit and a suit for $375,000 damages in a "civil fraud" case against Reese— this for tricking me into signing away my interest in our Holmby Hills mansion. Jerry Geisler later talked me into dropping the "civil fraud" suit (that was his term, not mine) against Reese and I always suspected that Reese slipped him a few thousand to persuade me to change my mind. The real truth never came out.

Our so-called "sensational" divorce suit was well aired in the press. I testified in court that my husband had committed acts of violence against me and that I feared further harm from him. But I was not required to be too specific and I avoided mentioning our big fight and my fall down the stairs which I am sure caused me to lose my baby. The newspapers attributed my baby's so-called "premature" birth* and death to my being in a car accident, with Reese driving. I let it go at that. He was well known around town as a reckless driver and he had been in quite a few accidents, as the press noted.

Our divorce mess was sticky enough as it was and hit Hollywood like a bombshell. Our property battle was finally settled

---

* Actually, my baby was a nine months' child.

out of court. All I asked Reese for was compensation for my medical bills and for the working time I had lost at Columbia.

I thought it only fair that he should reimburse me for the amount I would have earned at Columbia if I had remained there working instead of marrying him. I asked for $20,000 tax free, which was approximately the amount I would have had left after taxes if I had earned $100,000. (I'm using round figures here; my lawyer took care of the details.) That's all I asked from Reese and that's all I got, in spite of the fact that he went around telling everyone that I was a golddigger and had taken him for a million dollars. Now I wish I had. I got my interlocutory divorce decree on January 22, 1947, a little less than a year after we were married.

I was still in and out of the traction bed and steel brace for my injured back when my agent, Vic Orsatti, called and told me that Cyd Charisse had fallen and torn a tendon in her leg and was out of M-G-M's *Easter Parade* opposite Fred Astaire. The role was up for grabs and producer Arthur Freed was testing girls. Was I ready to try for it?

Was I ready! It was months since I had danced a step, but please God let me be able to do it. To be in a picture with Fred Astaire was every dancing girl's dream.

I swallowed my last ounce of pride and telephoned Louis B. Mayer. I don't know exactly what I expected of him. It would be unthinkable to ask him to get me the role. I still wanted to make it in Hollywood on my own talent. But I felt insecure because of the traumatic events of recent months, because I had been incapacitated and out of circulation for so long.

I knew that my agents could get me the test without Louis B. Mayer's help, but it was as though I needed reassurance from Mr. Mayer himself.

When I called him, he was polite and solicitous. He inquired about my health and said he was sorry to hear about my troubles. But I could detect a faint aloofness in his voice. He had told me that he could never feel the same way about me again, and I knew he didn't. But I finally got the words out. I told him that I knew about Cyd Charisse being out of *Easter Parade*, and I asked him if he could arrange a test for me.

He said he would talk to Arthur Freed and ask him to give me a test. But he added solemnly, "Yes, I'll do that for you, Ann. I'll see that you get the test. But if you don't do well in it, I can't help you any further."

I don't know how many girls auditioned for that role—but I got it! And I won it strictly on my own and not through my erstwhile friendship with Mr. Mayer, as some of the gossip columnists implied. It was Arthur Freed and Fred Astaire who made the decision, though for a while it was touch and go whether I was going to get the part, even after winning the auditions.

As it turned out, Fred Astaire was very hesitant about working with me, and it had nothing to do with my test. It had to do with my height. I was five-feet-seven-inches tall, really too tall for Astaire and there for a moment or two I was afraid he wasn't going to let me have the part. But he liked my test very much and finally agreed that I should do the picture—if I would wear ballet shoes in my dancing scenes with him.

It was decided that the scenes could be shot so that my feet wouldn't show. The scenes I had with Astaire were ballroom dancing scenes in which I should have been wearing high-heeled evening shoes. But these would have made me taller than Astaire. I remember all of us watching the rushes very closely to make sure that my feet didn't show in those flat ballet shoes.

I also had to wear my hair flatter than usual for this picture, with a low chignon, to make me appear shorter.

It was about this time that famed columnist Louella Parsons began giving "the little Miller girl" a big build-up, although she didn't have all her facts straight.

In her column of July 26, 1947, she wrote:

> Louis B. Mayer, who has discovered some mighty big stars for his company, M-G-M, and built them into powerful names, has

always believed in Ann Miller. Now he has personally signed her and will find stories for her. [Wrong]

I suppose you are thinking, "But Ann Miller isn't a newcomer." Right. She isn't. But she has never hit big in spite of the many movies she's made.

From here on you'll be seeing her in M-G-M's important musicals, dressed by the studio glamour makers, and dancing in beautiful settings. Then we'll see a "new" Ann Miller, or I miss my guess.

Again in her column of August 13, 1947, she wrote:

I don't believe for a minute the stories going around that Ann Miller is being groomed to take Judy Garland's spot at M-G-M in case Judy's illness is long-drawn out. Judy is a singer. Ann is a dancer.

But the parade of musicals to boost the little Miller girl starts impressively. She goes into "Easter Parade," the super-special Irving Berlin picture featuring his wonderful music—old and new numbers.

Then Ann will be "The Belle of New York" for Arthur Freed, with stardom straight ahead. I'm inclined to agree with M-G-M that she can click with the force of a "new" stellar personality, even though she has been on the screen for years.

I was in excruciating pain with my back all during the shooting of *Easter Parade*. I couldn't dance in a steel brace so I had to be taped up each day, from just under my bust to a little below the navel. And each evening I went through holy hell pulling that tape off. By the end of the picture my skin was almost raw. I had to take Darvon (pain pills) to get through my dancing scenes. I hate taking pills of any kind. Each night my mother strapped me back into my harness and the traction bed. But it was all worth it to be in a picture with Fred Astaire and Judy Garland.

Poor Judy. Such fantastic genius. Such a waste of talent. And the problems she created on the set! Sometimes she merely wouldn't show up and we had to shoot around her. Other times she would bring her baby daughter Liza with her to work, happily distracting the rest of the cast and crew.

I admired Judy very much and was so sorry for her. She would be given her pep pills before she came on the set, to make her emotional so she would cry easily in her scenes that called for tears. And then the poor kid got more pills at home at night so she could go to sleep. It all started so innocently but no wonder Judy got hooked on pills. She was also a very impressionable girl and became sophisticated way beyond her years, an old lady mentally at a very young age. She was mixed up in a clique of strange people and that certainly didn't help her very much.

Easter Parade came out in 1948 and got absolutely rave reviews for Fred Astaire naturally, but also for me. Typical was the one in the New York *Times:*

> Fred Astaire, who has no peer, is dancing at the top of his form . . . Although Judy Garland gets the top billing, she also gets stiff competition from the long-legged Ann Miller, who does an especially graceful ballroom dance with the master. Miss Garland is a competent trouper . . . but somehow we feel that Miss Miller pairs better with Astaire.

Then I did a movie, *Texas Carnival*, with Esther Williams and Red Skelton. What a ball we had on that one. I loved working with Esther Williams. She had a marvelous sense of humor, always smiling and laughing, never moody. And producers were forever chasing her all around because she was considered one of the sexiest actresses on the lot.

I'll let you in on a secret. Most of that sexy look Esther had on screen with her eyes half closed was the result of her being nearsighted. She had trouble trying to focus on her leading man or on the cameras and key lights. I always called her Esther Hazy.

Physical handicaps never seemed to slow down a star. Judy Garland had beautiful legs and big eyes. But she had a small hump on her back which dress designers had great trouble in camouflaging, though they always managed somehow . . .

Mario Lanza was blind in one eye. Clark Gable's ears were too big, Mickey Rooney was too short, and Jeanette MacDonald had to wear wigs—it cost M-G-M a fortune to keep her in wigs.

It also cost them a fortune to keep me in opera-length hose because my legs were so long and there were no pantyhose at that time. A dancer is supposed to wear sheer silk stockings, not those thick colored tights that ballerinas wear. Besides, I was always too tall and long-legged to fit into ballerina tights. So all my long dancing silk stockings had to be custom-made—and I always had to be sewn into them! It was one helluva job for the wardrobe ladies, but even worse for me.

Most chorus girls worked bare-legged because they couldn't afford the hose. They just wore leg make-up. But a featured dancer couldn't get by with that. Her legs looked best in silk stockings.

How well I remember the misery I went through standing for hours and hours on end all those years with two wardrobe ladies sewing my silk stockings into the underneath elastic seams of my tight panty briefs. I couldn't wear garter supporters in the underpants because my costumes were always so tight that the garters would make lumps. So in every picture I made the stockings had to be sewn onto the pants, and I had to stand while it was being done. The stockings always had seams down the back and I had to stand straight and tall in order to get the seams straight.

Well, you can imagine the problems it created if one of my stockings popped a run during a take, which they often did. Off I'd go to wardrobe again, holding up production while the whole cast and crew waited for me to be sewn into a new stocking. I'd have to stand there, hot and tired and panting from exhaustion under the big lights, with the wardrobe ladies sewing like mad so I could get back on the sound stage.

It wasn't easy for them getting their needles through my

elastic tight pants, and it wasn't easy for me with those needles forever pricking and sticking me. What a mess.

The studio ordered my extra long silk dancing stockings—at $12 or $15 per pair—from a man named Mr. Willy de Mond—the number one stocking man—who had a shop on Highland Avenue (Willy's of Hollywood). It turned out to be terribly expensive for my studio. The hose had to be perfect and I was always getting runs. Well, I understand it was Mr. Willy who later invented pantyhose and I was told he got the idea from the way his hose had to be sewn into my dancing underpants.*

It was my great good luck to have my dear friend Hermes Pan as my choreographer again in some of my M-G-M musicals, in-

* Willy de Mond is a Hollywood institution. For fifty years he has designed stockings for stars, celebrities and socialites from Hollywood, Broadway and Paris. He stockinged Marilyn Miller in *Sunny,* for *Ziegfeld Follies of 1921;* inaugurated sheer stockings, called "Black Bottom" stockings, for *George White's Scandals.*

When Ann Miller was twelve years old and "trying to pass for eighteen," as Willy says, he sold her her first pair of opera-length hose. "I'll never forget that first time she came in here with her mother," he recalls. "Such legs!" He's been a fan of hers ever since, and admits it was Annie who inspired him to invent pantyhose when she asked, "Why don't you make stockings and underpants all in one so I don't have to be sewn into them?"

In 1946, Mr. Willy, as he is known, presented Annie with the annual "Golden Calf Award" for the most beautiful legs in the world. (He presented the first award in 1935 to Marlene Dietrich.)

Ann has introduced many of Mr. Willy's "firsts" in the leg department. She was the first to wear mesh stockings in 1940 in *Edie Was a Lady.* In 1947, Ann wore—really a revelation—the first pair of seamless (or seam-free as Willy calls them) opera hose, knitted to the perfect measurement of her beautiful symmetrical gams—8½ inch ankle, 12½ inch calf and 19½ inch thigh. Ann also was the first to wear the elaborate sequined and embroidered stockings which Mr. Willy designed. And, of course, the pantyhose.

When he saw Ann in the TV special *Dames At Sea,* he commented that her legs are still as spectacular as when he persented her with that gold trophy for the most beautiful legs in the world—N.L.B.

cluding one called *Lovely to Look At*, which was the movie version of Jerome Kern's Broadway musical, *Roberta*. It also starred Kathryn Grayson, Howard Keel, Red Skelton, and Zsa Zsa Gabor. Zsa Zsa and I became good friends during the shooting of this picture, even though she had been piqued at first because I was dating one of her ex-husbands, Conrad Hilton. But after all, she was divorced from him and no longer had a monopoly on the man.

Among my favorite films for one reason or another during my M-G-M era were *Small Town Girl* because in this I did a Busby Berkeley number—"Gotta Hear That Beat," one of his last— which was merely spectacular and typical of the genius of Berkeley; Cole Porter's *Kiss Me, Kate* because I think it was one of my best; and Vincent Youmans's *Hit the Deck* because I had a couple of fabulous numbers choreographed by Hermes Pan. One was called "Hallelujah!" It was done on board ship with about a hundred sailors behind me, all marching and keeping time with their feet while I did a very staccato tap number to the rhythm of their feet.

I loved working at M-G-M. Sometimes I pinched myself to see if it was all true. Here I was actually eating lunch in the same commissary with Clark Gable and Spencer Tracy and all the big name stars of that fabled era of Hollywood. I even saw Greta Garbo there once, when she came to visit George Cukor.

Strangely enough I rarely saw Louis B. Mayer on the M-G-M lot. His wife had finally divorced him (they had been separated for years) and he had remarried in December of 1948. His new wife, Lorena Danker, was the widow of an advertising man, a tall and very pretty lady who was, I think, very good for him. I often saw them around at parties and out dancing at the Mocambo or Ciro's. I always found her very warm and friendly.

But about the only times I saw L. B. Mayer on the M-G-M lot were on those occasions when he would gather all of his stars together—those under contract to his studio—for a group photograph, a "family" picture, as it was known.

And what an illustrious family it was: Spencer Tracy, Hedy Lamarr, Clark Gable, Lionel Barrymore, Greer Garson, Debbie Reynolds, Kathryn Grayson, Robert Taylor, Lana Turner, Ava Gardner, Elizabeth Taylor, and on and on. We were all a part of the most powerful motion picture empire in the world, the Rolls-Royce, Tiffany, and Dom Perignon of studios.

And the M-G-M stars were all treated like L.B.'s prize-winning race horses.

Louis B. Mayer really considered his stable of stars his "family" and psychologically it worked. But as in all families, his "children" frequently misbehaved, creating grave problems for him. There was Judy Garland and her nervous breakdown and the time she nicked her neck in the bathroom with a piece of broken glass. There was the star lady who used to shack up with a Negro and she finally got pregnant. It wasn't becoming to do that sort of thing in those days and Mr. Mayer was fit to be tied. Another star lady was constantly drunk and in bed with everyone on the lot, down to the grips and electricians.

There was always great jealousy among the lady stars regarding their set dressing rooms and their permanent dressing rooms in the main buildings as well. They were all decorated like small luxurious apartments. But when Lana Turner had a portable toilet installed in her set dressing room, all hell broke loose. The other star ladies demanded equal privy privileges. Lana's john-john was subsequently removed to keep peace in L.B.'s M-G-M family.

No French poodle or race horse could ever have had more pampered treatment than L. B. Mayer lavished on his family of stars. But he had rigid standards of decency and propriety. And his key man, Howard Strickling, had a full time job keeping the scandals of the pampered M-G-M set out of the papers. If Strickling were ever to write a book about what he knows went on behind the scenes, a lot of people would have to leave town.

Poor L.B.! What a stable of stars' headaches he had. Many more than he had with his race horses.

How sad it was to see the "changing of the guard" in that great M-G-M lion's den, and the tragic demise of a studio that had once represented all the power and the glory of that era known as the Golden Years of Hollywood.

Although Louis B. Mayer's power had diminished considerably in his later years as the "new guard" took over, an age had been completed and *finis* written with the passing of this greatest of all movie moguls on October 20, 1957.

He died a bitter and lonely man. But he gave so much happiness to the world. And to a young girl named Johnnie Lucille Collier whose golden memories of him can never be tarnished. I wish I could have given him even a little of the happiness he yearned for, or an iota of the happiness he gave to others.

On a sunny day in May of 1970 I sat in tears on a big M-G-M sound stage watching all the star wardrobes and properties of those Golden Years being sold at a public auction. This truly was the death knell for a Hollywood that is no more. And oh the echoes of the past, the memories and ghosts that paraded out of a golden bygone era as countless treasures went up on the auction block . . .

The ruby slippers worn by Judy Garland in *The Wizard of Oz* were sold for $15,000. The "lucky" trenchcoat that Clark Gable wore in several pictures went for $1,250, and Elizabeth Taylor's wedding dress from *Father of the Bride* for $625.

Up on the auction block went Jean Harlow's nightgown, Lana Turner's bra and panties, Marlon Brando's coat and Charles Laughton's hat from *Mutiny on the Bounty*, Norma Shearer's costumes from *Romeo and Juliet*, and *Marie Antoinette* and Ava Gardner's dresses from *Show Boat*. Even the famed old show boat itself, the *Cotton Blossom*, was auctioned off.

There were Eleanor Powell's dancing costumes from her *Broadway Melody* musicals and mine from *Easter Parade, Kiss Me, Kate, On the Town, Texas Carnival* and *Hit the Deck.*

Did I buy my costumes? No, I bought Esther William's bull fighter suit from *Fiesta.*

Debbie Reynolds, bless her heart, bought many of the props and hundreds of costumes—including some of mine—to put in the Hollywood Museum she is planning to establish. She spent more than $250,000 at the M-G-M auction in order to preserve some of these priceless treasures here in Hollywood where they belong. True, they are a part of Hollywood history that is past, but shouldn't historians know the past in order to build a better future?

It is one of life's little ironies that my so-called reign at Metro-Goldwyn-Mayer started after my courtship with Louis B. Mayer was over. It spanned approximately a ten-year period, from 1948 to 1958, when I married my second husband. But those in between years were the happiest of my life, because my career was in full bloom and so was romance once again, this time with the one true love of my life. But he was a man I couldn't marry because though long separated and later divorced, he couldn't get a Catholic dispensation to marry again. Oh, the mess I've made with my life in the romance department!

Chapter 12

LOVE FINDS ANNIE MILLER

I want to set the record straight right here and now. I was *not* having an affair with Conrad Hilton, as all the gossipy headlines implied. True, I was his dancing partner all over the world and at many of those fabulous Hilton Hotel openings which were as glamorous as Hollywood premieres in the old days. But we were always just good friends, and, I might add, marvelous friends. We had a wonderfully warm unromantic relationship.

Truth to tell, Connie Hilton was my second-best beau all during the years I was with Bill O'Connor. It was Bill, not Connie, who was the one and only genuine true love of my life. It was Bill who introduced me to Connie, and my name was linked romantically to both of them—as well as to many more—throughout my M-G-M years. After all, these were my personal "golden years," too—the years from twenty-five to thirty-five, an age when a girl had jolly well better start taking stock of herself and her affairs of the heart if she is to find any security for her future.

I didn't expect then to keep dancing all my life. Although it looks now as if that's my "star of destiny." But in my twenties, I was still looking for a Prince Charming who really was a Prince Charming. I was grown up finally. Or so I thought. (Now I'm not so sure.) At least I'd been married and divorced and had my share of heartaches. I had worked hard all my life. I deserved a fling. And boy, was I making up for lost time!

I was in perfect position for it. Mama-Kat had loosened the reins on her kitten. At least a little. She couldn't go with me everywhere.

I was a part of World War II Hollywood, playing all the Army camps, and Navy and Air Force bases. Martha Raye and I once did thirty shows in one day at the Coral Gables Hotel in Florida which had been turned into an emergency hospital . . . Linda Darnell and I each received citations for our work with the war wounded. We were all set to go to Bataan and Corregidor but our tour there had to be canceled due to the bombings.

The late-fabulous-forties and early-fifties were years of War Bond drives, the Hollywood Canteen, movie promotional tours, fast overseas junkets for premieres and openings. It was all a whirlwind of glamour and excitement and I was right in the center of it. As M-G-M's new "dancing queen" my name was up there in lights all over the place. The "new" and always "little" (five-feet-seven!) Annie Miller was in constant demand for public appearances and social functions. I went anywhere and everywhere I was asked. I was having a ball and I was the belle of the ball wherever I went. I lived every minute of it, making up for lost time.

I was pretty and popular and deliriously happy in those long-ago golden years of my life. I was meeting men, men, men by the dozens—from Shahs and Maharajas to Spanish bull fighters and international playboys. I'm not boasting. I'm just trying to give you an idea of the whole big wide world of masculinity I might have had to choose from if I'd had sense enough to play my cards right. I knew Prince Rainier before he married Grace

Kelly, and Aly Khan before he married Rita Hayworth, and
Aristotle Onassis before he married Jacqueline Kennedy. And I
was dating André Dubonnet, the apéritif king, before he married
Elyce Hunt, and the Shah of Iran before he married Soraya, and
Tony Martin before he married Cyd Charisse.

Just for openers, among my serious beaus were Ernie Byfield,
Jr., whose father owned the Pump Room in Chicago; Jack
Seabrook, who owned Birds Eye Frozen Foods; Gilbert Swanson
of Swanson's Frozen Foods; Jim Kimberley of the Kleenex clan;
Randolph Churchill, Winston Churchill's son and one of Eva
Gabor's ex-husbands, Charles Isaacs.

With such plums to pluck, leave it to me to fall madly in love
with a man who was not free to marry me.

I met William V. O'Connor through my good friend Margaret
Pereira, wife of the famous architect William Pereira.

Bill was an attorney, who eventually became Chief Deputy
State Attorney General of California and Governor Edmund
"Pat" Brown's right arm. His prominence in politics was one
reason our relationship had to be a very discreet one. The other
was his religion. He was Catholic and there was little chance that
his wife would ever give him his freedom to marry me. Nevertheless, I continued to hope—for nearly twelve years of my life.

Actually, Bill and I were seeing each other long before we
became an "item" in the society and gossip columns. We had
met soon after the break-up of my first marriage with Reese
Milner. And we had a psychic rapport from the very beginning.
In fact, at the risk of sounding completely dingy, I am going to
tell it like it happened. I fell in love with Bill O'Connor's picture in the Los Angeles *Times* before I ever set eyes on him or
knew anything about him. And my psychic antenna flashed
the message to me that I was going to meet this man and that he
was going to be the great love of my life.

Remember, my great-grandmother who was a medium predicted that I would inherit her psychic powers. And remember,
I said I also believe in Ouija boards.

So without telling my friend Margaret Pereira about the picture, I called and asked her to come over and work the Ouija board with me. Sure enough, the Ouija board told me that I was going to fall in love with a tall, dark, and handsome man, and that he was an attorney, and I was going to meet him in a private home.

Then I took Bill O'Connor's newspaper picture out of my purse, showed it to Margaret, and said, "I hope this is the man."

Margaret laughed and said, "Bill O'Connor, oh sure! He'd be a real catch for any girl who can get him—*if* you can get him."

She said she knew him well. He and his wife were legally separated and she would invite him to dinner at her home sometime when I could come.

She set the date for the dinner party. When I accepted her invitation, I didn't know that Bill and his wife were still seeing each other once in a while. Apparently Margaret didn't know it either. I went alone to dinner at the Pereiras, all a-flutter inside at the anticipation of meeting this new man in my life who was going to sweep me off my feet. I had already decided. You can imagine what a let-down it was when he showed up with his wife, Adele.

I must say, she was a very attractive person. Bill and Adele O'Connor were among Hollywood's most popular couples, very social and "in" on several levels—the society-film celebrity-political crowd. They gave posh parties at their beautiful Bel Air home, but Bill also maintained an apartment in Beverly Hills, where he spent a great deal of time—especially during those "off-again" periods when Adele would go globe-trotting off to Mexico or elsewhere for the opening of the opera—or whatever. Their friends accepted the O'Connors' lifestyle. After all, this was Hollywood where anything goes.

The next time the Pereiras gave a dinner party and invited both of us, Bill came alone. Margaret very cleverly seated us together. That was the beginning of a twelve-year romance from which to this day I haven't fully recovered. Meeting Bill was like Kismet. We had been drawn to each other the moment we first met on the evening his estranged wife was with him. And now, on our second meeting we both knew without putting it in words that it was meant to be.

In the early stages of our romance, we agreed not to appear in public together. In spite of their religion, Bill and Adele had agreed on a divorce but it was not yet final. In addition, Bill was an extremely devout Catholic, and even with a divorce he knew that he could not remarry unless his former wife passed away or signed the papers permitting him to remarry. Otherwise he would be excommunicated from the Church. Also, he couldn't afford to take a chance on any type of scandal that might hurt his fine reputation in politics. (At one time he wanted very much to become governor, and almost did.)

In all honesty, I must admit that in the early years of our relationship Bill never promised that he would one day marry me and he never encouraged me to hope that he would. But I hoped anyway. At one point I even began taking catechism lessons studying to be a Catholic in hopes that he would marry me. I knew that he loved me and I still know it. Out of three marriages and numerous romances, Bill O'Connor is the only one who gave me true happiness.

Looking back over my scrapbooks, it is amusing now to see how we fooled all the columnists. We were forever turning up at the same parties and I was always with someone else . . . so many that I had even forgotten some of them until my scrapbooks refreshened my memory . . . Ann Miller with Freddie de Cordova . . . Ann Miller with Gilbert Kahn (son of Otto Kahn, noted New York financier) . . . Ann Miller with Greg Bautzer . . . Ann Miller with the Maharajah of Cooch Behar . . . Ann Miller with Ernie Byfield, Jr. "This steady twosome seems to be getting serious," said Louella. (Ernie was then a screenwriter at M-G-M.) . . . The columnists were always marrying me off to someone. The three most mentioned bridegrooms-to-be were Ernie Byfield, Jr., Conrad Hilton, and Eddie Lasker—although

columnist Walter Winchell had me about to marry Bob Rhoden-
berg, former owner of the Baltimore Colts.

Well, columnists have to keep cooking up something to keep
their readers happy, and I was grist for their mill. It seemed to
make good copy even when I denied all the marriage rumors. I
don't know how many times I said, "No, I am not going to marry
Conrad Hilton . . . I'm not marrying anyone . . ."

Bill and I often laughed at all my romantic flings in the gossip
columns.

It wasn't until 1949 that our romance came out in the open,
and he became my escort at many of the important social-polit-
ical-film industry functions during my M-G-M years.

But we still made it a point not to be identified as a "steady
twosome." My mother kept nagging me that it was wrong to be
so devoted to Bill. She reminded me constantly that he was a
devout Catholic and would never marry me. She insisted that I
have other boy friends and not go steady with Bill. And deep
down I knew she was right. So, I continued to date other men.

Bill also dated other women, of course. He was very popular.
Topmost on the list were Joan Crawford and Rhonda Fleming.
It broke my heart every time he went out with someone else, but
I knew better than to try to hold too tight a rein on him. I simply
put a smile on my face and went my own merry way.

And among the merriest times I had admittedly were with
Conrad Hilton.

How that man could dance! He still can. And we are still
good friends. Everytime we meet at a party, he always says,
"Here comes my favorite dancing partner."

He always tells people, "You know Annie and I have danced
together all over the world. She's the best dancing partner I
ever had."

Connie, of course, is also much older than I. He must be in his
early eighties but he still looks great. He still has that glint in
his eye and his high good humor and his love of pretty young
girls. I'm sure that's why he left the Church to marry Zsa Zsa

(as I was hoping Bill O'Connor would be able to do for me), and why at one time he was infatuated with Virginia Warren, the pretty daughter of former Governor of California and Chief Justice of the United States Supreme Court Earl Warren. And I'm sure it's why he always wanted me around as a dancing decoration at his fabulous Hilton Hotel openings . . . Will I ever forget the Istanbul Hilton opening? . . . Connie and I were always the first ones out on a dance floor. Our theme song was "Varsovienna"—the one that goes: "Put your little foot, put your little foot," et cetera. Connie considered that his lucky tune. He always held rehearsals with his orchestra and leading lady for his hotel openings.

All three of the older men in my life—Louis B. Mayer, Connie Hilton, and Arthur Cameron—were superb dancers.

I was considered one of the best rhumba dancers in Hollywood (having learned it from Desi Arnaz), and Connie Hilton was one of the few who could keep up with me. He could dance better than most men half his age. I think it's because he always liked to be in the company of younger people. He looked young, he acted young. And he still does. He always comes to my Christmas Eve parties, which I've given every year for thirty years, and he's always the life of the party. He thinks young. I don't think he'll ever grow old.

Connie has remained a marvelous friend through the years, and a very dear friend. But he was never a romance. He was, as I mentioned, my favorite date during my romance with Bill O'Connor, and, as I also mentioned, Bill introduced me to Connie. They were good friends. I'm sure Connie knew about our relationship and why it must be carried on with propriety. I'm sure he also didn't mind taking me out when Bill couldn't because we always had such great times together.

There was the Havana-Cuban Hilton, the Hong Kong Hilton, the Tokyo Hilton, the Continental Hilton in Mexico City, all the Hiltons in the Caribbean, Cairo, Madrid, and Istanbul . . . I was at them all and probably some I've forgotten.

But romance? Forget it. Connie just loved to dance and so did I. And we loved going out on the town together. We often double-dated with his son, Nicky, and Elizabeth Taylor, when they were courting. Elizabeth was under contract at M-G-M at the same time I was. The four of us were together the evening Elizabeth and Nicky broke the news to his father that they were going to be married.

Connie, of course, was delighted at the prospect of having such a beautiful daughter-in-law. He was probably a little jealous too. Knowing how he loved beautiful young girls, I'm sure the thought must have crossed his mind that he'd like to be in his son's shoes.

Nicky was a cute boy that night. I remember he turned to me and said, "Gee, Annie, if you marry Dad, just think what a glamorous stepmother I'd have."

And I remember looking at Elizabeth and Nicky and thinking how lucky they were, and how beautiful it all was . . . a marriage made in heaven. They were the most gorgeous young couple in the world and they had the world by its tail. Here he was, the handsome heir to the huge Hilton dynasty, a young king; and here she was, the world's most beautiful woman, so lovely and so talented.

I went to their wedding (May 6, 1950) and the reception they gave at the Bel Air Country Club and it was like something straight out of Louis B. Mayer's most romantic films . . . Almost unbearably beautiful . . . And then unbearably painful to see that marriage so quickly disintegrate. (She married Michael Wilding on February 21, 1952.)

As for Annie Miller's marriage plans, they were also slowly disintegrating. I think my great good friend and lady society columnist Cobina Wright was the only one of all the columnists who knew how deeply involved I was with Bill O'Connor, although of course our close friends knew. When I gave a birthday party for him on June 12, 1949 (he was a Gemini),

Cobina mentioned it in her column, along with the speculation that "the next cake they cut will be their wedding cake."

But the years went on. Bill finally gave me an engagement ring, a beautiful star sapphire in a gold basket weave setting of twenty large diamonds. It was beautiful. He had finally found a way to have his Catholic marriage annulled, he told me, so off he went to Rome and London to take care of all these little details that would permit him to be remarried in the Catholic Church to me.

But it didn't work out. There were certain papers his wife wouldn't sign. Don't ask me why. But without them we could not be married in the Catholic Church, as Bill wanted.

When he returned to California, I gave him back his ring. I knew that he would never leave his Church to marry me.

It was soon after this that Bill Moss came into my life and I was ready for him, a twice-disillusioned damsel in search of a Prince Charming, and in the very vulnerable position of about to be making the same mistake twice.

William Moss was a big oil man from Odessa, Texas (something in common right off the bat), and he had once been married to my friend, Jane Withers. Something else in common. He looked a lot like Red Skelton.

More important, he looked a little like my first husband, Reese Milner. Don't ask me why we always do this. Only psychiatrists know the answer, but they say we always marry men who remind us of our fathers or first husbands.

Bill Moss was reddish-blond, blue-eyed, tall and handsome and smoked cigars with the same mannerisms that Reese smoked them, and I was soon to find out the two of them had a lot of other things in common also. Both were virile men who had an eye for women, who loved expensive homes and pretty playgirls.

Bill Moss didn't want me to work. He wanted me to give up my career. "I want to take you away from all this business.

You'll never have to work again. All I want is for you to be my wife."

It was Reese all over again. I was getting nowhere with Bill O'Connor. I finally said yes to Bill Moss.

We were married August 22, 1958. (Look, I don't really remember all these dates. My collaborator, Norma Lee Browning, checks them out.)

That was one wedding I won't forget. Bill and I had planned a beautiful church wedding at a little Congregational church by the sea in La Jolla, California, and some wealthy Texas oil friends of his, Ve and Gordon Guiberson, were giving us a beautiful reception at their home. but while Ve was helping me into my wedding dress, the telephone rang. It was a long-distance call for me. It was from Bill O'Connor.

He begged me not to marry Bill Moss and pleaded with me to stop the wedding. He was going to leave the Catholic Church and marry me, he said. I couldn't believe my ears. Was he actually saying that, after all these years? But no, he couldn't really mean it. "I'm driving down to get you," he said. "I'll be there as soon as I can."

I took a deep breath and said, "It's too late now, Bill. The people are already at the church . . . I'm marrying Bill Moss. Goodbye."

"But you're not in love with him. You belong to me . . ."
I hung up on him.

I was heartsick and confused. I knew that I belonged to Bill O'Connor. But it *was* too late now . . . And as I walked down the aisle of the church I could still hear that telephone ringing. And all the time I was taking my wedding vows with Bill Moss, I could hear that telephone ringing, ringing, ringing. It was like an omen.

And I could still hear Bill O'Connor's voice begging me to call off the wedding and telling me finally after all these years that he would even leave his Church to marry me. I had waited twelve years to hear those words. They came too late.

Why are men like that?

When Bill Moss and I walked out of that church, man and wife, they didn't play the traditional "Wedding March." At Bill's special request they played instead, *Around the World in Eighty Days.* Yes, in true Texan style we were doing it up big.

And in the background, as we ran through all the rice and confetti, I could still hear the ringing of the telephone.

That marriage was doomed from the start.

Chapter 13

TEXAS HIGH LIFE

My marriage to Bill Moss really might have worked—if it had not been for Bill O'Connor, Arthur Cameron, a Dallas heiress, too many drinking parties, and a few other hindrances.

Although I was born in Texas and lived there as a child, I had never been initiated into the wild and woolly world of Texas oil men until I married Bill Moss.

His father was a judge in Odessa, Texas, who had bought up a lot of real estate which later turned out to be literally soaked in oil. The family had millions.

I must say our wedding in La Jolla was beautiful. I still have my wedding book with our bridal party pictures, and a list of all our guests—which reads like a Who's Who of Hollywood and Texas oil millionaires.

One of the photos surely must be a collector's item. It's a picture taken of my husband with his best man, Gordon Guiberson, and his ushers—including another Texas oil multi-millionaire, Arthur Cameron, who was to be my next husband.

Rehearsing a dance number
with the fantastic drummer,
Thurston Knudson, for
Columbia's *Hey, Rookie!*
in 1943.

My last Christmas Eve with
Sonja Henie (Mrs. Neils
Onstad) at my annual party
(1967). The fabulous
ice-skating champion and
film star died in Oslo,
Norway, on October 12,
1969.
(*Photo by Sylvia Norris*)

In *Hey, Rookie!* I did an Egyptian nautch dance, which is another name for the belly dance. My costume was a copy of my childhood "Egyptian-Nella" costume which I wore when I was seven years old and performed at the **Big Brothers Club** in Houston, Texas. (*Columbia photo*)

Dancing with the fabulous Fred Astaire in the M-G-M production of *Easter Parade*. Unfortunately, it was the only time I had the privilege of dancing with Mr. Astaire in a motion picture.

Above, a scene from
Easter Parade (1948). (Left
to Right: Dick Simmons,
Ann Miller, Fred Astaire,
and Judy Garland)
(*M-G-M photo*)

Right, another picture of
me dancing with Fred
Astaire in *Easter Parade*.
(*M-G-M photo*)

It isn't every girl who gets her present and future husbands in the same wedding picture.

Among my bridesmaids were Linda Darnell, who had also been a bridesmaid at my first wedding with Reese Milner; Margaret Pereira, who had introduced me to Bill O'Connor (her husband Bill Pereira, gave the bride away), society columnist Cobina Wright Sr., who was to become like a second mother to me (not that I needed another!) and who had a secret crush on my future husband Arthur Cameron, and Betty Bloomingdale, whose husband Alfred (of the Bloomingdale department stores) had once been an ardent suitor of mine.

Heading our wedding guest list was California Governor and Mrs. Edmund G. Brown. Both Connie and Nicky Hilton were there, as were Mr. and Mrs. Clint Murchison and a lot of other rich Texas oil men I didn't know; Mr. Warren Leslie, one of the vice-presidents of Neiman-Marcus; Mr. and Mrs. Nat Dumont (he's a wealthy industrialist) who were to be my attendants at my next wedding; Ginger Rogers, June Haver and Fred MacMurray, the Art Linkletters . . . and on and on.

With a guest list like that it wouldn't have been very decent of me to call off our wedding even for Bill O'Connor.

When Bill Moss and Jane Withers were married on September 20, 1947, they had one of the biggest weddings in Hollywood, there were over five hundred guests, and I was one of them. I remember thinking what a charming man Bill was and how much he looked like a tall version of Reese Milner. Actually, I had met Bill Moss then, but only briefly. So I don't count that meeting. I didn't really become acquainted with him until we started dating at the end of my Bill O'Connor romance.

When my engagement to Bill Moss was announced, Jane Withers called me and asked me to lunch. She said she had something to tell me that she thought I should know. In a nice way she tried to warn me that she didn't think the marriage would be a happy one, just as Harry Cohn and Vic Orsatti had tried to warn me about Reese.

But I didn't believe her. I thought it was just girl-talk. She was probably still in love with Bill and jealous of us, I thought.

My life has followed such a weird pattern. It's like returning to the scene of the crime. Maybe I'm a masochist. But Janie was right.

Ours was a very stormy marriage, though Willie, as I called him was never as violent as Reese, and I must admit that some of our fights were partly my fault. For one thing I simply couldn't keep up the pace with Willie and his wild and woolly Texas millionaire friends and their drinking parties. Hollywood has always been known for its wild parties but they're tame compared with those Texas binges that last for days.

Again I had given up my career completely to travel with Willie. I didn't know Texas oil men traveled so much but I guess that's the way they make their money on big oil "deals." We had a house on Summit Ridge Drive in Beverly Hills and an apartment in Dallas, and we were constantly commuting between the two places. As oil man Willie Moss's wife, I was expected to entertain lavishly as is the custom of all Texas oil millionaires. And I did. I love parties and I love Texans. I must say that being married to that Texas wildcatter Willie was never dull, and in many ways I adored him, but I simply didn't have the energy or the patience to keep up with him, especially when we went out to parties that lasted two or three days. What a life! Texans are the world's greatest party people and fabulous hosts.

We would usually start off at a party at a friend's elegant home, where the liquid refreshments flowed like water and everyone whooped it up.

And then we'd wind up two or three days later at the Cepango Club, then one of the most popular night spots in Dallas.

Our troubles usually started because I couldn't keep up with Willie and I would ask to go home, especially when I knew he was drinking too much. He would become angry with me and then the fights would start.

But we always kissed and made up, and in between our little battles we had some marvelous times. We did a lot of traveling together all over the world. We had been married only a few months when Conrad Hilton invited us to attend the opening of the Cairo Hilton Hotel in Egypt. As a special second-honeymoon present for me, Willie arranged for us to sail up the Nile in a private boat which had once belonged to King Farouk to visit the Valley of the Kings. I could hardly contain my excitement at the thought of finally seeing all those places I had always dreamed of and the great temples of the Pharaohs, especially those of the Thutmoses and Hatshepsut, the only lady Pharaoh who ever ruled as a "king."* She was the one whose bearded face I had gazed upon in a New York museum all those years ago, the one whom seers have told me I was supposed to have been in a previous incarnation.

One of the big regrets of my life is that I never got to make that trip because I became very ill and had to be flown out of Cairo.

But before this happened, I did have the unusual opportunity of meeting President Gamal Abdel Nasser who was in power at the time. He was tall, handsome, personable, and very athletic, an extremely charming man but there was one thing he did to his country that I didn't like at all. He had ordered all belly dancers to wear mesh netting between their bras and their skirts. The reason for this was President Nasser wanted their belly buttons covered. He felt it was immoral to show this area

---

* Thutmose I (1540 B.C.) was third king of the XVIII dynasty of ancient Egypt. He had two sons, Thutmose II and Thutmose III, and a daughter, Hatshepsut, the only one born of a royal mother, which made her heir to the throne in spite of her sex. She married her brother, Thutmose III, who seized the throne from his aged father, but before long Hatshepsut gained equal power with her husband-brother, relegated him to the background and called herself "king." (From the Columbia Encyclopedia.)

of the body. Personally, I thought such an edict was perfectly ridiculous because there's nothing more beautiful than this dance when it's done right and it certainly can't be done right if you're wrapped up in mesh netting. It's perhaps the most exotic dance in the whole world.

Willie and I remained with the Hilton entourage as far as Athens, where there were ground-breaking festivities for another Hilton Hotel. But I was put to bed with a high fever. Between Bill and Connie they managed to get the monarch's (King Paul I) doctor to take care of me. But I insisted on getting up out of bed to go and see the Acropolis, though I practically had to be carried. After that my temperature shot up to 105 and I was flown out in a special plane to the American Hospital in Paris with a severe case of pneumonia. I guess I almost died. When I had recovered enough to be moved again, Willie took me to St. Moritz in Switzerland where I was bedded down in the Palace Hotel for five weeks. St. Moritz was the only place in Europe where the sun was shining at that time of the year.

In spite of our problems, we did manage to make it through the first year of our marriage—which at least was a better batting average than I had in my first one. And Willie very thoughtfully took me back to La Jolla to celebrate our first wedding anniversary. We stayed at the lovely El Charro Inn. We had only been there a short while when suddenly one night I awakened and sat bolt upright in bed with a psychic flash that something terrible was happening to Bill O'Connor. As I have mentioned, there had always been that psychic rapport between us from the time I first noticed his picture in the newspaper.

Somehow a message was flashed to me that Bill O'Connor was going to die.

I awakened Willie and told him we had to go back to Los Angeles.

When he asked why, I wouldn't tell him at first. But finally I did and he was furious with me. I couldn't blame him. But I began weeping and wailing and begging him to take me home. He told me I was crazy and he was livid with rage as he got up and started tossing things in his suitcase. He should have tossed me out on my ear right then and there. But I couldn't help myself. I simply never had gotten over Bill O'Connor, though I had not seen him since I married Bill Moss. I am not the type of person to violate a marriage contract—something that couldn't be said of any of my husbands.

We headed back to Los Angeles.

I was still crying and trying to get up the nerve to turn on the car radio. Bill turned it on for me. The first thing we heard was that Bill O'Connor had died of a heart attack. The date was August 27, 1959.

It was a long sad ride back for me. Willie relented a little and wasn't as angry with me as he might have been. He had known Bill O'Connor also. Everyone knew Bill O'Connor and everyone loved him. Bill Moss had known of my devotion to him. He knew how I felt now, he understood and I will always be grateful for that.

We arrived home at dawn, and as soon as the maid heard us, she came and told me that I was to go over to Cobina Wright's house immediately because Cobina wanted to talk to me. Cobina's house was directly across the street from ours on Summit Ridge Drive. She always used to have her head hanging out the window so as not to miss anything in the running battles of "little Annie and Willie." None of it surprised her. She was a wise and wonderful little old lady, my second-best Mama-Kat, and she knew all about my romance with Bill O'Connor. We both knew, too, that he had started going downhill after my marriage to Bill Moss. He began drinking too much and seemed not to care about anything.

Naturally, I was having dark thoughts . . . What if I had listened to him when he begged me to call off the wedding? Would he really have married me? It was another of those little ironies of my life that Bill O'Connor should die while Bill Moss and I

were celebrating our first anniversary. And I blamed myself for
leaving him to marry Bill Moss.

I flung myself into Cobina's arms, sobbing.

She said the reason she sent for me was that she knew this was
going to happen.

She tried to reason with me. "Look, child, you can't hurt
Willie. Bill O'Connor is dead and you have a husband who is
alive . . . You can't carry on like this or you'll lose Bill Moss,
too. You mustn't let him know how deeply this has affected you.
Now, just clean up that face of yours and go back over there and
stop crying . . . And don't let your husband see you with
those red eyes . . ."

Well, I did go home, and though I tried to mop up my face as
best I could, I still couldn't hide my red eyes from Bill Moss. He
looked at me sternly and said, in his best wild-and-woolly Willie
true Texan style, "Tell you what I'm gonna do, Twinkle Toes.
(That was his pet name for me.) I'll take you to Bill O'Connor's
funeral but I don't want you to cry one tear."

As soon as Willie had left the house, I called the wife of Bill
O'Connor's brother and asked her to take me down to the
funeral home. I had never seen anyone I loved lying dead before, and my first thought was, how peaceful he looks. I remembered a habit he had of always combing his hair. He had
one wisp of black hair that tumbled down over his right eye
and he was constantly trying to comb it back into place. So I
took a comb out of my purse and stuck it in his pocket and I
told his sister-in-law, "Now, wherever he goes in Heaven, he'll
have a comb to fix his hair. That will make him happy."

I didn't cry there and I didn't cry at his funeral services—
probably because I had taken half a bottle of Miltowns and I
was in another world. Like a zombie.

I picked up my marriage with Bill Moss but it never had a
chance. There were too many things against it from the beginning. He began going off more and more on his own. I found
that being married to a Texas oil man wasn't all it was cracked up

to be. Sometimes he called on the phone but for the most part it was a rather lonely life.

Finally he packed his bags and said he was going to Texas and wouldn't be back. So I filed for divorce—on Valentine's Day, 1961, exactly fifteen years to the day after Reese Milner and I obtained our marriage license in 1946.

Bill Moss and I were married August 22, 1958, and separated February 13, 1961. My divorce action filed the next day charged him with extreme cruelty and at my hearing on May 11, 1961, I testified that he had frequently struck me and once broke my hand.

It wasn't too long after Bill O'Connor's death that Bill Moss and I—after another big argument—had decided to try a temporary separation. It just so happened that Ve Guiberson, who had been matron of honor at my wedding, was also having problems, and so the two of us decided to go on a little mutual-sympathy fling in Hawaii.

I had no idea where Bill was. He had been gone over a week and I'd had no word from him. Ve and I were staying in the Royal Hawaiian Hotel in a huge suite with all the luxuries, but instead of having the time of our lives as we had anticipated, we were in all truth a little sad and miserable—because we would have preferred to have our husbands with us.

We had been there only a few days when it happened again— my psychic antenna sending me a message about Bill Moss in the middle of the night. I saw him with a beautiful blonde in a red dress at the Cepango Club in Dallas.

I knocked on Ve's door, awakened her and told her about it. I said I was going to call the Cepango Club and find out if Willie really was there. She urged me not to be a fool. I was merely "hallucinating," she said. But I put the call through and they finally got Bill Moss on the phone. When I heard his voice, I came right out and asked what he was doing in that night club with a blonde in a red dress.

He was stunned into a moment of silence. Then he said, "You're having me followed, aren't you?"

I said, "No, I've got something better than detectives."

Of course he didn't know what I was talking about. "How could you be in Hawaii and know that I'm here at the Cepango? As a matter of fact, yes, I am here with some friends. So what?"

I said, "Thank you very much," and hung up.

It wasn't until later that I learned he had been out with the wealthy Dallas heiress that very night. And she was indeed wearing a red dress.

Not that any of this truly mattered. As I said, this marriage was doomed for so many reasons. Though technically it lasted nearly three years—from August 22, 1958, to May 11, 1961—it was really finished after our first anniversary fiasco. We both kept trying—off and on—to make it work, but it was like trying to patch up busted tires.

Still, there will always be a soft spot in my heart for Willie. He saw me through the grand finale of the one great love of my life and into my next Mack Sennett episode with our mutual great friend, Arthur Cameron, the most colorful and flamboyant of all the men in my life. And he was to come back into my life later.

Chapter 14

CAMERON OPUS 1

Arthur Cameron was the comic opera era of my life. I still don't believe him.

He was the first one to phone when word leaked out that Bill Moss and I were having problems. I had known Arthur Cameron for twenty years. I considered him an old family friend. My mother adored him. He had known Bill O'Connor and both my husbands. He had been an usher at my wedding with Bill Moss.

So you can imagine my surprise when Arthur Cameron came over to our house and told my mother and me that he had always been in love with me and wanted to marry me.

He told me I had made two mistakes and it was time I should settle down with a man who really loved me and wanted to take care of me without trying to possess me.

Mistakes? I don't remember whether it was his fourth or fifth, but he had just recently gone to court for an interlocutory degree from his latest wife, Jean Lawrence, and he wasn't any more free to marry than I was. In those days we had to wait a year and a day before the divorce became final, meaning we could not remarry in California in the meantime.

I reminded him that I hadn't even gone to court yet for my interlocutory degree, though Bill Moss and I were separated.

Arthur Cameron was older than I. He was sixty and I was thirty-eight. But he looked and acted much younger. And he did have an irresistible charm—as all his wives and mistresses I'm sure would testify. He was terribly handsome, by far the best looking of all my husbands. Most people thought he looked a lot like Cary Grant. I thought he looked a lot like Bill O'Connor. And that was my downfall. He also adored Bill O'Connor.

I began going out with him. I call that period of my life my Mack Sennett comedy days. I was constantly being trailed by detectives. I hadn't bothered to go to court yet for my interlocutory degree from Bill Moss and when he learned I was going out with Arthur Cameron, he began having me tailed. When Arthur found out about it, he hired his own detectives to keep an eye on Willie's sleuths. So every time I left the house I would always look back to see if everyone was ready to go before I took off—with two cars full of detectives following me. I thought it was very funny. Probably they did too.

The detectives followed me right down to Mexico City, when Mother and I accepted Arthur's invitation to be his guests for a week's vacation. My mother went along as our chaperone to prove that I was not having an affair with Arthur.

Actually, there was nothing but a good twenty-five-year friendship between us at this stage. Arthur spent most of his time taking us sightseeing and trying to convince Mother and me that I should marry him. He proposed every ten minutes and he told everyone who came along that he was going to marry Ann Miller. He was trying to sweep me off my feet with his constant attention and romancing, and he was doing a pretty good job. At least I was enjoying every minute of it.

Until—enter Bill Moss. His detectives had tailed us all the way to the top of the elegant Tecali Hotel where we were having dinner (and where we had separate suites) . . . There was a big scene. If you've never seen two Texas oil millionaires tangle, you can take my word for it—it's some confrontation!

Though it started off rather violently, they wound up having a friendly drink together and talking it out. I don't know what kind of an agreement or arrangement they made between them, if any, as neither Bill Moss nor Arthur ever told me, and I had quietly excused myself (being half scared to death) to go to the powder room, and then went back to my suite.

It was only after we came back home that I finally told Arthur I would marry him—when we were both free to do so.

He said we didn't have to wait for our divorces, that he could arrange for us to get our divorces in Mexico and be married there. I wasn't so sure I liked this idea. I knew that with his money he could probably arrange anything he wanted at any place any time.

Arthur Cameron, as everyone knew, was an extremely wealthy man, a multi-multimillionaire, whose real estate holdings and oil wells were supposedly bringing him in $25,000 a day without turning a finger. He lived at 910 Benedict Canyon in the home that Louis B. Mayer once owned. He had a fleet of six Cadillacs all painted "Cameron white," as everyone called them, and he owned a six-acre, walled-in paradise estate in Palm Springs, one of the biggest in that desert resort.

He was reputed to be worth $100,000,000 and I guess no one ever doubted this. At least I didn't. But Arthur wore his money well, and I liked that.

His biggest fault so far as I was concerned was that he was mad for pretty women.

But he promised me faithfully over and over again that he would definitely end all his philandering if I would only marry him. I was beginning to weaken.

Then one afternoon a mutual friend of ours, one of his attorneys, Arthur Crowley, came to my home and begged me not to marry Arthur Cameron.

"For God's sake, Annie, and for your own sake, stop being a romanticist and get your head on straight. I've known Arthur for years. When he sees something he wants, he goes after it because he has the power and he has the money. Now he wants you. But don't be a fool. If you get married in Mexico, the marriage will be legal there, all right, and probably elsewhere in the world, but not in the United States.

"Eventually you will have to be married again in California—after your divorce is final."

I told him that was fine with me.

Then he hit me with a real zinger.

"What makes you think Arthur Cameron would marry you again in California at the end of your year's waiting period? He's the most unpredictable man in the world. Please, Annie, listen to me. In order to protect yourself, don't rush into this with a Mexican divorce and marriage. Make him wait for you a year, until your California decree is final. Then marry him—if he hasn't changed his mind by then. You know how he is with women. He gets bored pretty fast. If he's still mad for you at the end of that waiting period, then you know you have a real marriage."

"You're absolutely right," I said firmly. "If he really loves me he should be willing to wait." I promised Arthur Crowley that I would take his advice and at the time I really believed it.

Two days later, I got my interlocutory decree in California. That was on May 12, 1961. And thirteen days later, on May 25, I became Mrs. Arthur Cameron in a ceremony at the Tecali Hotel in Mexico City.

To this day I don't really know what made me say yes to Arthur, except that he was a haven in a storm of unhappiness. And maybe it was because I'm an Aries and I have my moon in Pisces and my heart rules my head. That's why my mother has always called me the headless wonder, I let my heart rule my head and love rule my life. When I'm in love I just never listen to anyone and I do all these bird-brained things but I can't help it because I'm an Aries and that's the pattern of an Aries.

Arthur Crowley got wind of our plans and called and begged me not to go through with it. "Annie, you're going to regret this," he warned. "I told you Arthur Cameron gets bored with women very quickly. I know Arthur."

Cobina Wright called, too, and warned me that Arthur probably would not go through another ceremony in California a year later if I married him now. But I thought she was only jealous because she'd had this school girl crush on him for years.

So Arthur and I flew to Mexico City, and Valerie and Nat Dumont came along with us to be matron of honor and best man. Our friend Miguel Alemán, former President of Mexico, had helped arrange for Mexican divorces for both of us.

And so we were married. It was a beautiful ceremony, performed by a Mexican justice of the peace, in a fantastic suite at the top of the Tecali hotel, overlooking beautiful Chapultepec Park and Maximilian's Palace. And Miguel Alemán sent me a lovely bouquet of flowers and a letter on my wedding day, wishing me much happiness.

Well, now the fun really began. There's one thing Arthur Cameron had over my other husbands. He had a wonderful sense of humor and he was most generous with his money. So it was agreed that we would take my mother and Cobina Wright with us on the first lap of our honeymoon tour of Europe, and our first stop would be the famous Niehans Clinic in Lausanne, Switzerland.

Mother, Cobina, and Arthur were all anxious to take those marvelous rejuvenation shots of Dr. Niehans that are supposed to prolong your life and restore your fountain of youth. I guess everyone has heard about Dr. Paul Niehans and his treatment, which is called "cellular therapy." He liquefies certain organs from embryo lambs and injects them into your system. Many VIPs have had the CT shots, as they're called, including Hedda

Hopper, Konrad Adenauer, Pope Pius XII, and Somerset Maugham.

Well, Arthur took one look at the size of the needles used for the shots and decided he couldn't go through with it. I'll admit the needles were frightening to look at, about five inches long.

Finally Arthur said, "Okay, Annie, why don't you be my guinea pig? You take a shot first and if it doesn't hurt you, then I'll take them." I thought he was joking. Some joke. But he wasn't.

Dr. Niehans explained to him that I was too young and active and didn't need them.

But I secretly wanted Arthur to take the shots. He had suffered a mild stroke a few years earlier and I was hoping the cell therapy would help him. Actually, I didn't mind being his guinea pig. I've always known that men are bigger sissies than women when it comes to taking injections of any kind.

I took two or three of the shots and when Arthur saw that I didn't scream about it, he pulled himself together and submitted to the ordeal. And, of course, Mother and Cobina were having a ball throughout the entire treatment series.

The treatment did help all three of them, but Arthur would have been helped more if he had obeyed the rules that went with the CT shots—no cigarettes, no liquor, no sex for two months! Cigarettes were no problem, he didn't smoke, but anyone who thought Arthur Cameron could ever give up booze and sex until the day he died had another think coming. Two days after he finished his shots he was all over the place chasing the chambermaids—and me.

When the treatments were finished, Mother and Cobina returned to California and Arthur and I moved to the Beau Rivage Hotel, a fantastically beautiful place overlooking the lake in Lausanne. I developed an allergic reaction to the shots and developed a fever of 104 degrees. Dr. Niehans said it was nothing to worry about but I had to stay in bed a few days.

It was during this time that Arthur, in one of his most engaging and generous moods, decided that I deserved a beautiful diamond ring for being such a good girl and taking the shots for him—and for letting my mother and Cobina come along on our honeymoon.

"You're a very unselfish girl, my darling. I know you've had other rings but not like what I'm going to buy for you," he said.

And right then and there, he picked up the telephone, called Harry Winston in New York, and told him to send a man over immediately with a nice selection of diamond rings. The Winston man arrived the very next day with his little black satchel and in it was every size and shape of diamond you can imagine . . . Pear shapes, marquises, square and emerald cuts . . . the most fabulous-looking diamonds I had ever seen in my life.

The truth of the matter is that I was upstairs in bed with my 104-degree temperature, when I heard the Winston man arrive downstairs—we had a two level suite at the hotel—and I overheard Arthur tell the man that none of those stones would do because there wasn't one really long enough for my finger. When I heard that, I got out of bed and practically crawled downstairs on my hands and knees because I was so weak—but I just had to see those diamonds! And when I saw them, I told Arthur that any one of them would do, they were all so beautiful. But he ordered me to get back in bed, saying, "No, they're not long enough or graceful enough for your hands."

Arthur had always told me I had beautiful hands, and I do have very long tapering fingers. I thought any hands would have looked good in any of those diamonds.

But Arthur sent the man away and called Harry Winston again. Mr. Winston said he would have a virgin stone cut especially for me, in exactly the size Arthur ordered. That stone was flown to me clear across the world, and it was the most fabulous 20-carat blue-white diamond I'd ever laid my eyes on. It had just a tiny flaw and Arthur paid $125,000 for it. If it had been perfect, it would have cost $650,000. I still have it. I call it my Arthur Cameron diamond. I keep it in my bank vault along with my other valuable jewelry and take it out to wear on only very special occasions. The insurance on it is $15,000 a year.

As soon as my fever was gone, we went on to Paris for a few days to see all our friends and to take in some of the French couture collections. Then on to Rome, where we had a marvelous time—except for one memorable argument.

We had gone to dinner at the Villa Camilluccia, the house that Mussolini had built for his mistress, and hanging from the ceiling of the restaurant were two quite fabulous chandeliers that immediately took Arthur's eye. He called over the maître d' and asked where they came from, explaining that he wished to buy two just like them for his Benedict Canyon home. The maître d' told him they were from Moscatelli in Milan, the world's greatest chandelier maker. Right then and there, Arthur decided that we were going to Milan to buy some chandeliers. Then, having made that momentous decision, he said now we should celebrate. And he meant with real booze, not wine.

I reminded him again that he was not supposed to drink hard liquor so soon after his Niehans shots. But a lot of good it did me to argue. He said he was tired of wine, he wanted some good old Texas bourbon, and he proceeded to order some and sit there and get stoned while I twiddled my thumbs. I really have never learned to be a heavy drinker in spite of all my hard-drinking husbands and Texas oil-rounder friends. I prefer wine.

So like a spoiled child I pouted all the way back to the Grand Hotel, where we were staying, and when we entered the lobby, Arthur raced up the stairs ahead of me and locked the door to our suite so I couldn't get in.

I pounded on the door and begged him to let me in. He yelled back at me, "No, all you'll do is nag at me not to drink. I'm pouring myself another bourbon. You can go downstairs and get the key to your own room but I'm locking off the rest of the suite."

He was really quite smashed. I had no choice but to get the bellboy to open my door for me. When I awakened next morning I was hurt and angry. I tiptoed over to the door between our rooms and listened. I didn't hear a sound. Apparently he was sleeping it off.

So I'll tell you what little Orphan Annie-girl did. I quickly and quietly got gussied up in my best finery, went downstairs, called a cab, and asked the driver to take me to Balestra, one of Rome's top fashion designers. And there, with all the aplomb of a Texas oil multimillionaire's wife, which I was, I bought $10,-000 worth of clothes and charged them all to Arthur Cameron.

By the time I got back to the hotel, Arthur was up and around and cold sober. I informed him of what I had just done and presented him the bill. At first he was furious. He nearly went up in smoke. But he started to laugh. I must say he really did have a fabulous sense of humor. The whole situation suddenly struck him as hilariously funny, and he said, "Annie, you're a good girl and I've been a bad boy. I deserve to be spanked for what I did. That was no way to treat you. Now, I'll tell you what I'm going to do. I'm going to surprise little Annie and just buy you all those clothes." And he paid for them. I still have them upstairs in my wardrobe. They're fabulous clothes and they are still fashionable. They fill one huge closet which Mother and I call my Arthur Cameron dynasty.

We returned to Paris after a few days and Arthur offered to treat me to a special hairdo from the great Alexandre, hairdresser to Elizabeth Taylor, the Duchess of Windsor, and countless other celebrities. I'll never forget walking into his hair salon and seeing all those marvelous French women sitting there in their pink robes and with French poodles in their laps. The great Alexandre came over to me and asked how I wished my hair coiffed.

"You're the expert," I said. "I'll let you decide. But make it something romantic."

"*Mais oui*," said he. "I design you someteeng called Romance of the Seventeenth Century, and I dedicate eet especiallement *pour vous*."

Well, that dedication ceremony was something else again. It took an entire day. First I went through a whole line-up of salon operators and underlings who brushed my hair, then shampooed it, then brushed it again, then finally put it in rollers and stuck me under a dryer. When it was dry—and this took forever—the great Alexandre pirouetted out from somewhere, went into some Pavlovian leaps, turns, and ballet sprints, with comb and brush in his hands. I think the great Alexandre really missed his calling. He puts on quite a show. When he claps his hands, all work in the salon stops and all his operators stand around him in a semicircle to watch him work.

He swept my hair up, wrapped something around it—the something turned out to be a bunch of little braids wound with ribbons—flared it out in back and somehow twisted it in the shape of a heart. Then he made little spit curls around my ears. And there I was—with my spit curls and this big black heart-of-hair on the back of my head. "*Voila! Pour vous, pour vous*, eet ees Romance of the Seventeenth Century," said the great Alexandre.

Everyone applauded and a photographer popped up and started taking pictures. With all the other ladies looking on, it was a little embarrassing—but even more so when Arthur Cameron walked in. I turned and showed him the big heart on the back of my head, and he broke into loud laughter.

"Annie-girl, that's the funniest damn hairdo I've ever seen," he said.

He didn't think it was so funny when he was presented the bill—$150! I must say I nearly went into a state of shock, but Arthur was quite gallant about it. He paid the bill and gave generous tips without creating a scene, as some men might have done. I'm sure he figured what's done is done. And I assured him that once I put on the proper dress and jewelry to go with it, he would think my Romance of the Seventeenth Century hairdo quite divine.

I asked the great Alexandre to put lots of spray on my hair because I wasn't going to take it down for a week.

And I didn't, either. But what a mess that turned out to be.

Arthur had promised to take me to Venice, a place I had never been, before going on to Milan to buy his precious chandeliers.

In Venice we stayed in the Aga Khan's suite at the Bauer-Grunwald Hotel and we fell in love with the city.

When it came time to undo my Romance of the Seventeenth Century hairdo, guess what. None of the hotel's beauty salon operators could get a comb or brush through my hair. They tried everything to loosen the sticky mess and then they told me they'd just have to cut the heart off. Cut my hair! I broke into tears. But I had no other choice. At first, when I saw myself in the mirror I thought I looked like a French poodle in drag. But after it was set it turned out fine and the great Alexandre caper provided my husband with his favorite story to tell on me until the day he died.

Arthur was very kind to me in Venice. He sometimes affectionately called me his little duck, and he took me over to one of the glass blowing factories in Murano and had a little glass duck blown especially for me . . . We went on to Milan where Arthur purchased two of the chandeliers at $5,000 each, but after he came home and had them hung he liked them so well that he ordered two more to be shipped from Italy . . . The little duck and the chandeliers had a sad ending for me. After Arthur died in March 1967 an auction was held to dispose of many of his belongings from his estate. I went, and I saw my little glass duck on the auction block. I was determined to have it and I bid for it. But the bids kept going up and up until they were way out of line. It was auctioned off for far too much money, and I was heartbroken to have to give up the little glass duck that had been so much a part of my precious memories of Arthur Cameron.

The chandeliers were also auctioned off for far too much money but that I didn't mind so much. They were not as personal as the duck, only insofar as they would always remind me of that night at the Mussolini-mistress Villa-restaurant where Arthur had first seen them and decided to buy them and then began to celebrate with real Texas-style booze . . .

Ah, so many happy memories of that honeymoon . . .

And then the dawning and the not-so-happy memories.

When we returned to California, we divided our time between his famous house at 910 Benedict Canyon and his Palm Springs estate. I still had the house that Bill Moss and I had shared on Summit Ridge Drive, and when Arthur Cameron was away on business I would sometimes stay there. With our Mexican divorces and marriage I trustfully considered Arthur Cameron to be very much my legally wedded husband, but he reminded me that neither of us yet had our final divorce decrees in California and so we should behave with a certain amount of decorum as it really was illegal for us to be living together in California. He advised me to put up a front of still living part-time in the Summit Ridge Drive house so that our ex-spouses couldn't "get" anything on us to hold up our divorce proceedings.

Oh, I tell you, it was all as mysterious and romantic as a James Bond whodunit.

But I was in love again and I was putty because my moon is in Pisces, and anything Arthur Cameron said to do I did. Anything for you, my love, my dove, my Don Juan, my dear darling who loves me enough to buy me a $125,000 diamond and a little blown-glass duck.

All our good friends, of course, accepted our Mexican marriage. We entertained frequently with beautiful dinner parties at both his Benedict Canyon mansion and the one in Palm Springs. Arthur was a very charming and gracious man who thoroughly enjoyed living like a king. And he treated me like his queen. Until, as Arthur Crowley had warned me, he became bored.

I finally began to realize that he was spending a great deal of time away from the house. He would say, for instance, that he

was just going out for a walk and then not come back for
hours.

But somehow he always soothed my hurt feelings by doing
something nice for me. And I was absolutely ecstatic the night
he told me that he was giving a lavish big luncheon for me to
announce our wedding date in late May, after my divorce from
Bill Moss would become final. He gave the luncheon. He planned
it all himself, ordered the flowers, the food, and took care of the
minutest details of the entire event. It was, as might be expected
of anything Arthur Cameron would plan, a most elegant luncheon at his Benedict Canyon home, and Arthur announced to one
and all that we were going to be married in California as soon as
my divorce was final.

But I had begun to suspect something not quite copacetic in
his comings and goings. Those CT shots apparently were working overtime. He was leaving me alone far too much. Then I
began listening in on his telephone calls and my fears were confirmed. He had a whole swarm of sweeties on the string.

I confronted him with the evidence and issued an ultimatum,
"Either those pussycats go or I go."

To my surprise and horror he said, "Okay, pack your bags."

Could this be the same sweet man I had married in Mexico
City, the same man who had ordered Harry Winston to fly over
a special-cut $125,000 diamond, the same man who had bought
me the little blown-glass duck in Vienna? Indeed it was.

I packed my bags and went back to my Summit Ridge home
in the hills that night, called my mother and told her where I
was, and then proceeded to cry my heart out. Two days later,
Mother called me and said I must come down to her house (also
in Beverly Hills) immediately because our living room was a
disaster.

I was horrified at the sight which greeted my eyes. Everything
I owned—clothes, hats, suitcases, even my bicycle—all my personal belongings from Arthur Cameron's Palm Springs and Benedict Canyon homes were dumped into my mother's house on

Alta Drive, just dumped there by Arthur's chauffeur and gardener who had come in two limousines and tossed everything inside the house on the living-room floor and then left. My mother was in tears. And I was ready for a nervous breakdown.

But would you believe I went back to that man?

As I said from the start, he was irrepressible, he was irresistible, he was totally devastating with women—and he knew it. And being an Aries (always my alibi) love springs eternal and I went back with him.

Then one day the Aries fireworks exploded. I was upstairs in my room at 910 Benedict Canyon when the buzzer buzzed and it was one of the maids saying that Mr. Cameron wanted me down at the pool.

Dutifully I went.

Aha, he was having a party. I heard the fun and laughter as I approached the pool and I thought perhaps he was throwing a surprise party for me. It was a surprise all right.

Arthur was sitting there like a potentate watching a whole pool full of bikini-clad bathing beauties frolicking around and obviously having a grand time.

Life was anything but dull with Arthur Cameron.

When I could get my voice back I asked him who all these women were.

"They're your little sisters, darling," he said, smiling broadly.

"What do you mean, sisters?"

"Now, now darling, you don't have to worry about them. After all, you're the one I married," he said.

By this time, I had counted seventeen who were all strangers to me.

"You mean I'm queen of the harem?" I asked, not too sweetly.

"Don't be like that, darling. Just smile and be sweet to them and show them what a great lady you are," he said.

As I have mentioned, Arthur Cameron had a marvelous sense of humor but if this was his idea of a joke, it certainly went over my head. He had assembled seventeen mistresses for a pool party—all for my benefit. I don't know what he was trying to prove except that he was doing his own thing his own way and I could either take it or leave it.

One at a time would have been enough to make a wife flip her wig. But seventeen was too much even for an Aries with her moon in Pisces! I left his poolside benefit party, stalked out of his house and never went back again.

Arthur's problem was he fancied himself the Maharajah of Beverly Hills. I couldn't take being his Maharini knowing he had all those pussycats.

Chapter 15

CAMERON OPUS 2

Soon after I left I received a telegram from Arthur that read: I AM BREAKING MY ENGAGEMENT TO YOU. SORRY ABOUT THE WHOLE THING.

I couldn't believe he would do this to me.

And where did that leave me regarding a divorce?

His telegram must mean that he was refusing to admit we had been married in Mexico. I still considered myself his wife, and though I wanted nothing more to do with him, I couldn't file for a divorce in California because that state doesn't recognize a Mexican marriage as valid. Would I have to go back to Mexico to get a divorce from him?

Meanwhile, in California I was still technically married to Bill Moss. My divorce from him wouldn't be final for nearly two months. I thought oh dear God, what have I done? Here I am married to two men and that's bigamy, isn't it, and they arrest people for bigamy, don't they? It's either that or if Arthur refuses to marry me then everyone will think we've

Dance number from M-G-M's *On the Town* with Alice Pearce, me, Betty Garrett, Frank Sinatra, Jules Munshin, and Gene Kelly (1949).

Above, Busby Berkeley staged the extravagant production number I did in M-G-M's *Small Town Girl* in 1953. The number was called "The Beat." Film starred Jane Powell and Farley Granger with S. Z. Sakall, Robert Keith, and Bobby Van. (*M-G-M photo*)

Above right, clowning with Red Skeleton in M-G-M's *Texas Carnival* in 1951. (*M-G-M photo*)

Below right, Kathryn Grayson and I were kidding between scenes on the set of M-G-M's *Kiss Me, Kate*. The 1953 film version of Cole Porter's hit Broadway musical also co-starred Howard Keel. (*M-G-M photo*)

When you go to Egypt, you have to ride a camel. So here is Annie Miller perched on top of you know what as I visit the Giza Pyramid in 1955. (*Al-Hilal photo*)

been living in sin for ten months. How did I ever get myself into such a mess?

I telephoned him repeatedly and left messages with his secretary but he never returned any of the calls. I had no intentions of going back to him this time but I had to discuss what our situation really was and how to get it untangled.

I called his house but was told he wasn't there. I called both the El Presidente and Tecali hotels in Mexico City but he wasn't registered at either place.

Finally I swallowed my pride and telephoned our mutual friend, Arthur Crowley, and asked him if he knew anything about the telegram.

Matter of fact he did. He was the one who sent it, at Arthur Cameron's request. No, he was not permitted to tell me where Arthur was. But he made it very plain that Arthur definitely was not going to marry me in California just as Mr. Crowley had predicted. And furthermore, he confirmed my worst fears. "Arthur wants out. He's denying everything. He says he is not married to you, has never been married to you, and has no intention of marrying you," he said. "You can't say I didn't warn you, Annie. Arthur is a restless soul."

"We most certainly were married in Mexico, and I have witnesses to prove it. We also took my mother and Cobina with us to Europe on our honeymoon," I told him.

"You'd better find yourself a good attorney," Arthur Crowley advised.

Valerie and Nat Dumont, who had been our witnesses at the wedding in Mexico, were very upset when I told them the latest news. They recommended Jacques Leslie for my attorney. He was a former judge, now practicing law.

I told him the whole story, even about the pussycats in the pool.

He said I would have to file suit against Arthur Cameron, claiming that he had led me into a fraudulent marriage.

I told him I knew nothing about legal matters and that all I wanted was for Arthur to admit to our marriage and tell the truth about it so my reputation wouldn't be ruined.

"Since you know about these things and I don't," I said, "I'm going to leave it all up to you. I'm sure you'll do what is right and for my best interests."

"Fine," Mr. Leslie said. "You're in good hands."

As it turned out, my break-up with Arthur Cameron made the biggest headlines of any of my marital rifts, beginning with banner headlines on the front page of the Los Angeles *Times* (Thursday, April 5, 1962) ACTRESS ANN MILLER SUES LA OILMAN FOR $7 MILLION.

I was absolutely stunned when I saw the headlines, and even more so when I started reading about myself. Actually, according to the report, I was suing Arthur for $7,150,000! . . . "Movie actress Ann Miller filed suit for $7,150,000 Wednesday against Arthur A. Cameron, Los Angeles oilman, on a claim he induced her into a fraudulent Mexico City marriage . . . Miss Miller, 38, in a petition filed in Santa Monica Superior Court, also asked for a division of community property . . ."

I was in such a state of shock that my first thought was: What's the $150,000 for? Why pick a dumb figure like that? Why not just leave it in round numbers? Read on, Annie, read on . . .

> Her suit charged that as a result of Cameron's "fraudulent misrepresentations" her career as a singer, dancer and actress in motion pictures and television suffered severe damages. For this, she is asking $5 million damages.
>
> Other damages sought were $150,000 for loss of valuable "marital rights;" $1 million for "great pain and mental suffering and mortification" and $1 million in punitive damages.
>
> The suit asked that the Mexican marriage be declared valid on grounds that once "someone induces another into a fraudulent marriage he cannot later claim immunity from the responsibilities of matrimony."

I called my attorney Jacques Leslie and told him I didn't want Arthur Cameron or his money. I wouldn't have them on a silver platter. All I wanted was for Arthur to admit to the marriage. I didn't want all the people my mother and I knew to think that I had lived with Arthur Cameron and traveled with him all over Europe without being married. I didn't want his money. I only wanted him to acknowledge our marriage.

My attorney reassured me. "Leave everything to me, Annie."

Arthur called me from Mexico and said I wasn't going to get away with this, and then he hung up without letting me say a word.

Also he hired detectives to follow me night and day from the minute my divorce suit was filed.

I later learned that Arthur Cameron had a detective's report on every day in the life of every woman he was keeping.

It is difficult to write about this man with any credibility. He was simply an unbelievable phenomenon. There will never be another like him. He had, for instance, given me $10,000 to furnish and decorate our bedroom at 910 Benedict Canyon. Only the bedroom. I even had a closet in the room filled with another $10,000 worth of lingerie. He could be so kind and so cruel at the same time.

I really must digress for a moment to tell you a little more about Arthur Cameron and that house at 910 Benedict Canyon which played such an important role in my life. Arthur had permitted me to go ahead and buy the $10,000 worth of negligees and night gowns at Saks Fifth Avenue. I had bought the night gowns especially to look glamorous for him, only to be told that he hated night gowns and I never got to wear one, not even one. For breakfast he liked me to wear only a negligee and a ribbon in my hair. So I was up to my royal derrière in night gowns. I still have them, as well as a whole closet full of Arthur Cameron negligees in my house in Beverly Hills.

The famous house at 910 Benedict Canyon is now nothing but a memory. It has long since been razed to the ground and the five-and-a-half acres divided into ten lots. But strangely enough not one has been sold. The property, which is close behind the plush Beverly Hills Hotel and one of the choicest spots in the city, is known as the Cameron Estate. I hear the lots are up for sale for $160,000 each, which is quite expensive even for such choice property. And perhaps that is the reason they're not selling.

But personally I've always felt there was a curse on that 910 Benedict Canyon place. The house itself, as I have mentioned, was originally the fourteen-room "bungalow" built for Marion Davies on the M-G-M lot which became the center of social affairs for that studio—as well as Miss Davies's "dressing room."

It was later moved to the Warner lot and then to the Benedict Canyon address, and became known as one of the Hearst estates.

I first knew it when Louis B. Mayer lived in it.

And such wonderful memories I have of those happy times —the Sunday-night dinner parties and screenings of new films in that marvelous projection room. And such ghoulish memories, too, of the time when I shared that same house (off and on) with Arthur Cameron, and he had all the seats ripped out of that beloved projection room and converted it into a storeroom for the antiques he was constantly collecting and a business office for his oil business.

Not that he really needed an office. He already had one in the Kirkeby Building on Wilshire Boulevard—a huge suite with four secretaries. But he never went there. Sometimes in the afternoon he would drive over to the golf course just across the street and down a few blocks from his Kirkeby office building (he owned quite a few blocks of real estate for quite a few miles along Wilshire Boulevard) but he never bothered to go to his office. He conducted most of his business (oil and real estate), when he thought about business, from his home on Benedict Canyon. Somewhat in the Howard Hughes image.

Anyway, I'll never forget the projection room in that house and the wonderful memories it held of so many good times and great movies—and then Arthur Cameron's two teen-age boys kept bashing golf balls against that movie screen and tearing it to pieces. They were rather unruly boys. Whenever I tried to say anything to them, they would retort, "You're not my mother!" And I would choke back the tears. I had a real affection for his children. (He had four, two boys and two girls.)

Such strange memories I had of that house—first that it was forever haunted by the spirits of Marion Davies and William Randolph Hearst, but it bore the stamp of Louis B. Mayer's personality even more. At least for me. When I was in that house with Arthur Cameron, I could feel L.B.'s spirit around us. Both Arthur and L.B. were Cancer-born, L.B. on July 4 and Arthur on July 15. Both loved that house. And both loved music. Somehow I have always associated L.B. with music. Arthur Cameron liked music, too, but he leaned more toward gypsy violins or Mexican music, especially that at the Villa Fontana in Mexico City where we had our wedding dinner and the orchestra feted us with "Cu-cu-rru-cu-cu, Paloma."

Ah, Arturo, my love . . . But all things come to an end.

My court battle with Arthur Cameron finally started and what a field day the reporters had with that one.

In a separate maintenance suit filed pending trial of my $7,000,000 damage and divorce suit against Arthur, I supposedly asked for $10,000 monthly expenses—including $50 a month to care for my French poodles, which of course made headlines. ($2,500 a month for clothes, $1,000 for entertainment, $500 for travel, $50 for club dues, $450 for beauty aids and care, and $300 for food.) Why not? It really wasn't my idea. Plus, of course, $100,000 for his fees and $25,000 court costs.

Arthur and I finally met again face to face, with our lawyers. I told him I would make a deal with him—I would drop the lawsuit against him if he would admit to our marriage.

And I remember so well his response, "Would you really do that, little duck?"

Perverse as it may seem, there was still an affection between us and it was obvious to everyone throughout our bitter court battle. It was all so incongruous. During the course of the testimony, so many memories came back . . . for both of us. Gradually, during our court sessions we became on friendly terms again. I even brought some bananas and cookies to court, a snack for Arthur. He wasn't accustomed to being up so early in the morning, as he usually slept until one or two o'clock in the afternoon, and, of course, these court sessions started at nine o'clock in the morning. Arthur never functioned very well until noon at least. I would feed him the bananas and cookies to try to keep him awake and coherent.

At one point both our lawyers suggested that we call the whole thing off and have a reconciliation.

"Not on your life," I said. "If it takes $7,150,000 to get Arthur Cameron to admit to our marriage, it's going to stay that way, buster, until he admits it."

My lawyer could not track down any official recording of the marriage, which I thought was rather weird, but my friends Valerie and Nat Dumont came to court and testified that they had been at our wedding in Mexico City.

After all the testimony in court, Arthur and I were called in to the chambers of Judge Edward R. Brand whom we had both known for many years. He tried to talk me into dropping the suit.

I repeated my stand to Judge Brand. "I'm not going to drop the suit until Arthur admits we were married."

I told him I didn't approve of the sum of money my lawyer chose, it was not my decision, and I wasn't interested in Arthur Cameron's money but I would not drop the lawsuit against him until he admitted our marriage.

Arthur was sitting there listening. Finally he said to the judge, "I'll tell you what I'll do. I'll let Annie keep her ring. I'll go ahead and give her mother the $50,000 I was going to give her to put in trust for Annie when I married her. And I will sign an agreement to have our marriage annulled if Ann will drop the suit."

I said, Fine, Whooppee, that's it, and walked out. I had made my decision. Arthur was admitting to our marriage by agreeing to an annulment and that was good enough for me. I told Jacques Leslie to drop the suit.

I remember Arthur and I went back into the judge's chambers and Arthur swooped me up and literally turned me over his knee and spanked me, with Judge Brand looking on.

The press made a big deal of our annulment and settlement. They described me as wearing an "all is forgiven smile" and reported (from the Los Angeles *Herald-Examiner*, May 10, 1962):

> "I'm glad it's all over . . . Arthur and I are the best of friends. He is one of the kindest and most generous men I have ever known. All I wanted from the beginning in this thing was to clear my good name. I never intended to ask for $7.5 million and $10,000 a month temporary support and alimony. That was just when I got my Irish up," she explained.
>
> She also said she was "still in love" with Cameron, with whom she "lived for ten months," and that she would continue to see him on a friendly basis.

Newsmen also had a field day with the fact that my annulment from Arthur Cameron was granted only a day before my final divorce from Bill Moss.

According to the Los Angeles *Times* (May 11, 1962):

> When reminded by newsmen her final divorce from Texas oilman William Moss would not be final in California courts until today, Miss Miller said: "Heavens, does that mean I'm still married to him?"

The Los Angeles *Herald-Examiner*'s version is (May 10, 1962):

> When informed by newsmen that she was still technically married to Moss, the perplexed beauty turned to her attorney and asked:
>
> "Goodness—when am I going to be free from all this mess?"

Arthur Cameron and I walked out of court arm in arm, went out to dinner together that night, and remained friends until the day he died.

Don't ask me to explain it. Some people just get along better when they're not married. We dated constantly after our annulment and he did many nice things for me and my mother. He installed a burglar alarm service throughout my mother's home. He bought us a new color TV set which was delivered one Christmas Eve. He gave lavish Christmas parties in our home. And when my mother fell and broke her leg in five places, it was Arthur Cameron who got her a hospital room and paid the hospital and nursing bills. And when she left the hospital, he put her in a beautiful suite at the Beverly Hills Hotel for six weeks, with nurses around the clock, so she could rest and relax. Arturo liked my mom. He always called her "Clara-Girl" (her name is Clara) and me "Annie-Girl"—or "Little Duck," and referred to us as his two "showgirls."

He showered me with presents—a $50,000 diamond necklace, a fabulous floor-length white mink coat and a sable stole. Unfortunately, the necklace and stole were stolen during an engagement in Chicago at the Pheasant Run Playhouse. I have always felt that the burglars were really after my 20-carat diamond ring which I was wearing that night. Arthur always told me that ring was my security against the future because it would go up, up, and up in price and if one day I was desperate I could sell it.

He also told me never to sell my mother's home unless it was absolutely necessary because the price would continue to go up.

"Keep these things for your little nest egg," he always told me.

Ah, yes, but he was a wily one, too. I put my little Summit Ridge house up for sale—the one I lived in with Bill Moss across the street from Cobina—wtih a price tag of $80,000,

including the furnishings. When I received an offer of $65,000
I decided to take it. I needed the money at the time. The real
estate agent told me that the person buying it didn't want his
name revealed and I thought it was probably Howard Hughes.
I learned later that it was Arthur Cameron who bought the
house—for one of his prize pussycats to live in while she was
in this country. She is very well known, apparently happily
married now, so let sleeping dogs lie. What really burned me
up was that I let my house go for such a low price—to Arthur
Cameron, no less. If I'd known he was buying it I would have
tripled the price.

Nevertheless we remained friends.

We often went to the Monseigneur Room at the Beverly
Hilton because Arturo, as I sometimes called him, loved violins.
There we could dance to an entire orchestra of violins. He loved
that. And we frequently went to the Bistro. That's where all
the movie folk go. It's where we had our last date.

I knew that Arthur wasn't well. It was getting more and more
difficult for him to walk without being dizzy.

Our last night at the Bistro Arthur asked me to take him down
to Acapulco, with a nurse and a doctor, so that he would get
well. He told me he still had other women but I was the only
one he trusted. I believed him. He promised to take care of me
and my mother if I would only help him. And of course I
said yes. I knew he was a sick man. I made all the arrangements
for us to stay at the El Presidente Hotel. (He actually preferred
it to the Tecali.) I talked with his doctor, and I hired a nurse.

But we never made the trip because two days later Arthur
Cameron was dead.

Apart from my personal grief, it also hurt me to know that
this man who loved life so, who loved music and fun and
dancing, died all alone in his bedroom at 910 Benedict Canyon.

I'm sure that in the back of my mind I always hoped that
Arthur and I would eventually get together again. And I think

we would have if I had been able to get him well. But it wasn't in my karma to save my third marriage. So I blew another one. And nice girls don't blow three marriages. I must admit I was not too proud of my track record.

Chapter 16

THE OTHER MEN
IN MY LIFE

I believe in being nice to your ex-husbands. If they're nice enough to marry you, why not stay on friendly terms with them? The truth is that I got along much better with both Arthur Cameron and Bill Moss when I was no longer married to either of them.

Incredible as it seems, I got my annulment from Arthur and my divorce from Bill only days apart—a free woman twice within the same week.

And before long I was dating both of them again. Bill always called me when he came to town and I went out with him a great deal.

Contrary to popular belief, none of my millionaire husbands showered me with million-dollar settlements. All I got from Reese Milner was $20,000 tax free to compensate for my loss of work at Columbia. From Bill Moss I got the Summit Ridge house, a car and $30,000 cash over a period of three years. And from Arthur Cameron I got my $125,000 diamond ring and a settlement of $50,000. I promptly went out and blew it all on art objects at auctions. I became a nut on auctions, simply adored them and still do though I have become somewhat saner in my bidding than when I was having a spree spending Arthur Cameron's money. For a while there I was known as "Auction Annie." I didn't want that $50,000 from Arthur Cameron. It made me feel cheap. That's why I blew it on auctions— like throwing it out the window.

I moved back with my mother in the house I had bought for her on Alta Drive and began to think about reactivating my career. I had given it up completely when I married Bill Moss. My time was spent promoting his career rather than mine, traveling with him and entertaining his Texas oil friends.

But strangely enough it was Bill who came to my rescue after my Cameron fiasco and offered to help me get started with my career again. He was appreciative of the fact that I had given it up to marry him, and now that I was no longer tied down by marriage he encouraged me to get back into show business. More important, he urged me to take singing lessons, and even offered to pay for them himself. I knew I could dance but I didn't think I could sing. Bill Moss had great confidence in me.

"I know you can make it again, and make it big," he said, "if you'll just learn to sing as well as dance. You're a great dancer but there will be more doors open to you if you'll develop your voice. And you can do it. I know you can."

He insisted that I take singing lessons. He pushed me into it and he did pay for my lessons with Harriet Lee, one of the finest voice coaches in the business.

Bill knew that I had spent all my Arthur Cameron "loot" at the auctions. He also knew my other extravagant spending habits and probably figured that my funds were running low or that I would never get around to taking voice lessons if I had to do it with my own money. So good old Willie, my ex-husband, made all the arrangements and paid all the bills.

He made a bet with me. He said, "If you go at this thing seriously you can become as well known as a singer as you are a dancer—and I'll bet you land something big on Broadway. If I lose the bet you can keep the money. If I win, you can pay me back someday if you want to."

I thought he was absolutely mad, but could anyone wish for a more gallant gesture from an ex-husband?

And I will be forever grateful to Bill Moss because he won his bet. He is the man responsible for my third and strongest comeback in show business—my role in recent years as *both* a singing and dancing star of big book musicals on stage.

First *Can-Can* in Houston . . . and at a big dinner held in my honor I stood up and announced proudly that I wished to give full credit to my ex-husband Bill Moss for encouraging me to take singing lessons which landed me the role.

And within two years to my own amazement I did indeed land something big on Broadway, as Bill had said I would. And that, as the whole world must know by now, was *Mame*. What a tumultuous and memorable opening night that was. More on this later. I'm sure the proudest person in the audience that night, next to my mother, was my ex-husband Bill Moss who had faith in me. I'll always love him for it.

I have not married again though I confidently expect to because all the seers have told me I will.

One of my problems is that I loved too deeply and not wisely. I am intensely emotional and romantic and I have to be very deeply in love with a man before I can have any physical contact with him at all. I also have strong mental control and the ability to turn off, literally put myself in deep freeze, if a man does something to hurt me. I can either be the coldest person in the world (they call me Miss Deep Freeze) or if I'm in love, I love a man to death. There's no in between. I'm Miss Overboard.

In my work and travels I've met scores of fascinating men. Most of them were only dates, not heavy romances. Many have been Europeans or Latins. We seem to have a mutual attraction for each other.

One of my biggest crushes was Antonio Vega, the most exciting man in all of Brazil. Next to Cary Grant I think he's the most handsome man I ever met—tall, with black hair and brown eyes. When I met him he was being chased by every woman in the country. But he was my constant escort during one of my film junkets to Brazil. The Brazilian jet set is the wildest in the world and during Carnival time everyone goes mad. Antonio took me to wonderful parties but one I especially remember was a divine dinner party in the fabulous showplace home of some rich friends of his. And I mean rich. When we sat down at the elegantly set dinner table, we noticed that all the plates were turned over. Soon a line of servants filed in and gracefully moved around the table turning the plates right side up. Surprise! Under each lady guest's plate was a ring—an exquisite aquamarine and diamond set in platinum.

For little Johnnie Lucille Collier inside the Ann Miller mold, this exotic world she was living and traveling in was almost too too much. It made me feel that I was on an Oriental carpet in the *Arabian Nights* and afraid to open my eyes for fear the dream would end . . . Antonio eventually married a beautiful Brazilian girl and for all I know has lived happily ever since . . .

And then there was my Spanish bull fighter, Mario Cabre. How can I ever forget him? He once saved my life from a switch-hitting bull. I don't know whether this was before or after his romance with Ava Gardner. I had enough trouble keeping track of my own. But Mario was one of Ava's *toujours l'amour* romances and appeared in a movie with her, *The Barefoot Contessa.*

I met Mario in Madrid during one of my early movie junkets

to Europe, and he invited me to be his date at a birthday fiesta in his honor at the ranch of a very wealthy Spaniard who was famous for giving luncheons for visiting celebrities. I've forgotten his name (if I ever knew it) but Mr. Rancher was known as a man who enjoyed entertaining his guests with a little bullfight—and with the visiting celebrity in the bull ring. That's the Spanish-type sense of humor, I found out.

Well, Mario Cabre took me out to this elegant luncheon, filled me full of marvelous Spanish wine, and then dressed me up in a toreador outfit, a real one. I had never worn one before and it was a beautiful thing, with the bolero, the cape, the hat, the works.

I remember Mario and his Spanish friends flattering me, telling me how great I looked, and saying, "You're such a graceful dancer. Please why don't you go out into the ring with a little baby bull?"

No one bothered to tell me that Ava Gardner had been out in the bull ring with a little baby bull not long before and ended up with twelve stitches in her face.

I was feeling quite good on all that Spanish wine, so I raced out into the middle of the bull ring, carrying my beautiful cape of white satin lined in red, and decorated with beads and embroidery . . . All the guests at the luncheon came and sat around the bull ring which had a tall fence around it.

Well, someone opened the corral gate and out came this thing which must have weighed 2,000 pounds. Talk about a gringo. I dropped that cape and I ran like a bat out of hell. Never have I run or danced that fast, before or since. I'm supposed to be the world's fastest tap dancer but I'm sure my tap speed was nothing compared with the speed I built up as I ran clear across that bull ring and finally hid myself safely behind one of those big boards that always decorate bull rings. The bull fighters escape behind them.

That bull hit the board with such an impact that he had a

very hard time pulling his own horns out, and I was shaking with fear.

I remember seeing Mario leaping out into the ring, grabbing my cape, and somehow fighting the bull away from me. He knew that I was in real danger. But all the other Spaniards were laughing because they thought it was hysterically funny. They said I looked like a female Charlie Chaplin.

Personally, I didn't think it was so funny and neither did Mario. He told me that even he, a professional bull fighter, could have been killed because this animal was a switch-hitting bull —meaning that he hooked from the left as well as the right. This kind of bull is dangerous. The bull fighter can easily be killed because he doesn't know which way the bull is going to hook and so can't prepare for it. And that's the kind of bull they sent me out in the ring with.

I think it was during this same trip to Europe that I met Claude Terrail, who owns the Tour d'Argent restaurant in Paris . . . he loves to dance and is a great connoisseur of food and wine . . . and André Dubonnet, the apéritif king. André invited me to be his guest at the annual Red Cross Gala at the palace in Monte Carlo, where I met Prince Rainier and the darkly handsome Aly Khan who flirted with me like mad.

One of my best beaus at one time was the big financier, Frank Ryan, who built a million-dollar home in Spain and knew some of the most exciting people in Europe. It was he who took me to a small dinner party at the home of J. Paul Getty in Paris, and if Mr. Getty is as stingy as people say, I certainly saw no signs of it that evening. He was a charming host.

Among the guests at the party was Aristotle Onassis. I can understand why Jackie Kennedy fell for him. He's not movie-star handsome but he has great animal vitality and a love of life and a marvelous sense of humor.

I once deliberately stood up a very important date at the last minute—the Shah of Iran. I had met the Shah's half-brother, Prince Hamid Reza Pahlavi at a party given by Sir Charles and Lady Mendl, then the reigning hosts of Hollywood. They always entertained beautifully and their guests invariably included the most glamorous international celebrities, as well as famous authors, musicians, and the film world's top directors, producers, and stars. I used to be invited to many of Sir Charles and Lady Mendl's soirees and it was there one night that Prince Hamid told me the Shah was coming to Hollywood and would I do him the honor of going out with him while he was here? The Prince said I was just the right type for his brother because the Shah loved to dance and he liked tall brunettes.

I said of course I would be thrilled to go out with the Shah of Iran. Who wouldn't? Imagine, even meeting the Shah of Iran, much less going out on a date with him! I could hardly wait.

Sure enough, not long afterward there were headlines in the papers saying the Shah had arrived in Los Angeles and was staying in the royal suite at the Ambassador Hotel.

And sure enough, I received a call from Prince Hamid asking if I were free the next night because the Shah wanted to take me out to dinner and dancing at the Mocambo. He said that he—the Shah's brother—would call for me in a limousine at eight o'clock and that it would be a black-tie party. I assumed he meant the Shah was hosting a small dinner and dancing party at the Mocambo, but I was the lucky girl chosen for the Shah's date.

I was so thrilled and excited that I dashed out to Saks and bought a new dress, all beaded. It was divine and it should have been. It cost me a week's salary. But I wanted to look extra-special and glamorous for the Shah of Iran. Or at least try to.

Came the day of my big date and I started early in order to be ready for the Shah in plenty of time. I had my hair coiffed, my nails manicured, took my best jewels out of the bank vault, and was all dressed up in my divine new dress and waiting when I picked up the evening paper and read the headlines.

There was a big front-page story about the Shah—and it quoted him as saying he was not here to date the fleshpots of the West but to buy farm machinery for his country.

The nerve of that man!

I was boiling mad and I still hadn't simmered down when the doorbell rang ten minutes later. I peeked out of my bedroom window and there it was all right, the limousine waiting in front, so I knew it was Prince Hamid at the door.

I didn't even bother to go downstairs to greet him. I wrote him a note and sent it down with the maid. I simply said I would be unable to dine with the Shah tonight. I didn't give any excuse.

Naturally, the next day Prince Hamid telephoned me and this time *he* was furious. What happened? Had I been taken ill? I explained to him that I felt just fine but that I had read the interview in the newspaper, that I was rather a well-known Hollywood personality, and if I had gone out with his brother it surely would have been in the newspapers. And, I added sweetly, I certainly wouldn't want to make a liar out of the Shah of Iran.

The Prince said the Shah had been misquoted and that I was entirely wrong in breaking the date.

Not long after that, the Shah married Soraya, but many years later, after they had separated, the Shah made another overture toward me, this time through my dear friend Hermes Pan, who has been very close to the royal family of Iran for years. Hermes called one day to tell me that the Shah and his family had asked him to invite me to be a guest at the palace for one week. I don't remember what the occasion was but there was to be a tremendous festivity of some kind, climaxed by a big ball, and Hermes said the Shah very much wanted me to go. But at that time I happened to be right in the middle of making

Kiss Me, Kate, one of my best M-G-M pictures, and the director, George Sidney, wouldn't let me go. He said they couldn't shoot around me without wasting millions of dollars. So I had to decline the invitation.

I sometimes wonder what might have happened if I hadn't broken my date that night—and if I had been able to accept the second invitation from the Shah of Iran. He later married his present wife, Fara.

I often went out with the Maharajah of Cooch Behar when he was in town. In fact, I'm the one who introduced him to Nancy Valentine, the girl he later married . . . And then there was the Maharajah of Baroda, a terribly nice man, and very brilliant and fascinating. I could sit enthralled for hours listening to him tell stories of his life in India.

Another of my more serious romances was with one of our town's top obstetricians. This almost ended in marriage. But I didn't like his always being on call morning, noon, and night, and dashing off to the hospital in the middle of a party, leaving me to get home the best way I knew how. Not that I ever had any problem with this. There were always plenty of men ready and willing to escort me home. Many times I would be all dressed up and ready to go on a date with my handsome doctor and he would call and cancel at the last minute. An emergency. Babies can't wait. I don't think I'd like being a doctor's wife.

I lean more toward oil men and politicians. I've always found them vital, stimulating people. Bill O'Connor, my one great love, would have been a great politician if he had lived longer. The seers tell me that my next husband is going to be another oil man and/or a politician. I'm still waiting.

Meanwhile, I can't resist telling here about my one date with President Nixon's adviser, Henry Kissinger. Not that it's any distinction to go out with him, since he's dated every starlet in town.

In the fall of 1971 my good friend Arlene Dahl and her

present husband, Skip Schaum (whom she married after Alexis Lichine), arranged for Mr. Kissinger to be my dinner companion at a party which also included my close friends, Bill and Margaret Pereira. We drove down to the home of the Pereiras' son in Newport Beach, not far from San Clemente where Mr. Kissinger was staying as a guest of President Nixon in the West Coast White House. He met us there and from the moment he walked into the room, we hit it off well.

But I had certain reservations about him because of something I had seen which made a deep impression on me.

Not long before our meeting, I had spotted Henry Kissinger having dinner at Trader Vic's in Beverly Hills, with a beautiful, glamorous girl-about-town, a well-known starlet. But he was not only having dinner with her, he was actually necking with her quite openly.

Heaven knows I'm no prude, and under other circumstances I might have thought, my, how romantic. But in my opinion a man of his political stature and prominence should do his romancing in the privacy of someone's home, not in a public restaurant.

And I proceeded to tell him so. I don't know why, I just couldn't resist it. He probably felt it was none of my business, although he took it rather well, I thought. I was seated next to him at the dinner table, and that's when I told him how I felt about his behavior. I think I did it in a lady-like manner, quietly so that the others couldn't hear.

He accepted it like a gentleman and even thanked me for my friendly advice. But I'm sure right then and there I squelched any chances I might have had with that politician. I don't think he's the one the seers have in mind anyway, as he isn't my type.

I know Mr. Kissinger is a brilliant and learned man and a very scintillating dinner companion. But sometimes even the most brilliant men can be very naïve when it comes to women.

Naïve? Listen who's talking! But it's been wonderful to meet all these glamorous, interesting men. If it weren't for Annie Miller, little Lucille Collier from Houston, Texas, would never have known this kind of life. Perhaps she would have been happier back in Houston married to a bricklayer and with fifteen kids running around the house. Who knows, who knows?

Chapter 17

MY DATE WITH THE INVISIBLE BILLIONAIRE

Yes, I even had one date with Howard Hughes. Only one. And that was enough. Let me make it clear, I was not one of Howard's "girls" or girl friends. He only asked me for the one date on behalf of his girl friend of the moment, my friend, Linda Darnell.

Strangely, two of my very closest friends, Linda and Kathryn Grayson, dated Howard Hughes—during separate periods of time, of course—and I knew him mainly through their eyes.

He dated Linda first and she was madly in love with him. And I do believe that at one time Linda was Howard's biggest crush since Billie Dove, who was said to be his greatest love. Linda looked very much like a young Billie Dove and I would assume this was why Howard fell for her.

Linda seemed positive that Howard Hughes intended to marry her although I was never so sure about that. Linda wasn't free to marry anyway. She was only separated from her husband, who was still begging her to come back to him. But she really idolized Howard Hughes and had her heart set on marrying him.

All the time she was dating him, I never met him. This was during my early Columbia years and even then he was eccentric. He kept the weirdest hours.

One night I was awakened from a sound sleep by the ringing of the telephone. It was two o'clock in the morning. The caller was Howard Hughes.

"Hi, Annie. This is Howard Hughes. (We were both from Texas.) You've got to help me. I've got a problem with Linda," he said. "I have to talk to you. I want to ask you to do a favor for me. I know you and Linda are close friends and I don't want to hurt her. When can I see you?"

Tomorrow night, I said.

He said he would pick me up around nine o'clock and take me to dinner.

So the next night I got all dressed up in a pretty cocktail dress and waited. Nine o'clock came. Then ten, then eleven, and still no Howard Hughes. Finally about a quarter of twelve the doorbell rang and there stood Howard.

I couldn't believe what I was looking at. He was wearing a dirty old coat with grease spots all over it and patches on the elbows, a beat-up shirt, wrinkled trousers, and old tennis shoes.

He walked into the hallway and I said, "Is that what you're going to wear to dinner?"

He said, "Yes." So I told him, "Well, I'm not going out with you dressed like that." He really did look awful, and I have always had a reputation of being chic, well groomed, and fashionably dressed, if I do say so myself.

He didn't seem to mind my insulting him. He sort of grinned out of the side of his mouth and asked if he could use my powder room to change.

"I have another shirt and a pair of trousers in the car," he said, "if you want me to change."

I said fine. And he went out to the car to get his clothes. I didn't know his habits at the time—none of his girl friends ever talked much about things like that, I guess. But apparently he always kept a supply of fresh shirts in the car and a pair of clean trousers. He had been working late that night, he said, and didn't have time to go home and change. I was to discover later that he also always carried a paper bag full of sandwiches in the car to nibble on when he got hungry.

Howard disappeared into my powder room and came out looking very neat, with a clean shirt and a marvelous pair of trousers. But he still had on that awful jacket and the tennis shoes. I didn't know then about his reputation for wearing sneakers. After all, I was traveling in a little higher class society and most of the millionaires I knew liked to dress well. Since Howard Hughes had offered to take me out to dinner, I naturally assumed he would be wearing a dark suit and a normal pair of shoes. When he asked, "Well, how do I look? Any better?" I blurted out, "Yes, but I don't like the shoes."

To which he replied, "You're going to have to take the shoes. Come on. It's very important and I don't have time to argue with you. Let's go."

Actually Howard Hughes at that time was a very good-looking man, tall and lanky, and charming. I could see why Linda—or any girl for that matter—would be attracted to him.

We left my house and got into the most beat-up battered old Chevrolet I've ever seen and drove to the old Perino's, which was and still is, considered one of the most elegant restaurants in town. We were shown to our table and as soon as I was seated, Howard said, "Excuse me for one minute." He disappeared through a door at the back of the room, and into the kitchen of the restaurant.

He was gone for quite a while. I thought, my God, what's happened to him? And I was absolutely famished.

He finally reappeared, carrying a huge bowl of salad to our table.

My bridesmaids—Betty.
Bloomingdale (center) and
Marjorie Reynolds—watch
me cut the cake at the
wedding reception following
my marriage to Reese Milner
on February 16, 1946.
(*Columbia photo*)

Reese Milner and I drink
a toast after our
marriage ceremony at
All Saints-by-the-Sea
Church in Montecito,
California. (*Columbia photo*)

Bill Moss and I just after I became his wife in La Jolla, California, on August 22, 1958.

The male members of the wedding party line up at the reception following my marriage to Bill Moss. (Left to Right): Best man Gordon Guiberson, Ross Brunner, bridegroom Bill Moss, Don Heard, Warren Leslie and Arthur Cameron, who was to be my third husband.

Two of my dear friends—Linda Darnell (left) and Ginger Rogers—wish me well on the day of my wedding to Bill Moss.

Arthur Cameron, husband number three, and I went to the famed Lido in Paris during our honeymoon in 1961.

"I mixed it myself. I never let anyone else touch food that I eat," he explained.

Then he asked the waiter to bring a toaster to the table, along with a loaf of bread, and he made his own toast. I guess he thought either someone was going to poison him or that he might be contaminated by other people's germs.

We finished our toast and salad, and then he began to talk to me about his problem with Linda. One reason he confided in me about it, I think, was that he knew she was my closest friend— and also all three of us were from Texas. I suppose he figured we could all trust one another.

"Annie, you've got to help me with Linda," he said. "I think all the world of her but I don't want to get married. I know that she's becoming very serious and really thinks I'm going to marry her. I haven't encouraged her in this at all. I'm not ready to get married yet. Maybe it would work out if she'd let me think about it for a while . . ."

But there was another more important problem he wanted to talk about.

"Linda's husband wants a lot of money from me to let her go. That's why her divorce has been held up. I don't particularly like this sort of thing," he said. "It's like a robbery, a stick-up. I'm not going to let any man do that to me."

I didn't blame him. I was shocked at what he told me. I knew Linda's husband. I wouldn't have thought he was that kind of man—but then, look at how little I knew about my own husbands.

"I don't know exactly how to tell Linda about this," Howard said, "or even whether she should be told. I am still very fond of her and I would do anything not to hurt her. She is a lovely girl and I think I do love her but not enough to marry her yet. And now, with her estranged husband demanding money from me, well, it has sort of turned me off. I want no part of it. Do you think you can talk to her and help her realize without hurting her too much that marriage is out. I'll leave it up to you how to tell her . . ."

I promised him I would talk to Linda, though I dreaded it. I said I would try to explain the situation to her the best I could. That was all I could do.

I was still starved after our dinner of salad and toast, but when Howard asked me if I'd like to go with him to his projection room at Goldwyn Studios to see the rushes of his latest film, I agreed. We got back into that beat-up old car and started off. But halfway there, we ran out of gasoline. He forgot to fill the tank.

"What are we going to do now?" I asked.

He replied, "I saw a filling station about four blocks back there. You wait here in the car and I'll walk and get a can of gasoline. Then we'll have to push the car and get it started."

And that's exactly what we did. It was two o'clock in the morning but Howard didn't seem at all perturbed. In fact he acted as if this was the sort of thing that happened every night. So I sat there in the car and waited while he went to get the can of gasoline. He poured it into the tank, then slipped under the wheel and turned the key. The motor wouldn't start.

"Come on, we have to push," he said.

Would you believe Miss Twinkle-Toes and Mr. Billionaire out there in the middle of the night pushing a beat-up, rust-buckety rattletrap of a car to make it start? Well, that's what we did. When it finally started, we jumped in real fast, drove back to the service station to return the gasoline can, and then on to Goldwyn.

With all the other fascinating things to remember from that night, will you forgive me for not remembering the name of the movie we saw?

Howard had gone into moviemaking by then and was a producer, and obviously it would have been one of his films. But what impressed me most was his private projection room.

For one thing, the seats.

"Wait till you try these seats," he said. "They'll surprise you. But don't be scared. When you sit down, a flap will come out automatically under your legs—and, well, you'll see."

Sure enough, the instant I sat down a big flap came out from under the seat, tilted me back and raised my legs up so that I was sitting there like a queen in a huge overstuffed chair. In other words his projection room seats—which usually are similar to the seats in any movie theater—had been designed by him for easy conversion to a comfortable chaise longue-type viewing throne.

Also along one wall was a dashboard apparatus with a jillion knobs, switches, and assorted gadgets I didn't understand. But I learned that some of the dials were there so he could turn up the sound as loud as he wanted it. And he wanted it loud. Howard was hard of hearing. He could hear fine in a car or an airplane or even on the telephone, he told me, but in most normal situations he was terribly deaf. He turned the sound up so loud he nearly blew me out of the projection room, chaise longue and all. But I lived through it, probably because I had learned to adjust to my mother's partial deafness.

As we were driving home Howard explained to me why he was a night person. He said he works better at night and is able to think more clearly then—mostly because the phones never ring. That was a big thing with him—the ring, ring, ring of the telephones. It bugged him, he said. So it was in the quiet of the night that he did his best work.

When he arrived at my house, he walked me to the door and said good night. I told him not to worry about Linda, that I would talk to her.

"You don't know how much I appreciate that, Annie," he said. He thanked me and off he drove into the night.

That was my one and only date with the man who was to become known as the world's richest recluse.

I went to see Linda the next day and broke the news to her as gently as I could. I assured her that Howard was in love with her but wasn't ready for marriage just yet. And I thought it best to tell her about her husband—that he was demanding a money settlement from Howard before he would free her.

Linda broke down and was completely hysterical. It almost broke her heart to hear what her husband was trying to do to Howard. Later when she had recovered from the shock and sadness of it all, and could maintain her composure, she discussed it with Howard and told him how sorry she was. I could understand why Howard had wanted me to talk to her first and prepare her. It wasn't nearly so hard for them to talk about it together as it would have been had he broken the news directly.

Some years later, while I was under contract at M-G-M, Howard borrowed me to make a picture for his own studio, RKO. It was *Two Tickets to Broadway*, and also starred Janet Leigh and Tony Martin. During shooting of this movie, I fell and hurt my back quite severly and a big production number I was supposed to do had to be cut. The set had already been built and I'm sure my injury cost the studio a lot of money. Howard called to tell me how sorry he was that I had been hurt and my number had to be cut. Otherwise, I never really had any contact with him while I was working on the picture but I suspected that his real reason for borrowing me from M-G-M was to thank me for the favor I had once done for him.

Incidentally, at RKO, Howard was known as "The Shadow" because no one ever saw him.

Jane Russell, also a friend of mine, is the girl Howard Hughes catapulted to stardom in his famous movie, *The Outlaw*. She still has an income of $1,000 per week from the Hughes company. Instead of asking for and getting a huge sum per picture while she was under contract to him, Janie played it smart and insured her future by settling on a lesser amount over the longer haul. I've never ever heard Janie discuss anything personal about Howard Hughes. During the celebrated Clifford Irving "authorized autobiography" Hughes book hoax, Janie was asked by newsmen to give her views on the seemingly unending brouhaha and she said, "No way. He's still my boss and my friend." She's a smart girl, Janie.

I have had only one indirect contact with Howard Hughes in recent years, and that was while he was still in Las Vegas and after my success in *Mame* on Broadway. My agent told me that both Howard and Bob Maheu (before their break-up) wanted me to star in *Applause* at one of the Hughes hotels, but the producers of the musical thought I was too young for the part.

The last time I talked to Howard Hughes was in Palm Springs a long time ago. I had gone down with a friend for a long weekend of lolling in the sun. About two o'clock in the morning the telephone rang and it was Howard, calling my friend. I got on the phone for a minute or so just to say hello to him. He asked me how everything was going. We had the usual chitchat—the kind any two Texans might have at two o'clock in the morning. And that's the last time I ever heard Howard Hughes's voice.

Chapter 18

STARDUST FLASHBACKS

What a potpourri of memories from those golden years. And Howard Hughes wasn't the only one with strange eating habits.

Today many Hollywood stars eat nothing but organically grown foods. But my first encounter with a big star health food addict occurred several years before the health food fad really got under way. And it was rather disconcerting to me.

I had planned a lovely all-girl luncheon for about twenty of my friends in the Garden Room at the Beverly Hills Hotel. I ordered flowers, place cards, wine, the whole works. I was doing it up right. Perle Mesta was in town and she was one of my guests. So was Cobina Wright, of course. The day before my luncheon party Cobina called and asked whether she could bring Gloria Swanson. Could she! Gloria Swanson was a name I had heard since I was a little girl because she was one of my mother's favorite stars and I was thrilled to pieces at the thought of meeting her.

Miss Swanson walked in with Cobina. We were introduced

and I showed them their places at the table. I noticed with some puzzlement that the petite Miss Swanson was carrying a large wicker basket on her arm. But one doesn't express open curiosity at a big star's accessories.

When the waiters began serving the first course, I overheard Miss Swanson tell one of them, "No, thank you, I brought my own."

And to my amazement she proceeded to open her wicker basket and pluck from it an assortment of fruits and vegetables which she placed on her plate.

She began nibbling away and chattering like a chipmunk. I was shocked and highly insulted that she would not touch one bite of anything on my luncheon menu which I had gone to such trouble to plan and order.

I turned to Perle Mesta, who was sitting next to me, and said, "What on earth is that lady doing?" Frankly, she reminded me of a happy rabbit crunching away on those vegetables.

To my enormous embarrassment, Miss Swanson heard me from her place farther down the table. She turned to me and very graciously explained that she never ate anything that wasn't organically grown. Since then, of course, Gloria Swanson's bring-your-own-health-food habits have been widely publicized. And I'll bet one of the reasons she looks so spectacular today is that wicker basket of organically grown goodies she always carries. Carol Channing is another who takes her own food with her, no matter who her host and hostess are.

Ginger Rogers and I became very good friends during the filming of *Stage Door*. I have always felt that I owe her a special debt of gratitude because I wouldn't have been given that role if Ginger hadn't agreed to wear higher heels and a higher top hat in our big dance number. But I adored her for other reasons as well, and one was that she had a real honest-to-goodness soda fountain in her house. I was only fourteen when I did *Stage Door* with her, and I loved going up to her house because she would go behind the bar and make ice cream sodas and malted milks for her guests. Anything we wanted, she could make.

Ever since then I have always wanted a soda fountain, too. But I never had one. I guess in some ways all of us remain kids at heart forever. Ginger was always like a little kid, and she used to give great fun roller skating parties at a rink on Sunset Boulevard which she rented especially for her friends.

Ginger still looks fantastic today. In fact, at the 1972 Golden Globes award everyone was talking about how great Ginger looked—far more glamorous and younger than many of the young starlets on the Hollywood scene today. She has an extremely youthful figure, beautiful clear eyes and complexion, and enormous energy. She is a practicing Christian Scientist, doesn't smoke or drink—she never has—and takes great care of her figure by swimming, playing tennis, and watching her diet.

But, like me, she didn't do too well in the marriage department. One of her husbands was Jacques Bergerac, a handsome French actor who loved rich spicy foods and good wines and smoked a lot. Jacques himself told me that one of the things which broke up their marriage was their difference in eating habits. He couldn't really enjoy all the marvelous French foods he was accustomed to, he said, with Ginger sitting there eating nothing but a lettuce leaf. It annoyed him. And vice versa.

I have mentioned earlier that *Stage Door* was one of my favorite pictures not only because it introduced me to Ginger Rogers and also to Hermes Pan who has remained one of my longtime dearest friends. And speaking of being kids at heart, Ginger's soda fountain somehow reminds me of Hermes's tree house. That's right, I said a tree house. He had it built in a big old oak tree at his place in Coldwater Canyon, and he actually uses it himself as a retreat when he wants to get away from people, or when he wants to get rid of them. You may have heard about our Hollywood parties, how they go on and on. Not at Hermes

Pan's house. When he decides the party has gone on long enough, he just takes his pitcher of martinis and goes up in his tree house and stays there, and eventually his guests discover he's gone. They know where he is and they know that's their signal to go home, the party's over.

Errol Flynn was famous for his wild, wild parties and the women he wooed all over the world. It was the custom at Errol's parties for all his guests to get drunk and fall into the pool. I never did but John Barrymore fell in regularly.

To me Errol Flynn was an absolute paradox. For all his flamboyance he was a man with rather old-fashioned ideas—or at least one that I became quite well acquainted with during an M-G-M junket in South America. Errol was married to Pat Wymore at the time and of all his wives Pat was a thoroughbred.

Errol and Pat took their six-weeks-old baby along with them on the trip and for the life of me I couldn't figure out why. He was an adorable baby and I loved him but I thought what a drag to have an infant along on a fun-and-work film junket. It also worried me because I never heard a peep out of the baby. He never ever cried and I couldn't understand why. One evening Errol, Pat, and I went to a big cocktail party and right in the middle of it, quite suddenly, Pat excused herself and said she had to leave. I asked her where she was going. She took me aside so the others couldn't hear and whispered, "I have to feed the baby. Would you believe my husband insists that our baby be breast-fed. So that's what I have to do."

And that's why they took the baby with them everywhere they went. It was probably one of the world's most widely traveled babies.

But to me it was incongruous that one of Hollywood's most virile, boisterous, hard-drinking, high-living, girl-chasing glamour boys would insist that his wife breast-feed her baby.

Not only that, he also insisted that his wife join him in martinis at the cocktail hour. Everyone knew how Errol loved to drink but he hated to drink alone. So Pat dutifully drank along with him. Not as much, of course. No one could keep up with Errol Flynn.

But it slowly dawned on me why their baby never cried and was always so quiet. He was probably happily tranquilized on martini milk!

When I sprang that on Pat and Errol they got a huge chortle out of it, Errol especially. He had a superb sense of humor.

Speaking of babies, I loved the way Arlene Dahl planned her last baby so it would be born under the proper astrological signs. Show business people, as you've probably heard, are very superstitious. Many of them also are astrology buffs and never make a move unless it's okayed by their personal astrologer. But there's no one more avid than Arlene Dahl. She knows astrology well, has written books on the subject and writes an astrological beauty column. When Arlene became pregnant by her last husband, Skip Schaum, she told her obstetrician that she would tell him exactly what day she wanted her baby to be born, since she was to have a Caesarian anyway.

Her O.B. man was Dr. Blake Watson, who is known as the attendant of the royal court of Hollywood celebrities and socialites.

When it was almost time for the baby to be born, Arlene began working diligently on her astrology charts, and when she had it all figured out, she called Dr. Watson, gave him the date she wanted and said the baby had to be born at 10:30 in the morning.

He said he would call the hospital and arrange everything. But then Arlene called him back the next day and informed him the time had to be changed to eleven o'clock—because she wanted the baby to be born with the Moon in Aries, so it would coincide with her husband's moon and his sun and rising sign, which is Aries. Well, as Arlene told me, her doctor was somewhat annoyed because after all a Caesarian is a major operation and

everything had been set for 10:30 A.M. But Arlene has a way
with men. Her doctor switched the time to half an hour later and
Arlene's baby was born under the most perfect astrological
conditions. A lucky baby, that one.

As I have mentioned elsewhere, a great deal of the seamy side of
Hollywood was hushed up by high-powered publicity men who
were paid a lot of money to keep stars' names out of the papers.
But some of the most scandalous "incidents" have become classics within the trade. For instance, Harry Cohn's rage at a big-
name star who always came to work in filthy underwear. (The
wardrobe ladies complained.)

I was making my first picture at Columbia, *Time Out for
Rhythm*, when a very famous and much older star lady came and
watched me do a big production number in which I wore sheer
black stockings and a fabulous costume made of black and silver
beads. I thought she was watching me in a rather strange way,
but I was too young to know what it meant.

The next day I received a note from this great star lady saying
how much she had enjoyed watching me dance, and would I
care to have lunch with her in her private dressing room. I was
thrilled. I knew that she was considered a very important star and
Harry Cohn had given her a beautiful suite of rooms to use.

I sent a note back saying that I would be delighted to have
lunch with her. Then she sent me a dozen long-stemmed red
roses with another note saying how much she was looking forward to our luncheon. They came while I was having my hair
done.

Well, the hairdresser told the wardrobe lady and she told the
costume designer, and he told someone else who told someone
else who told Harry Cohn that little Annie Miller was going to
lunch with the great star lady *alone* in her dressing room.

But I never did have that lunch—that day nor any other. I
learned much, much later that Harry Cohn himself sent down
orders that under no circumstances was I to be allowed to have

lunch with Miss Star Lady in her suite. That day and each day throughout the remainder of shooting the film—or at least my part in it—I was kept on the set rehearsing during all my lunch hours. My lunches were sent in. I didn't understand it and I was terribly disappointed because she was one of my favorite movie stars. It wasn't until years later that I learned Miss Star Lady liked girls better than men and Harry Cohn wasn't about to let young naïve Annie Miller be involved in anything like that.

When I had been around long enough to learn a few of the facts of life, I could appreciate Harry Cohn's concern for me. And I guess the rumor was true because some years later I met one of Miss Star Lady's dates in Paris, a beautiful "boy" who was really a girl and one of the most famous Lesbians in Paris . . . The great Star Lady is still living and working and she looks great but she's been "face-lifted" all over and is still going strong.

I was still at M-G-M when two of that studio's biggest star ladies were caught in bed together in Palm Springs . . . And then there's that elegant hotel in Madrid that won't accept Hollywood celebrities as guests because one of our town's most glamorous stars, three sheets to the wind, lifted her skirts and piddled on one of the potted plants in the hotel's front lobby. Right in front of a group of important guests.

None of these "incidents" from the golden years would so much as lift an eyebrow today in a town that now accepts all forms of sexual activity as normal. Filmlandia's morals have changed considerably since the days of Ingrid Bergman and Roberto Rossellini. Now it's considered chic to buy a house and live together without getting married, equally chic to have your baby first and then get married (à la Mia Farrow and André Previn) and even more chic to have your baby and *not* marry its father, à la Vanessa Redgrave or Juliet Prowse.

Maybe it's considered tacky today but I guess I'm still an old-fashioned girl with old-fashioned morals and though the Hollywood I grew up in had its vices and its dens of iniquity, it also had a class, a quality, an elegance and sheen that are nonexistent today.

I think the thing I miss most about Hollywood is the glamour of those bygone days. And to me one of the stars who was most typical of that glamorous era was Sonja Henie. Cigar-chomping Darryl F. Zanuck made Sonja into the Queen of Ice. She might also have been called the Queen of Diamonds. She loved things that glittered. Her dresses were always beaded and they sparkled like the sun; and always her fingers, arms, neck and ears were covered with big diamonds. She always wore all-white outfits and drove a white Cord car. She reminded me of a big Shirley Temple doll. From a little girl on skates in Norway, she skated her way to one of the richest, brightest star-thrones in Hollywood and she ruled like a queen until the day she died.

Quite in contrast but spectacular in her own way was that darkly beautiful Spanish spitfire, Lupe Velez. I became acquainted with her in the '40s when I was dating Harry Karl. He sometimes took me to the boxing matches at the Hollywood Legion, and our seats were right next to Lupe's. She always became very excited and emotional, and would stand up screaming "*Arremba! Arremba!* (Attack!)" or "Keel him, keel him!" I remember one occasion especially when she got so excited she completely forgot herself, started jumping up and down and pounding on the man in front of her until she knocked his toupee off. You think that stopped her? She just leaned over and kissed has bald head and went right on yelping.

I never think of Lupe without remembering a funny story she told me once about her bust pads. I had mentioned to her how I hated wearing bust pads when I was a teen-ager. I was always afraid something dreadful was going to happen—either they would slip and show or fall out in my soup or something. As it turned out, Lupe Velez wore bust pads too. And she told me about the time a big pompous producer took her out to dinner but had too much to drink and on the way home in the car he started making passes at her, grabbing her by the bosoms and so on. Lupe was getting madder and madder but she couldn't very well jump out of the car.

When they arrived home, he walked her to her door, started to crush her to him, saying, "Oh, let me have just one more squeeze before we say good night."

She said, "Okay, you son of a beetch, you want them? You can have them."

Whereupon spitfire Lupe snatched out both her bust pads and threw them in his face.

I'll always have a special spot in my heart for Ann Sheridan—another Texan, and the most big-hearted girl I ever met. I only did one movie with her, *The Opposite Sex*, but I loved her. Everyone loved her. She was a real champion among women, and she died a slow painful death (from cancer) long before her time.

I have a special place in my heart too for Anita Ekberg—but for different reasons. I'll be forever grateful to her for something she did for me. I met Anita on one of our South American film junkets. There was quite a large group of stars on this one—Lana Turner, Rhonda Fleming, Anita, and I, and probably more whom I can't remember. Anita's current husband was with her. He was a very handsome British actor who drank too much, and like some other men I could mention he could get quite nasty and violent when he drank too much. He had a habit of going on rampages and beating her up. Their stormy marriage frequently made headlines in the newspapers and in fact Fellini's *La Dolce Vita*, which starred Anita and Lex Barker, was based on her real-life marriage with a man who here shall be called Robert, which is not his real name, of course.

Robert gave her a rough time on the trip and one night she came knocking on my door at 4 A.M., begging me to hide her because she was afraid he was going to kill her this time. She was

all roughed up and I took her into my little bungalow and hid
her in the closet.

It wasn't long until Robert came pounding on my door looking for her and yelling that he was going to kill her. Both of us
huddled in the closet, not making a sound, and he finally went
away.

When he sobered up they always kissed and made up. But it
would always happen again. I remember in Rio de Janeiro it happened several times, and the last time she was so badly bruised
that I felt she was lucky to get away with her life. I always
took her in and hid her and after the last time it happened
she came to see me the next day—while Robert was sleeping
off his big drunk—and said she was so grateful to me for
helping her, wasn't there something she could do for me?

I asked her to come in but said I couldn't talk to her much
right then because I had a jeweler in my suite who was showing
me some semi-precious stones—aquamarines, amethysts, tour-
malines, topazes, and others. Anita came in and looked over
the stones too. They were reputed to be the biggest of their
kind in the world. One was a 365-carat aquamarine and another
a 300-carat pink tourmaline. The jeweler told us—and I don't
know whether it was true or not—that both were strictly show-
piece stones and not for sale. They were to be presented to the
President of Brazil who was going to present them to President
Eisenhower as gifts from Brazil.

Well, the moment I saw the aquamarine, I knew I had to
have it. I wanted this beautiful thing with a passion and I
offered the man $800 for it which was all the cash I had on
hand. He just laughed at me and said he couldn't possibly part
with the stone because it wasn't really his. It was promised to
President Eisenhower. And besides, he said, it was worth much
more than $800.

I was heartbroken. But then I saw Anita wink at me and she
told the jeweler she would like to talk to him about several of
the stones, and could he bring them to her room? That night

she told me that she and Robert still were not speaking and she was going out to dinner with the jeweler.

Robert came around looking for her. I was quite worried. I didn't see her again that night, and only briefly the next day. She was on her way to the airport and said she was going back to Sweden and divorce Robert.

But on her way out, she handed me an envelope. Inside was a note which read: *Ann, I have arranged for you to have your aquamarine. I have the other one. All you have to do is pay the jeweler $800 in cash and the stone is yours. Love, Anita.*

I don't know what it was she did to that jeweler, but whatever it was she swung the deal, and President Eisenhower never saw those two stones. I had my aquamarine made into a necklace which is now one of my most prized possessions. (The Maharajah of Baroda once tried to buy it from me for his wife but I wouldn't sell.)

And I might add that Anita divorced her husband the moment she arrived back in Sweden.

Sometimes when I look at other people's husbands, I'm inclined to think mine weren't so bad after all.

Chapter 19

MILLER ON TAP

I've been mentioning the movie junkets we went on. This was another glamorous facet of the golden era of Hollywood that is gone now, along with the star system. The two went together, hand in hand, the stars and the junkets. The purpose was plain and simple—to promote and sell the product, movies.

In those days the studios actually created their own stars, designed, fashioned, and molded each one like a piece of valuable jewelry to glitter and shine not only on screen but as personal representatives of the movie studio. This was a basic part of the Hollywood dream factory.

In those days, too, America's biggest export was films. This was the reason for so many overseas junkets. The need for it doesn't exist any more because now so many movies are being made all over the world—both American and foreign. There was a time when the only motion pictures made abroad were almost entirely art films, and many countries all over the world were hungry for the Hollywood dream factory product.

Moreover, the people in foreign countries always went wild to see the stars themselves—in person. Since M-G-M was the largest studio, turning out the most movies and most glamorous movie stars, there were always junkets and film festivals. M-G-M had more overseas film distributors on its payroll than any other studio, as well as more theater exhibitors regularly receiving M-G-M products.

Now we come to the reasons Annie Miller was always on tap for these junkets. First of all, let's face it, some of our biggest screen stars were nothing but problem ladies off screen. There were certain stars M-G-M couldn't afford to send as its representatives, maybe because they drank too much or didn't get along with people, or for a variety of other reasons.

I got along with people. I didn't booze it up, sleep around, take pills, or smoke pot. I took my career seriously. I was always reliable. If they wanted me at six o'clock in the morning for publicity shots, I was there, Charlie.

On one of our early South American junkets, I made a big hit with Eric Johnston, who was the Jack Valenti of his day, because I was always on time and I was a good sport about doing whatever they wanted me to do, like a trained seal. I would sign autographs, pose for pictures, ride in parades, all the things they dream up for these junkets. Mr. Johnston said I was the best ambassadoress Hollywood had, and I became known as Hollywood's Traveling Ambassadoress. The studio sent me all over the world to spread good will and the good word about the movie capital.

But there was another more personal reason why I wanted to go on these junkets. I loved traveling, of course, but more important I learned that it could be the greatest education in the world. And I hungered for the education I had missed from being in show business at such an early age. Look, I don't like to scream it but I only went through the tenth grade. I still can't add worth a damn, I can't spell worth a damn and you'd have to take a Chinese Braille system to read my writing.

I didn't even know how to write a check until I married Reese Milner. I had always just turned my money over to my mother who took care of everything for me.

I *wanted* to go on those junkets not only for the fun and glamour but so I could learn. So I could make up for my lack of education and be able to converse with people intelligently. And the price was right. The studio, of course, picked up the tab on all our expenses.

That's why, whenever I was making a movie, I would rehearse twice as long and work twice as hard so we could shoot my part twice as fast and be finished—especially if there was a junket coming up. I knew that I would always be picked to go if I wasn't in the middle of a picture.

And, on all the junkets, wherever I happened to be, I was the first one up and out sightseeing—while the other star ladies were still asleep. Most of them never went out of their hotels except when they had to. They would spend hours in the beauty shop to look glamorous that night, and they wouldn't be caught dead taking an ordinary sightseeing tour or walking around in the shops.

I went out by myself and I went everywhere. And when people recognized me and gathered around me, I always tried to be gracious and friendly to them. I would ask them questions and try to learn as much about the people as I could in the short amount of time we spent in each place. As a result of all of this I was usually very popular with the natives of the country—as well as the local press corps. The photographers followed me everywhere.

Of course I met many interesting people and had many exciting adventures, but there was one cloak-and-dagger experience that I especially remember.

Actually, it was a combination of a movie junket and the Istanbul Hilton Hotel opening. And it involved a rather unpleasant experience with two of Hollywood's most celebrated star ladies, both much older than I, both Oscar winners, both living, still beautiful and glamorous, both married to wealthy men—and both will remember the incident when they read this. I prefer not to use their names, as I do not hold grudges and I wish them both well. But this will fill them in on the details of what happened to me after we said our goodbyes.

Conrad Hilton, as usual, had personally invited me to the Istanbul Hilton Hotel opening in June of 1955. I assume that he also personally invited the other two great star ladies, who came with Louella Parsons. There were many celebrities at the opening.

When I told M-G-M that I was going to Istanbul, the studio executives asked if I would go on to Cairo after the Istanbul festivities, and they would arrange all the hoopla and launch another world tour for the studio—starting from Cairo, if that was all right with me.

I said fine, at that time I hadn't yet been to Cairo. The Cairo Hilton opening (mentioned in a previous chapter) was in 1958 while I was married to Bill Moss.

I packed up my glad rags and about $150,000 worth of furs and jewelry and off I went to Istanbul for my dinner and favorite dancing date with Connie Hilton.

One of the star ladies was a very devout Catholic, and she had somehow learned that I was studying to be a Catholic at the time. These were the years, remember, when I was so madly in love with Bill O'Connor. Toward the end of our Istanbul festivities the Catholic star lady asked me if I would like to join their party for a trek to the Holy Land. There was a war going on in Jerusalem but we would be permitted to fly to the Arab side.

Of course I would adore to go. I thought how wonderful it would be if I could go back home and surprise Bill O'Connor with the news that I had been to Jerusalem and had actually seen the place where Christ was born and lived. Apart from my own interest in visiting the Holy Land, the anticipation of telling Bill O'Connor all about it would have been enough to make me eager to take the trip.

Because of the flight schedules we would have to stay over-night in Lebanon. But from there it would be an easy hop on to Cairo, where my work for M-G-M would begin. The two star ladies were not with M-G-M and so of course were not going on to Cairo—or at least not for the M-G-M tour. I didn't know what their plans were after Jerusalem.

There were five of us in the party—Louella and the two star ladies, and Kingsbury Smith, a reporter for the Hearst papers —and myself. We took off in the plane and I sat with Kingsbury Smith. He was delightful. He told me about the many places to visit in Cairo and the time passed very rapidly.

We arrived in Lebanon at about two o'clock in the morning and just before we landed I touched up my lipstick and combed my hair—something I always do no matter what time it is or where I am because you just never know who you're going to see or meet. I had noticed that the two star ladies were sitting there with cold cream on their faces and their hair up in rollers. I was somewhat surprised when they didn't bother to do their hair and make-up. I suppose they figured we would get off the plane and go straight to our hotel and to bed without seeing anyone.

Well, when the plane door opened, there stood a battery of photographers and the flashbulbs started popping when I walked off. And then off came the two star ladies, with no make-up and all those curlers. I could tell they were simply seething inside. But it wasn't my fault.

I had informed the M-G-M representatives in Istanbul that I was going to Lebanon and the Holy Land first, and then on to Cairo. I wanted my studio to know of my whereabouts, which is customary for any star under contract.

But I had no idea that all those photographers were going to meet the plane at that crazy hour of the morning. I didn't even know we had an M-G-M representative in Lebanon. But we did, and he was there to meet me. He was a Lebanese man who knew the custom officials, and he got me and my luggage through customs very quickly without any hitch.

I was still surrounded by photographers. As we were about to leave, I looked back and saw that Louella and the two star ladies were having some problems, so I asked our Lebanese man please to see whether he could help them through customs. He dashed back and talked to somebody, then pushed me into a limousine and said the other ladies would be well taken care of. When we arrived at the hotel there were more photographers and reporters waiting. By the time I got up to my room I was exhausted.

I took off my make-up, tucked myself into bed, and was just about to fall asleep when the phone rang.

It was one of the great star ladies. I wasn't too surprised. I knew how humiliating it must have been for them. But they did know that I was an M-G-M star and that I was going on to Cairo for an M-G-M junket. And even if they didn't know there were M-G-M representatives all over the world, at least they should have known enough to fix their hair and make-up before getting off a plane anytime or anywhere.

Miss Star Lady was livid. She called me a little bitch and asked me how dared I not tell them about the photographers.

"We don't have a big studio behind us any more, the way you do," she hissed. "If we'd known about the photographers, we would have had our make-up on and our hair in place. The least you could have done was to warn us ahead of time. It was very cruel and unfair of you not to . . ."

I tried to explain to her that it wasn't my fault, that I had no idea this was going to happen, and I told her how sorry I was about it. I did understand their feelings and I made what I thought was a most sincere and elaborate apology to her. But this wasn't enough for the great Star Lady.

Again she called me a little bitch and publicity hound.

Furthermore, she added, "We're going on a holy trek and we don't want you traveling with us. If you're along, there will be nothing but photographers everywhere and that isn't the sort of thing one does when visiting the Holy Land."

Then she delivered the final blow. "If you're going on with this trip, you're going alone or with someone else. You're not going with us." She said goodbye and slammed the phone in my ear.

Wow! I didn't know anyone could be so vicious and vitriolic. I was absolutely crushed. I had my heart set on going. And I was so close to the Holy Land now. It hurt me even to think of not going. I spent the rest of the night—what was left of it—tossing in my bed, crying, sleeping fitfully, and doing a lot of soul searching. I knew that I should not go on alone, especially with all the troubles between the Arabs and the Jews—and especially with all the valuables I was carrying. But after wrestling with my conscience, I knew what I had to do.

Our M-G-M representative was shocked when I told him the next morning that I was going on by myself.

"There is much war, strife, danger. You must not go into that country alone," he warned me.

In the end he wound up driving me to the airport and putting me on the first plane out to Jerusalem. Alone.

He had, however, persuaded me to purchase a switchblade knife for protection before I left. (Guns were not permitted.) I put the knife in my make-up kit which I carried aboard the plane.

Halfway through the flight, I went to the ladies' room and when I returned to my seat, I noticed my make-up kit was open and everything in it was awry. I searched through it frantically. The only thing missing was the knife. I knew this was a bad omen. I was terribly frightened but what could I do? I did nothing but keep quiet and hoped for the best.

I had prearranged for a room at the American Hotel and a

car was to meet me at the Jerusalem airport. There was a car, all right, but not exactly the kind I had expected. There were two men in it who got out, grabbed my luggage, beckoned me to get in, and then started off at high speed. It was a wild ride—through the city of Jerusalem and on past, perhaps twenty or thirty miles outside the city itself. They finally stopped in front of a small, dark Arab hotel, jumped out, opened the door and brusquely told me to get out. I was so scared I could barely walk or talk but I finally managed to ask them as cheerfully as possible where I was.

Without answering my question, one of them snapped in broken English, "Miss Miller, you have a lot of explaining to do."

They escorted me and my bags into the hotel, obtained a key from the front desk, and took me to a room upstairs. Again, I asked them where I was and who they were. They said I would soon find out. Then they left the room and locked me in, a complete prisoner.

There was no electricity in the room, only a small candle. It was so dark I couldn't even read to take my mind off of what was happening. I didn't know whether I should unpack.

Well, I had always wanted adventure and I was getting it. I thought of my poor mother and there were a few times during those frightened hours when I longed to be just plain little Johnnie Lucille Collier back in Houston, Texas.

Eventually a man arrived with a tray of food for me but I didn't dare touch it. There was a pitcher of water in the room but I was afraid to drink it. Then, finally, another man arrived and it began to unfold why I was being held.

"Miss Miller, we believe you are here on the Arab side of Jerusalem as a spy for the American Jews. You're a movie star, you've worked for the Jews all your life, and you're here as a spy, aren't you?"

I told him as calmly as I could that this was not true. I was in the Holy Land because I was studying to be a Catholic.

Ann Miller *is* "Mame."

My favorite *Mame* dress
which I wore in the "Bosom
Buddies" number.

Above, my mother's house on Alta Drive in Beverly Hills where I live with her and my French poodle, Poochie. (*Photo by Lee Marcus*)

Left, Mama, Poochie and me relaxing at home. (*Photo by Julian Wasser*)

Right, when I played Mrs. Dolly Gallagher Levi in *Hello, Dolly!* on the Kenley circuit in Ohio the summer of 1971. I was forty-eight.

Below, a production number from the *Dames at Sea,* television spectacular, 1971.

Ann Miller today . . . still 500 taps a minute. (*Photo by Kelley*)

Then he asked me why I had come all alone, and I explained that my friends had deserted me. I also told him about my M-G-M tour which was to start in Cairo.

I begged him please to take me to a telephone and let me try to make contact with a theater exhibitor who could verify my story by calling M-G-M in Cairo. There must be a theater somewhere in Jerusalem.

Finally the men agreed to take me downstairs to the phone at the desk. I first called the operator and asked if there were a theater in Jerusalem. Luckily there was one—and only one! I asked the operator to try to locate the manager. I was lucky again. The manager was also the owner of the theater and he happened to be in his office when I called. He also happened to know me from having shown some of my movies in his own theater, and he was a fan of mine. I explained my predicament to him and told him there were some people accusing me of being a spy. I asked him if he would call M-G-M in Cairo and they would verify my story. As a theater owner-manager-exhibitor, he ran other films besides M-G-M's of course, but he was most cordial and co-operative, and offered to call M-G-M right away and see what could be done for me.

After permitting me to make the phone calls, the men took me back upstairs and locked me into my room again.

It seemed like an eternity that I waited, but the theater man finally arrived—with the police. And you should have heard the elaborate round of apologies from all sides that were like music to my ears.

That theater-owner-manager turned out to be an angel. If it had not been for him, I might have been shot as a spy or left to rot away in some Arab jail. As it was, the whole episode turned into a glorious adventure. The theater man took me to the head of the Catholic archdiocese who assigned a priest to give me a personally conducted tour of the Holy Land, following the life of Christ step by step. He explained everything to me in English. It was an awesome, spine-tingling experience to be walking where Christ had walked. I will never forget it.

And on my last night in the Holy Land the theater man honored me with a huge dinner party—and he held it in front of the Arab hotel where I had been locked up. He invited about two hundred guests, many of whom came on camels. And we sat on the ground and ate wonderful spicy Arabian lamb with rice and fine wine. All the while we were dining there was soft Arabic music playing . . . and I could hear the camels moving softly, restlessly in the dark, where they had been tied . . . It was without doubt one of the most wonderful evenings of my life. For a little while time stood still and I felt as though I actually was living a page from Biblical days and the time of Christ.

The next day I packed my bags to leave. And it wasn't until then that I finally told my theater manager and benefactor about the unpleasant "incident" with the other two star ladies —and the real reason I had come to the Holy Land alone.

He of course also knew the ladies from their movies and he didn't much like what they had done to me. It just so happened, he told me, that they were arriving in Jerusalem from Lebanon on the same plane that I was taking on to Cairo. Apparently they had lingered in Lebanon long enough to make sure I had left the Holy Land.

My theater man thought it would be a great idea to pull a little trick on them. He arranged to have a battery of photographers meet the plane—to test them. If they posed for pictures and welcomed the publicity, he said, then we'd know they had lied to me with their excuse that this isn't proper in the Holy Land.

He had the photographers out in full force when the plane touched down, and he took me to the little commissary which overlooks the airfield and sat me at a table where I could observe all the proceedings while drinking Arabian mint tea. I watched the plane approach and touch down. I saw the star ladies emerge—and this time they did have their hair done and their make-up on. At least they had learned something from me.

They seemed somewhat surprised to be greeted by a horde of photographers, but did they refuse to pose for them? Not on your life, buster. Those star ladies who had said one doesn't do this sort of thing in the Holy Land posed like no movies stars ever posed before and in all sorts of positions—with the wind blowing through their hair, big smiles on their faces, shaking hands, signing autographs, anything the photogs wanted.

If they wondered later why none of those photos ever got into the newspapers, I can tell them. And they won't know until they read it here—there wasn't a single roll of film in any of those cameras. My Arab theater-owner friend saw to that.

Moreover, he chose precisely the right moment for us to emerge from the commissary and look on with amusement at the picture-posing group. Then the great star ladies spotted me and probably half-died from chagrin. At least they should have.

My friend escorted me up to the ramp and said goodbye. "They're only aging movie stars, my child," he said quietly. "Go in peace and God bless you."

I had to walk right past them to board the plane. It was quite a moment, meeting them coming down the ramp as I walked up. The only one I spoke to was Louella Parsons, who was very kind. She had called both the American Hotel in Jerusalem and my hotel in Cairo and had been terribly worried and upset when she learned that I wasn't registered at either one. Louella was a very sweet person and I was grateful for her concern.

I arrived in Cairo filled with excitement because I was finally going to see the Pyramids and the Sphinx and all the things that had fascinated me since I was a child. But before I was free to make the rounds like a tourist, I had to do a frantic whirlwind of publicity activities for M-G-M.

One of my movies was playing at the biggest theater in the city, and I was introduced on stage and spoke a few words in Arabic to the audience. They loved it. I was also introduced to King Farouk's favorite dancer. She taught me how to do the belly dance and gave me a pair of little finger cymbals which I still have. She also told me that Arab men judge their women and horses on their endurance and stamina. They never take a mistress unless she can dance for three or four hours without stopping.

One of the most important pashas in Cairo arranged a beautiful dinner party for me on the top floor of a big hotel. The women were all heavily perfumed and beautifully made-up, begowned and bejeweled, and the men were dark and exotic looking. The pasha had told me that we were going to be served a very ancient dish, one of the most ancient in the world. I was trying to imagine what it would be like and how it would taste, when out marched the waiters carrying these marvelous little tureens containing the fabulous ancient dish. The tureens looked ancient and exotic enough, but you can imagine my disappointment when I lifted the lid and took a taste. Okra! Plain old okra. I was brought up on okra in Texas. And to me it's about as unexotic as anything I can think of.

But I loved Cairo anyway. And, of course, one of the first things I wanted to do there was to consult a seer. I had always heard that the Egyptians are very psychic so I asked the M-G-M representative to arrange for a good seer to come and read my palm. One afternoon he brought this woman to my suite in the Menna House Hotel near the Pyramid of Gaza. She was very well dressed, in her early fifties, and she didn't speak a word of English. The M-G-M man told me he had chosen her because of her reputation and because she didn't know who I was.

She took my hand, looked into it and then started speaking in

Egyptian, while he interpreted for me. She said she saw my name up in lights and that I would be very famous. Almost exactly the same words the old gypsy fortuneteller had said all those years ago in the bus station in Houston. But then the Egyptian seer suddenly stopped talking and just stared at my hand. Finally she said she didn't want to read my hand any further, that I wouldn't have to pay her and she wanted to go.

I was petrified. I figured she meant I was going to die soon or something awful was going to happen to me. I begged the interpreter to try to persuade her to stay and finish the reading. Finally, but very reluctantly, she consented to do so. This is what she told me:

"You will have many men come into your life and a number of these men will die. One will die of an uncurable disease. Another will die of a heart attack. Another has something wrong with his nose. Another will have a stroke . . ." (She went into more gory details.) ". . . All these men have been or will be close to you and most of them will die sudden or unusual deaths ahead of their time . . . I see you surrounded by death and this is your karma . . . Because in another period you have been an Egyptian queen and you had many men killed during your lifetime. You are being repaid in this life for the sins you committed in another life. I am sorry, my child, but this is what I have to tell you. You will have many hardships, much suffering, and emotional unhappiness, but you will come out of it. You need have no fear for yourself. But you will lose so many of the men you love by death."

Then she left.

Of course at the time I didn't know what she was talking about. But I later deciphered it because it all came to pass. Within a few short years—four to be exact—Bill O'Connor, the one great love of my life, was to die prematurely (August 27, 1959) of a heart attack when he was only forty-eight years old. Another beau, Charles Isaacs (who was Eva Gabor's ex-husband), died at a relatively young age, of an incurable blood disease. My O.B. doctor who wanted to marry me went to the hospital for a very minor operation for polyps in his nose but something went wrong and he died. And my last husband, Arthur Cameron, as I have mentioned, did have a stroke several years before he died . . .

All of this lay ahead of me, was still in the future, but it certainly was not a pretty picture of the future the Egyptian seer predicted for me. I felt like a black widow spider. I must have been a terribly cruel and evil queen-king-pharaoh or whatever I was in my Egyptian incarnation. How many times must I be reminded of it?

It was spooky. The reading haunted me during the rest of my stay in Cairo. I became ill—funny, on both my trips to Cairo I took sick with a virus and I almost never do. However, this time the M-G-M people took good care of me and I was soon well enough to continue my tour for the studio.

Before leaving Cairo, I met an archaeologist named Kamal who took me on a tour of the museums, the pyramids and tombs, and the shops in the city. I was always on the lookout for antique jewelry, precious gems and jewels, and in one shop I spotted a beautiful bracelet and matching clips, which the jeweler told me had once belonged to the royal family. They were part of the Farouk collection, he said. I didn't really believe him, but I wanted them anyway. We were not allowed to take jewels out of the country but the jeweler told me he was going to be in New York soon, and he would call me if I was seriously interested in his collection of jewels. I said I was and he did call me in New York. And as it turned out I did indeed buy that beautiful bracelet and the two clips from the Farouk collection.

They were obviously very old, with rose-cut diamonds, emeralds and rubies and Egyptian hieroglyphics on them.

I'll never forget the night I wore them to a party in Hollywood where I met the exiled Egyptian Queen Mother Nazerlie, who had been thrown out of Egypt by her own son, King Farouk. When we were introduced I started telling her that I had been in her country and how wonderful it was. But then I noticed she wasn't listening at all. She was standing there staring at my Egyptian bracelet and clips. She finally asked me where I got them, and I told her. Then she said, very softly, "Those are mine. They once belonged to me."

I felt terrible. If I had been a terribly wealthy woman, I would have taken them off right there and given them back to her. Instead, I merely told her that I would treasure them forever, and I have.

That was the beginning of a good friendship with the Queen Mother of Egypt and with one of her daughters, Princess Atti and her husband, Riad Ghali. They are dear friends of mine to this day. All three of King Farouk's sisters, as well as his mother, were tossed out on their ears. One of the sisters, as most everyone in Hollywood knows, later became one of Arthur Cameron's girl friends. The Egyptian Queen Mother Nazerlie was brokenhearted to be banned by her son from her own country. She became a convert to Catholicism and I happen to know that she prayed for her son, King Farouk, until the day he died.

Now, whatever happened to those other two great star ladies who left a sour note in my memories of this junket?

Well, the one who made the telephone call that night and called me a bitch and a publicity hound, came backstage to see me at my Los Angeles opening of *Mame*—after I'd been a big hit on Broadway—and wished me lots of luck and all the et ceteras. She didn't mention that long-ago Lebanon incident but I knew she was thinking of it. How could she help it?

And the star lady who put her up to it (she's the one really responsible for the whole episode) ruled the roost for years in top international jet-set society, until recently her so-called billionaire husband went broke and they've hung up the FOR SALE shingle on their palatial digs.

All I can say is, everybody gets their comeuppance.

Chapter 20

ANNIE MAME:
HALLELUJAH DAY

After my annulment from Arthur Cameron, I decided to take a good long look at Ann Miller, at where I was going and what I wanted from life. I felt I couldn't continue making mistakes by desperately reaching out for love and marrying the wrong person. I must grow up and take stock of myself, my ideals and the real values in life. So far, I hadn't found happiness or real love—only madcap adventures that ended in sadness and divorces and a loss of time, tears and energy that I could no longer afford.

I did a lot of soul-searching and finally decided to withdraw from the human race—meaning men, mostly—and concentrate on the one and only thing in life I seemed to know how to handle well enough—my career. I obviously hadn't done very well in the marriage department.

So it was back to my career for Annie Miller. But what career? The Golden Years were over. And leaving my career repeatedly to get married had done nothing to enhance my standing at any of the movie studios—even if I had wanted to return to motion pictures, which I didn't. Not with the kind of pictures the moviemakers were making in the '60s.

I wouldn't be caught dead doing nude scenes or some of the other vile things they've started doing in the so-called "new" Hollywood. What's new about sex? I'm one who feels a leg in a black lace stocking is much more sexy than nudeness. The movies today—it's like watching someone go to the bathroom. What's fun about that? Louis B. Mayer would turn over in his grave.

Yes, indeed, the "new" Hollywood was different and I wanted no part of its obsession with pornography.

I do not delude myself that I was ever a Big Star. I never played politics, I never slept with producers, and I was never on call to entertain the bankers who flew out from New York. I kept my legs crossed when I wasn't dancing and so I ended up neither a Big Star nor a little one, but a happy medium—in pretty pictures like *Easter Parade*, *Kiss Me, Kate*, and *Hit the Deck*, pictures I'd be proud to show my own grandchildren if I had any.

Except for doing *George White's Scandals* in 1939 on Broadway, my entire career had been in motion pictures, and principally as a dancer. No one ever thought of me seriously as a singer or an actress because it was always my dancing that was featured.

In reactivating my career I had to make a serious decision. What direction was I heading? If I didn't go back into movies, where was I going. Where was the future for a dancer—*just* a dancer? Not a singer-actress-dancer, but only a dancer.

In some ways my reputation as a dancer was a handicap. How could I change my image from *Ann Miller, the dancer* to *Ann Miller, singer-dancer-actress*, and where could I go even if I changed the image? The era of movie musicals was over.

Deep down I knew I wanted to return to my career, to pick up where I left off, but I had sense enough to know that was impossible. Hollywood was a whole new ball game now.

While I was trying to find the answers within myself, my dilemma was resolved for me in a totally unexpected way.

One day out of the blue the telephone rang and the call was from the producers of the *Hollywood Palace* TV show, Bill Harback and Nick Vanoff, asking me to make a guest appearance on the show.

For years this was the most prestigious musical variety show on the air. Of course I said yes, I would do the show. I was terribly excited about it even though I had no idea of the kind of act I would dream up for it.

That night I was out with my ex-husband Arthur Cameron. I told him about the offer from *Hollywood Palace* and he was as excited as I was.

"Annie girl," he said, "this is going to be your big break and the beginning of a new career for yourself. And I'll tell you what I'm going to do. I'm going to stake you to the best damn' act that *Hollywood Palace* show ever had. You just tell me who you want to stage your numbers, do your musical arrangements, your costumes—whatever you want. But make it good so you'll knock 'em dead."

Arthur lent me his executive secretary to help figure out the budget and make out the various checks for all my expenses. I hired Nick Castle to stage my number, Louis De Pron to work with me on the tap steps, Bob Mackie to design my costumes, and Les Baxter for my musical arrangements—all tops in their fields.

We planned a number called "It Had Better Be Tonight." It was a Latin tune done with a tropical background. I sang it in Spanish and English and danced on big drums while the one and only Jack Costanza played the bongos. Well, I tell you, it brought down the house. *Hollywood Palace* was always a live TV show. My mother and Arthur were both out there in the audience, and when I finished they had tears in their eyes.

I was paid $7,500 for my guest appearance on the show. My mini-production cost Arthur $9,000.

But he loved it. And the producers loved it, too. The response was so sensational that they invited me back—not once, but three more times! Boom, boom, boom. Arthur was right. It was my big break in a new career. The second time around I did "Bill Bailey," again with Nick Castle's staging. Next, it was "Slap That Bass," an old Fred Astaire number which Louis De Pron helped me work out.

I was to save the best till the last. When they asked me to return the fourth time, I again hired Louis De Pron to work on an elaborate number called "Trapped in the Web of Love." (Arthur Cameron was still footing the bills, though I later paid him back every cent he had spent toward helping me reactivate my career.)

I had a chorus of boy dancers all dressed as big black spiders hanging on a huge web of rhinestones. And I was Little Miss Muffett. At one point the boy dancers crawl off the web and rip off my little girl costume and there I am—a black widow spider with a strapless leotard made of beads, a big red heart-shaped spot in the middle of my body, and beaded stockings. It was wild, and certainly the best of my four *Hollywood Palace* mini-productions.

But there's a dramatic story behind this one that might have been tragic. About a month before I was called for that fourth appearance, I developed a blood clot in my right leg. It became terribly swollen and the pain was so awful that I could hardly bear it. When the doctor came, he took one look at me and ordered me to the hospital. I didn't move from the bed for three weeks. They finally let me go home but a vein specialist told me that I was not to dance for a while until the injured vein healed and meanwhile I had to wear a tight rubber stocking on that leg.

I was so depressed. Annie Miller was known for her legs, and here I was wearing an unglamorous rubber stocking and not knowing when I could dance again. I didn't tell one soul about it, though, and when the *Hollywood Palace* producers called again for me to do a show—my fourth—I accepted in spite of the fact that I was absolutely forbidden by my doctor to dance again until my leg was perfectly healed. It could injure my leg permanently, he said.

Well, I got my little bird-brain to clicking and I figured that if I had to wear a tight rubber stocking on that leg anyway, why not?

So I talked Bob Mackie into designing for me a pair of rubber tights embroidered with sequins and beads. At first he was horrified and puzzled. Why would I want to wear something like *that?* But he did it anyway. Actually, it worked quite well for the spider number, and the costume looked great. No one could tell I was wearing rubber tights.

I danced merrily away in this number. And my leg healed up fine in spite of it. Of course I caught hell from my doctor, who happened to see me on the show and called to tell me what a terrible risk I had taken. I might have been injured for life. I might never dance again.

It reminded me of that other time when the doctors told me I would never dance again—after that horrible fall down the stairs and losing my baby, when I was married to Reese Milner.

Well, no doctor would ever slow me down again.

I was back in show business and facing a new career and a new life once again.

Fortunately, both of my last two ex-husbands came to my rescue, encouraged me, lent me money and really helped launch me on a whole new career in show business. As I have said earlier, it was my number-two husband Bill Moss who paid for my voice lessons during this launching period. And it was Arthur Cameron who pulled me through the *Hollywood Palace* prelude to my new career.

True Texans always stick together in time of need.

I hired a drama coach as well as a voice coach, found myself a new agent, Don Wortman, and told him I wanted to prove to people that I could sing and act as well as dance.

Don Wortman was another important man—besides my two ex-husbands—who had faith in me. He said he knew I could make it big on the stage. And then one day he asked me how I would like to do a stock engagement of the great Cole Porter musical, *Can-Can* if he could get me a booking in my home town of Houston.

With great trepidation I said yes, I would do it, but please give me time to work with my drama coach, Bill Tregoe and singing coach Harriet Lee, because I wanted to be well prepared.

I did *Can-Can* in Houston and it was a success. Annie Miller became the toast of the town in her home town where she had first started out in life as little Johnnie Lucille Collier, and where the old gypsy woman had told her she would one day see her name Up There in lights.

There are three places where those lights mean the most—Broadway, Hollywood, and your own home town. I had finally made it to my own home town with a splash. But could I make it to Broadway or Hollywood again?

The answer was not long in coming.

I took a crack at a non-singing, non-dancing straight role in Chicago, in a stage play called *Glad Tidings* at the Pheasant Run Theatre. I did it because I wanted to get all the stage experience I could. My reviews were very good—in a city noted for its rip-'em-up critics. But it was a very costly experience, for I was robbed of most of my furs, clothes, and jewels one night during my stay there. I sued the hotel and theater and won the first round, but the case is far from settled and these things always leave a sour taste in your mouth.

I was still feeling down in the dumps over this when some friends asked me to go with them to Sun Valley for a skiing weekend. Since my legs are my livelihood, I can't afford to risk breaking them on a pair of skis just for the hell of it.

So I don't ski. But I like other things that go with it—the *après*-ski parties, clothes, and especially the good-looking ski instructors.

So I went. It turned into quite a long weekend, as we got snowed in for ten days. It was a most memorable occasion. Actress June Allyson, who was in our little snowed-in party, developed kidney stones and had to be flown out as soon as we could dig out.

And I was willy-nilly dilly-dallying at the crossroads of my career while we were snowbound—and while my agent back in Hollywood was gnashing his teeth. He was on the long-distance phone with me every five minutes. The problem was— I had two very nice offers and couldn't make up my mind. One was to do the *Red Skelton Show* on TV. It was a firm offer and the pay was good—$10,000. I had done many movies with Red, he was a longtime good friend, and doing a TV guest spot with him would be marvelous exposure. Also it was a snap. I couldn't lose on this one. All I'd have to do was put together a tap number and get up there and do it. Same as I'd done millions of times before. People always seemed to get a big charge out of watching Annie Miller tap dance.

But the other offer was more intriguing.

My agent Don Wortman had persuaded New York producer John Bowab to sign me for a Florida run of the Broadway smash hit musical, *Mame*.

I had asked for it—a singer-actress-dancer role, that is. And I had done it successfully in *Can-Can* in Houston. But it wasn't quite the same. *Mame* was the current big hit on Broadway. Though there had been other Mames, Angela Lansbury had created the role, Angela Lansbury *was* Mame, and it was difficult for anyone to follow her—on Broadway or anywhere, including Florida.

I had to think twice before taking that one. So far I'd never ever had a bad review, and after all these years that's some kind of a track record. But so far the reviews had always concentrated on my dancing. And Auntie Mame was one helluva dame, a character rich in pizzazz as Patrick Dennis had drawn her and as Rosalind Russell first played her, and anyone who did the musical role had to have more than musical ability, they had to have real acting talent. I couldn't tap dance my way through that one. That much I knew. I could fall flat on my face, and then what?

It would be much safer to go with Red Skelton.

But I went with *Mame*.

It is a well-known fact that the majority of the bored, rich, top-hat society crowd in Palm Beach usually put in an appearance at a theater opening just to be seen and get their names in the society columns. And they usually leave at intermission.

It is all duly recorded in the press (and in my scrapbooks) that the wealthy society people of Palm Beach not only stayed through the intermission and to the very end, but gave me an almost never-ending standing ovation and made me an overnight musical-comedy celebrity. No one ever heard of those Palm Beachers standing on their feet that long to applaud *anybody*.

John Bowab, who was in the audience, of course, was very impressed. On the spot he signed me for *Mame* on Broadway. (He of course first checked with producer Bobby Fryer and Jerry Herman who wrote the music and lyrics, and both of whom had the last word on the role of Broadway's Auntie Mame.)

What a feather in my cap! But should I do it?

Mame had been a big hit but was in trouble at the time. Jane Morgan had taken over the role but the show was not doing too well. It was on "twofers"—meaning two tickets for the price of one. The contract at the Winter Garden had run out and the producers were on a week-to-week basis. I knew there were almost overwhelming odds against me. There had been so many Mames before me—Angela Lansbury, Sheila Smith, Celeste Holm, Janis Paige, and Jane Morgan.

I would be the sixth Mame on Broadway since the musical opened in May 1966.

With all the talent that had gone before me, I would be taking a big chance.

In Florida I had played *Mame* in both Palm Beach and Miami and my press reviews had been great. Typical was this one from the Miami Beach *Reporter:*

> We were flabbergasted by the calibre of Miss Miller's performance. She showed talents we never knew she had. Her dancing, of course, has never been questioned, but her style and quality as a performer has never had a chance to prove itself before. She is as good a Mame as they make and we fell in love with her from the first moment she appeared.

It is important to understand some of the events leading up to my success in the Broadway *Mame*, some of which was due to the much-publicized tap-dance number that was written into *Mame* especially for me.

You see, this was my idea to have the tap number written in, and when I suggested it to John Bowab, he thought it was a great idea. For my Florida production the number was choreographed by a young New York choreographer, Diana Baffa. Then, after hearing about the sensational choreography and the rave reviews I had in Florida, Miss Onna White, who happens to be the top lady choreographer in the business, offered to work with me on enlarging the tap number for my Broadway *Mame*.

Onna had won an Oscar in 1968 for her choreography in the movie, *Oliver*. It was a fantastic break for me to have her work with me on my Broadway *Mame*. She had seen all the Broadway Mames but had never staged a tap number for one before.

It wasn't all smooth sailing stepping into the Broadway company of a hit show that had been around for a while, especially because some veteran members of the cast and chorus were very bored and blasé about the whole thing after seeing so many Mames come and go. The tempo was so slow that they sometimes looked as though they were about to fall asleep on stage. At first they resented my order that the big "Mame" number should be done faster than the other Mames had done it, and they quite obviously resented the fact that a splashy big tap number, "How Young I Feel," had been written into the show especially for me.

But I was determined to put some life and excitement back into a show that everyone knew was dying and about to close. I told them all during rehearsals that if they wanted to work with me, fine. If not, go. Either wake up and shape up or get out. That's the way I felt about it and it worked. They turned out to be once again a great cast, and the whole show had a new drive and energy. There is always resentment when a Hollywood person takes over a Broadway show.

Even though I had to do it the hard way, I am proud of the fact that I was finally able to win their friendship and respect.

I have a huge bulging scrapbook of memories—all the press clippings from my two Broadway shows. Near the front of the scrapbook is a feature story from the New York *Journal American*, dated September 30, 1939. The headline reads BROADWAY'S MAGIC WAND TOUCHES ANN MILLER. There is a picture of me with the caption *"Scandals" tap dancer*.

And at the bottom of the page I had scrawled in my childish handwriting, a wistful comment:

"As I sit in my apartment looking out over New York, I think how wonderful to have such good fortune, to be a '*hit*' in a show. Maybe someday I'll be in a book show and sing and act, too . . ."

Well, someday is now, Annie. Thirty years later. Better late than not at all.

It was another opening night, May 26, 1969, the one opening night I shall never forget. It is indelibly etched in my memory, down to the tiniest detail.

We opened at the wonderful Winter Garden Theatre, only one block away from the Alvin Theatre where I had stopped the show with my Mexiconga number thirty years earlier. But it was different then. I was so much younger. All my life was ahead of me. How wonderful it had been to be in a hit show. But could I do it again? How well I remembered the words I had written in my scrapbok, "Maybe someday I'll be in a book show and sing and act, too . . ."

So here I was, thirty years, forty movies, and three husbands later, standing in tip-toed awe with my mother gazing upon that glittering block-long *Mame* sign on the roof of the Winter Garden Theatre . . . and my name up there in lights. The biggest, longest, most glittering sign in the Great White Way. Just like the gypsy woman said . . . It was choke-up time again . . .

Backstage I was so nervous I had the shakes. I can't remember when I've ever been so frightened. I suddenly felt so all alone. I could just picture all those people out there in the audience picking me to pieces, comparing me with Angela Lansbury, whispering "How old is she? Over the hill. She's gotta be fifty. How many times she's been married?" Three times, buster. And I just turned forty-six in April. How about that? It was that damn' fake birth certificate haunting me all of my life. Chin up, Annie. It's countdown for curtain time. There goes the orchestra. I wonder if Angela Lansbury was scared like this. That's one of the roughest things in show business, following a star who's made it big in a big Broadway hit. I could tap, sure I could tap, but I couldn't tap my way through *Mame*. Oh, dear God, why did I get myself into this? What would the critics do to me? What would Rex Reed write? He adored Angela Lansbury. We all know about first-loves. Who can follow that?

I peeked through the curtains and saw all the people pouring in. For one frozen moment I panicked. I thought I was going to faint. I felt like screaming. I wanted to run away . . . run, run, run. I almost did. How could I ever go out there in Angela Lansbury's footsteps—me, Annie Miller, the little dancing star of all those long-ago, faraway M-G-M musicals? Nobody cared about them any more. Such dark, dread thoughts I had in those last long moments before the curtain went up.

And then it happened. The curtain rose and there I was, poised up there high on the staircase in my solid gold-beaded pajama costume and with a gold bugle in my hand, all ready to sing the big "It's Today" number.

But something happened. That audience simply went wild. I got a standing ovation before I even began. It was the kind of ovation usually reserved only for curtain calls. The audience stood up and cheered and clapped and whistled and yelled "Bravo." It was unbelievable . . . I couldn't move or utter a word for those first few minutes. I would guess that this first tumultuous ovation lasted ten minutes or so. I remember just standing there frozen and incredulous, thinking this happens only once in a lifetime, it can never happen again, and finally I had to hold my hand up to stop the applause before I could sing my first song.

There are simply no words to describe my feelings on that opening night of *Mame* at the Winter Garden Theatre on that late May evening in 1969. The audience broke out in applause after so many numbers. I got another standing ovation after my big "Mame" number. But it was my big tap number, "How Young I Feel," in the second act, that really brought down the house. And at the end of the show another standing ovation you wouldn't believe. Many have said it was one of the most memorable opening nights in Broadway history.

It was like nothing I had ever dreamed of or expected. After the last standing ovation the aisles literally were clogged with people swarming down toward the footlights, and throwing flowers and lovebeads to me on stage. It was all a dream that would end if I pinched myself.

When I got back to my dressing room it was jammed with friends and well-wishers.

I couldn't believe my eyes or my ears. There was Rex Reed himself no less hugging me and telling me I was "simply fantastic."

And then came the reviews. They were great. They dispelled all my doubts and declared me as the new reigning queen of Broadway. The headlines proclaimed: ANN MILLER TRIUMPHS AS MAME . . . REVITALIZES MAME . . . IS A SENSATIONAL SMASH . . . A MAGNIFICENT MAME . . . STOPPED THE SHOW TIME AND AGAIN!

I don't like to seem immodest or toot my own horn but I just must record some of those reviews here for posterity.

Clive Barnes, New York *Times* (June 20) . . . Ann Miller brings zest to Mame. Her legs are the longest and loveliest in show business and she still dances superbly . . .

John Chapman, New York *Daily News* (June 1) . . . There have been six Auntie Mames in the Winter Garden production of "Mame" since the musical opened in May, 1966. I saw the newest one, Ann Miller, the other night, and she is the best in my fond heart . . . a Texas beauty . . . a good actress with exceptional personal warmth, and she can outdance all the other ladies on one foot.

William Hazlitt, *The Hollywood Reporter* (June 3) . . . It was Ann Miller's night Monday night at Broadway's wonderful Winter Garden Theatre. The bravos were never-ending. The applause, the whistles, the gee-whiz, was overwhelming. Maria Callas never had it so good . . . The applause was unbelievable, so deafening the expertness of the twirling taps was lost. . . .

Waves of hysteria swept the Winter Garden . . .

Radie Harris, *Hollywood Reporter* (June 3) . . . They gave her the kind of ovation at her entrance that is usually reserved for curtain calls. They stood up and cheered when she introduced a tap routine, especially created by Onna White, as part of her "How Young I Feel" (and looked) number toward the end of Act Two. And when the curtain finally descended to more cheers and a standing ovation, some of the more enthusiastic camp followers tore down the aisles as they do for Fonteyn and Nureyev. It really was *quelquechose!*

Drama critic William E. Sarmento wrote: . . . Ann Miller, I love you! I guess I always have . . . No one, not even Judy Garland at the Palace, ever was accorded the reception given to Ann Miller on her opening in "Mame" the other night. The ovation was thunderous. The audience went wild after each number . . . "Mame" belongs to Ann Miller now and always . . . She looks great. The hair is shimmering black, the figure terrific, and those dancing legs have never looked better. And when she tap dances, you just know that this lady is one of the all-time musical queens.

My good friend and syndicated columnist, Earl Wilson, summed it all up in his column of May 27 in the New York *Post:*

ANNIE MAME MAKES IT . . .
   It's going to be Ann Miller's town for weeks.
   The world's youngest quinquagenarian, opening as a replacement in "Mame" had the regular audience impersonating a yo-yo for numerous standing ovations. Then the ballet boys flew down to the footlights shouting "Bravo!"
   "Annie Mame" was a legitimate and sensational smash to that audience.
   There was a murmur in the crowd when she put on her dancing shoes to do a tap number created by Oscar-winner choreographer Onna White.
   Ann's dancing legs, dancing thighs and dancing derriere are as overwhelming as her energy.

One of my most favorite of all the reviews was the one in *The Wall Street Journal* (June 23, 1969) by John J. O'Connor.

   . . . The real point is that Ann Miller, modestly described in the program as a legend in her own time, has returned, and she is thoroughly delightful. She takes Mame and turns her into a warm, innocently sophisticated, immensely appealing creature, a bit daffy and forever smiling etc.—and it all works beautifully. Gorgeously costumed in Robert Mackintosh designs, she skitters, shuffles, glides about the stage, long fingers dangling from endlessly flapping hands, every moment bursting with vitality and good cheer. Her acting is excellent, her sense of time impeccable, and her singing of Jerry Herman's songs strong and pleasant.

Most of all, of course, there is the Miller dancing, and here the actress has the audience cheering with every step—or even the hint of one. She brings a barrelful of zest to all of the numbers, but she stops the show with a special tap number added for her own particular talent. . . . The cheers are partially wonderment, partially nostalgia, all deserved tribute.

Well, did you ever read such reviews?

Mother and I clipped them out of the newspapers, pasted them into my scrapbook, and as usual I penned my own comment: *The astronauts landed safely back on earth in Apollo 10, and I landed safely back on Broadway. Amen!*

Mame was the biggest love affair of my life. My Mame was a warm, happy-hearted one, and I played her with everything I had in me to give. Those who saw it will never forget one of Mame's most memorable lines: "Live, live, live," she cries. "Life's a banquet and most poor sons of bitches are starving to death."

Mame's philosophy fitted me to a T.

But I also always cried in the Christmas scene every night because it reminded me of my baby's death.

Professionally, I felt my biggest triumph was being accepted and applauded as a singer and actress as well as a dancer. To me this was the culmination of all my dreams. And never for one moment did I forget those who had stood by me and had faith in me—Bill Moss, Arthur Cameron, Valerie and Nat Dumont, my agent Don Wortman, and, of course, my mother.

It isn't easy doing the same show over and over, night after night, for weeks and months. Playing a stage show anywhere is a lot different from shooting a movie. But there's nothing more exciting than winning and wooing a new live audience at a Broadway show night after night.

With all its glorious fulfillment for me, *Mame* was also a very lonely period of my life. Between Florida, Broadway, Los Angeles, and summer stock, approximately two years of my life went into blood, sweat, and taps on theater stages around the country in *Mame*.

Romance was out. I had a new sweetheart-lover, *Mame*. And what a great tonic and therapy for me after all the mistakes I had made in my personal life. I felt like a tap machine but I knew this was best for me at the time. And incidentally, though it may sound immodest, I think I can safely say that it was my big tap number in *Mame* that revived the interest in tap dancing—which is a big thing today in our nostalgia era. Even Angela Lansbury sent me congratulations on my tap number and said it gave the show a whole new dimension.

Mame had a rather inglorious finale. It finally folded when I did—of double pneumonia. After eight months in the role, I simply collapsed with fatigue and a 104-degree temperature. It was all very dramatic. I was flown back to California and I was in bed for weeks . . . But when I recovered I opened again at Jimmy Doolittle's Huntington Hartford Theatre in Hollywood.

As I have said, the three places that count in show business are Hollywood, New York, and your own home town. My real home town was Houston where I had done *Can-Can*.

But Hollywood also had been my adopted home town for many years, and let me tell you, Hollywood is the toughest home town in the world, with all your peers sitting out there watching you, and some of them out of work and hoping you'll fall flat on your derrière.

Anything after my Broadway *Mame* has to be an anticlimax,

but I couldn't help being thrilled with the standing ovation and reception I was given on my opening night in Hollywood. There was a big party for me afterward and many of the top stars came, including Lucille Ball who had "discovered" me lo those many years ago at the Bal Tabarin in San Francisco . . . And the famous Star Lady who had crossed me off her Holy Land list on that unforgettable flight to Lebanon . . . and many more.

Again I got standing ovations at every performance, and to accomplish this in the jungle of Hollywoodlandia is quite a feat in anyone's book—as anyone who has ever tried it or achieved it can attest.

Hollywood columnist James Bacon wrote (Los Angeles *Herald-Examiner*, April 17, 1970):

> Ann is something to see in "Mame." She gets a standing ovation every performance, something that is rare in theatre after opening night when a star's friends fill the house.
>
> Annie does something in "Mame" that you don't see very often in musical comedy stars anymore—she sings and dances beautifully.
>
> Somehow, the musical theatre, of late, has cast people who either talk or croak beautiful music. Marilyn Miller must be whirling in her grave, along with Flo Ziegfeld.
>
> Ann, who has been "Auntie Mame" for the last 30 years, leaves the young chorus dancers puffing. None of them can match her energy.
>
> Her secret—pure honey and Vitamin E.

But that wasn't all. Ann Miller's real secret was pure love and devotion to a great role, the likes of which simply don't happen more than once in a lifetime.

There was another reason, too, besides the great role. I had simply fallen in love with the live theater. It had happened first with *Can-Can* back in Houston. The beautiful costumes, the lights, the people and the applause—it was all like a heady wine to my soul. Somehow on stage I became alive with a magic fire, a desire to win, to love and to please the audience. I've felt this way ever since. To me, when I go on stage, Ann Miller is lost and the part takes over. The show becomes real and the part I play becomes real, and every night is like opening night in my desire to win over the audience. In *Mame* I think some of the cast felt that I was obsessed with my role. Perhaps I was. I suppose you could compare it to being a convert to Catholicism. The convert takes it very much to heart and works harder at it than a person born into it, who takes his religion for granted. The stage never could I take for granted.

I played *Mame* to packed houses on the Kenley circuit in Ohio. I also played Mrs. Dolly Gallagher Levi in *Hello, Dolly!* the next summer. (Jerry Herman also wrote the music for *Hello, Dolly!*)

And in between I did that big Heinz Soup commercial for Stan Freberg, which made television history. It was my first television commercial. Stan Freberg is known as something of a wild genius in Hollywood. He spent $250,000 on that commercial—it lasted only one minute, the most expensive TV commercial ever shot. But it was great fun . . . Ann Miller dancing on top of a Heinz Soup can . . . in a Great American Soups Busby Berkeley type tap number . . . Soupedy-do . . . But do you know that more people saw me in that tippy-tippy-tap TV commercial than saw me in *Mame* during all those months on Broadway? It's astounding, the exposure you get on television.

Soon after this I was featured in a television special, *Dames At Sea* with Ann-Margret. This was a spoof of the Ruby Keeler-Dick Powell musicals of the '30s. I played the Mona Kent role. Again, my reviews were good.

But what can you do for an encore after you've made it in *Mame?*

Chapter 21

BUBBLES FROM
THE HIGH LIFE

Ah, memories, memories . . . I have so many of them and from time to time they surface, like the bubbles in a glass of champagne. So herewith is a potpourri of random thoughts, some of which come to mind because people are constantly asking me questions about all sorts of things.

For example: Are my legs insured? To tell you the truth, I couldn't possibly afford to carry full-time insurance on my legs and my jewelry, too. But when I'm working, the studios or independent producers take care of it.

At one time, when I was at RKO, my legs were insured for a million dollars with Lloyds of London. Not for their looks, mind you, but for their staying in one piece through the picture. It would have cost a fortune if I'd broken a leg halfway through a movie because they couldn't replace me without reshooting everything I had done.

As time went on, it became more and more difficult for the studios to get insurance on dancers, because of the chances we

were asked to take during our spectacular production numbers. I
never had a double and I did all my own steps, no matter how
dangerous they were. I had a few accidents along the way, and
I can't even count the number of bruised and scratched knees
and twisted ankles I've had.

When I was doing *Reveille with Beverly*, real flames of fire
were supposed to spring up behind me as I twirled my way
up and down a V for Victory platform. But sometimes the man
who controlled the fire turned a flame on in front of me and
I would have to leap out of the way. And once I didn't leap
quite fast enough and ended up with a singed costume, eyelashes, and hair after my big finale.

And then there were all those platforms and pyramids and
staircases that made the number super-special but which were a
real danger to dance on. When I was doing *Small Town Girl*,
I had to climb up a huge stairway and dance way up in the
air on a platform that was as high as a three-story building.
I get dizzy when I'm up that high and more than once, I
slipped and almost fell.

I've already mentioned the fall that landed me in the hospital
with a severe back injury while I was doing *Two Tickets to
Broadway* for Howard Hughes at RKO. That fall was from the
top of an enormous pyramid the studio had built for me. Nick
Castle had choreographed a spectacular number for me to do
on top of the pyramid. It was spectacular all right—and so was
the pratfall I took.

In *Kiss Me, Kate*, I was forever leaping around Kathryn
Grayson and Howard Keel—up on a table, down to the floor and
over the couch. That wasn't particularly dangerous but
it was tiring. I can't tell you how many times we shot those
scenes, because my shoe buckle would snag on Kathryn's wig
and knock it askew or I would jolt Howard Keel to one side.
It was quite an obstacle course.

When I did *Mame*, the producers had quite a time getting insurance on me—or any of the other Mames for that matter.

It wasn't for my dancing this time. Everyone who has seen *Mame* will remember that Mame swings across the stage, way up high, with a little boy at her side. Well, believe me, it's a long way down to the stage floor and we couldn't very well use circus nets! I don't know how the others felt about it but I wasn't particularly happy to play an amateur trapeze artist. Still, it was tame compared with other things I've done as a dancer.

I'm also constantly being asked how I keep so young-looking. Somebody came up to me just recently, when I attended Debbie Reynolds's opening night at the Cocoanut Grove and said, "You never seem to fall apart. You're always so well put together. You're like a walking eight by ten glossy."

I appreciated that because I have always taken good care of myself. I have never smoked and I don't like hard liquor so I've never been a very good drinker. I much prefer sipping a nice glass of wine or an ice cold beer.

I guess I learned to take care of myself from my mother. She's eighty years old now and still gets up at five every morning, puts on her make-up and dresses up as though she were going to a luncheon. She's a most remarkable woman.

It's most important to take good care of your skin, especially your face, otherwise it's going to dry and crinkle up. I always use a pure cold cream and use only cold cream soap. I wash my face in very hot water then splash cold water on it, before putting on a good night cream.

Forget all those high-priced lotions they're trying to push at you. You don't have to spend a fortune for good creams to keep your skin moist.

I also think it's very important to keep a good night cream or heavy oil around your eyes all the time. I even use it under make-up.

But health and good skin come from within. I recommend the use of vitamins but nutrition is the most important thing. Eat good lean meat, fresh vegetables and lots of leafy salads.

And don't forget exercise. If you're not athletic, walk, walk, walk. Walk briskly, with your shoulders back and your head up high. It's good not only for your weight, but for your circulation and heart. I also like to ride my bike around the block as often as I can.

I think if you're a star, you should act like one and look like one. I would never go out in public looking like those two star ladies when they arrived in Lebanon, or the hippie types who look like an unmade bed. When I go out, even if it's only to the local market, I put on my make-up, fix my hair and wear a pretty dress or pants outfit.

People are starved for glamour, because there is so much dullness in their everyday lives. They look to stars to provide it, off screen as well as on. That's why this wave of nostalgia has swept the country—because the thirties, forties and early fifties were a glamour era.

I think these young girls who go around today in gypsy dresses and bare feet and straggly hair look like a bad Halloween night. And women who wear anything that's in fashion —only because it's the fashion—even if it looks dreadful are idiots. The midis made most women look like London charwomen and the only thing worse are Hot Pants on ladies who are much too old or too fat to wear them. My fashion philosophy is—find a length and a fashion which suits you, stick to it and you'll never be out of style.

Of course it's not only clothes, it's also your outlook on life that keeps you young. I know girls in their middle thirties who resemble doddering grandmothers because they think old.

Ann Miller—Party Girl—that's part of my image in Hollywood. Sure, I love going to parties, after all those years of my youth when I was working and never went out. But I'm no playgirl and I don't go to parties to booze it up or look for men. I go because I like to get all dressed up in my frills and velvets and beaded gowns. I go because I like to see other people dressed up and looking happy and smelling so good.

I never went to parties when I was child or a teen-ager. I was always working too hard and always under Mama-Kat's thumb. Once I hit Hollywood, the fun wasn't to begin for a good long time. I guess that's why parties still mean more to me than they do to the average person. And I still get a thrill out of meeting famous people and movie stars. That's the Lucille Collier in me, I guess.

It's also Lucille Collier, who never forgot that her Christmas dinner one year was only a chocolate cake, who turned Ann Miller into a clothesoholic. Or worse—a spendoholic, not only for clothes. As I said, whenever I was unhappy, I would go out and buy, buy, buy, run up big bills spend, spend, spend, and get myself very deeply in debt. When I look back on this, I realize I probably did it deliberately. I'd worked so hard for so many years, and sometimes I think I was simply tired of working. But with those big bills staring me in the face, I would have to go out and work to pay them off.

I never went out on spending sprees without permission while I was married—except for that time in Rome. On my compulsive buying sprees, I spent my own money. That way, I punished only myself, and I had to work pretty damn' hard to earn it back.

I always spent more than I earned, which isn't a very good policy, because you should keep something back for a rainy day. But I never have and I just pray it doesn't rain too much. Although I do have my mother's house and my Arthur Cameron diamond just in case.

But being a spendoholic and piling up material possessions isn't as bad as selling your soul for money. I saw how those lady stars would throw themselves at Louis B. Mayer to get important parts and when I think back on what I've seen others do, I feel that being a spendoholic isn't so bad after all.

I'm always being asked whether I have any regrets. I'm not one to look back and mope and I don't believe in wasting time dwelling on the past. Perhaps I should have some regrets about moving in and out of my marriages the way I did. But to be truthful, I think the only part of my life I do deeply regret is the loss of my baby and the fact that I could never have another one.

For me, the saddest sound in the world is the tinkling music of the Good Humor ice cream truck. After each divorce, when I came back to my mother's house crying and miserably unhappy, I would hear that Good Humor truck coming down our street and it always seemed to be mocking me. Its happyhearted, merry-go-round music still reminds me of the sounds of all the toys that were given to me by friends at a baby shower.

I realize I've talked quite a bit about my clothes and my jewelry and furs—material possessions. But I want you to know there are some things which are as important to me as any of my jewels. They are my taps—the jingles I use on my tap shoes. I don't dare lose them. The jingle company went out of business, because there was no longer any demand for the large taps I've always used. Nowadays you can only buy the little ones. My jingles look like a washer which clacks against another little round disk. I have quite a few pairs and when I want to use a new pair of shoes for a particular number, the jingles have to be dug out of old shoes and put on the new ones . . . I also have a great sentimental attachment to that first pair of tap shoes, Joe and Moe, that nice Mr. Morgan gave me. They are among my most precious souvenirs.

Thanks to Mama-Kat and to my good old-fashioned Texas horse sense, I still have values which Hollywood hasn't been able to take away from me.

Hollywood has been good to me but there is one side of it that I've never liked. It is filled with superficiality and phoniness. Who you are and what you're doing are far more important than the real honest-to-goodness person you may be. When you've knocked around this town as long as I have, you know all about

The Look. I've had it both ways—when I've been Up There and when I haven't.

When you're up on top, people look at you with admiration and awe and believe me, it's thrilling. I've had it again, ever since I did *Mame,* and I have to admit that I enjoy that Look very much. It's pretty nice to be a success.

But there's another Look. It's reserved for those who have slipped from the top or who aren't working. I never got that Look when I was a star at M-G-M or when I was married to Bill Moss or Arthur Cameron, because everyone knew they were big oil men and millionaires and money breeds respect in this jungle. But after my annulment from Arthur, I would run into people I had known well during my reign at M-G-M and they would smile and shake hands and then look away. Or kind of look through me. Or look at me with an expression of polite dullness in their eyes. It hurts. Believe me, it hurts.

However, I've been luckier than most to have found some real friends in this tinseltown. Like the Nat Dumonts, the Bill Pereiras, the Art Linkletters, the John Tylers, Kathryn Grayson, and a few others. They helped me both materially and psychologically and were always around when I needed them. And as I've mentioned even two of my ex-husbands, Bill Moss and Arthur Cameron, gave me much needed support on many occasions.

These real people are those I call my funeral friends. If they outlive me, I hope they'll give me a good, old-fashioned Irish wake, because I want everybody to be happy at my funeral. I want them to have a drink and laugh, and remember me as Mame because Annie Miller is really a lot like Mame and her "Live, live, live, Life's a banquet" philosophy.

Some people would probably call me a square because I've managed to remain myself and down to earth. Perhaps if I hadn't, I'd be a bigger star or I'd have a lot more money. But I wouldn't want to have the things on my conscience that some glamour girls have. There's one star lady in particular—who lives like a queen in palatial splendor and everyone in Hollywood salaams to her. At the snap of her bejeweled fingers they all come running. Ha! If you only knew her true story! She was a full-fledged prostitute by the time she was fourteen years old. Three Maharajahs have told me this so I know it's true.

Yes, I am grateful to Mama-Kat for keeping me on the straight and narrow and instilling in me some of life's more worthwhile values, especially in a town that takes these values so lightly. Maybe this is the time to explain why I call her Mama-Kat. Ever since I've been twelve years old, people have always reminded me of animals. My mother has always reminded me of a large Persian cat. I used to say, Mother, I'll always take care of you. I'll tie a large satin bow around your neck, set you on a pillow and give you a bowl of cream.

My mother's given name was Clara. But all my beaus and husbands always called her Mama-Kat, except Arthur Cameron, who usually called her Clara-Girl and me Annie-Girl.

Reese Milner looked like a big bull to me, with his big neck and wide shoulders. So did Bill Moss—only he looked like the redheaded Hereford kind.

Bill O'Connor was my big rabbit. When I gave him a gift that had an inscription on it, I always put *To my big rabbit, Love, Annie*. He got teased about that a lot because I guess people thought it meant, you know, quick like a bunny. But I thought of him as a big jack rabbit, because he was always hopping around a room, shaking someone's hand, then hopping on to another table and on around the room. He was a politicking rabbit.

Arthur Cameron reminded me of a big black panther. He could mesmerize a woman merely by sitting back and staring at her with his fabulous dark eyes. She became like a little bird and when she least expected it, he would pounce on her.

And me? I always think of myself as a race horse. I'm nervous, high strung and temperamental the way a thoroughbred is. After

I finish a strenuous number I'm like a horse when he finishes the race. And brother!—stay away from me until I've had time to cool off.

I've sometimes been called a ding-a-ling because of the way I think and talk and also because of some of the things I believe in, like Ouija boards and reincarnation. I seem to keep coming back to this subject—but how can I help it? I want to tell you about two recurring dreams which I believe to be visions of experiences I've had in previous lives. (And I was dreaming these long before I ever went to Cairo.) I don't know what they mean and I find them disturbing—but very real nevertheless.

The first one begins out on a desert full of Arab tents, Camels tied to palm trees, fires burning here and there and the smell of heavy incense. In the biggest and most luxurious tent of all, there is a woman with long black hair. She is lying back against a mound of pillows. She has bare feet, gold rings on her toes and bracelets on her ankles. She is wearing a heavy breast-plate of gold and silver, inlaid with all different kinds of stones in brilliant hues of blues, greens, and reds. I see a band around her forehead, huge earrings and a gold Arabic necklace. Below her navel, there is a large, jeweled band, from which hang filmy veils or skirts of some kind. And on her upper arms are snake bracelets made of heavy gold.

I see a parade of people coming to her, bringing her all kinds of exotic foodstuffs on enormous copper trays.

And then I see two men, bringing in another tall, handsome man in chains. They throw him at the woman's feet. He says something which angers her and she suddenly leaps up and grabs a long, black whip and beats this man senseless. Then she calls the other two men and has him taken away.

There are always sentries standing by the opening to the tent and they do not like what she does. Yet they have fear in their eyes for they know she rules supreme. In these dreams, the woman seems to have great sexual strength and when she's bored with her lovers, she has them killed or beats them to death with her whip.

After the man has been taken away, she dances to drums. As the drums get louder and louder, she dances more wildly. And she's always laughing and demanding more wine to drink. Then she drops to the floor and sleeps.

And finally I see the long camel caravan moving away in the desert. It moves very slowly. I can even hear the camel bells tinkling and recognize the smells of myrrh, cinnamon, jasmine, and even camel dung. Then I awaken. What does it mean? I guess it's my karma catching up with me. It's always the same dream.

The other recurring dream also takes place in Egypt. I see a large pyramid with huge torches lit all around it. It is night. There is a long procession coming down the road. There are many priests with lighted torches and they are singing and chanting. They are carrying a golden slab and I feel I am lying on it, bound with golden chains.

I am surrounded only by men, no women, and they carry me into the pyramid and lay the slab on the ground. There are servants all around and a large chimpanzee of some kind which clings to me. There is an oppressive smell of incense.

Then all the priests depart and I am left alone with the servants. I see two huge doors closing and I can hear other exits being closed. The torches inside the pyramid begin to get dimmer and dimmer and I know that the oxygen is being all used up. Then it comes to me—I am being buried alive and I start screaming. Each time, in the dream, I cry out: How could this be? It cannot be by order of the Pharaoh, because I am the Queen, I am the Pharaoh.

Then it grows completely dark and I wake up screaming.

I've had both of these dreams many, many times. I'm sure a psychiatrist could explain them. But to me they are visions from other lives I have led. And they are a reminder of what the Egyptian seer told me about repaying my karmic debt in this life.

I adore men and I cannot possibly see myself being so cruel and evil. But if I did this in other lives, I hope my debt is now paid in full. I think it is. And now there's nowhere to go but UP.

Chapter 22

PLAY NO TAPS FOR ME

Here I go again. As Annie Mame says, "Live, live, live. Life's a banquet and most poor sons of bitches are starving to death."

So as I write this, I'm getting all my glad rags ready to go off on another junket to Iran and Munich, Germany, for some more hotel openings. Have eyelashes, will travel, that's me. Only this time it's the Sheraton chain. I guess Connie is running out of Hiltons.

Oops. Scratch that. The Iran trip was canceled. Now it's on again, only this time it's the Iranian Film Festival in Teheran. I spent weeks on the phone, rounding up stars for the press junket. Then came the big earthquake and that trip, too, was canceled.

I had asked my current most favorite escort, Henry Berger, to accompany me on this one. (Henry is former film star Anita Louise's widower.) We had both gone through all those painful shots—for nothing. Oh, well, I went out and bought some books on Persia, some peacock feathers, and some new Kenneth Lane jewelry to cheer me up, and as a consolation prize Hermes Pan cooked us a Persian dinner.

But Annie-girl never stays put for very long and as of this paragraph I'm up to my eyeballs in rehearsals for *Can-Can* again, this time for a tour of the John Kenley circuit in Ohio. After that I go to St. Louis to do Cole Porter's *Anything Goes* at the famous open-air summer Municipal Opera there. And then maybe take the show to Lincoln Center in New York.

Also I have just finished shooting my first straight TV acting role in a segment of *Love, American Style*. While I was doing it I could almost hear my dancing feet saying, "Thank God, she's going to let us rest in this one. Let's hope this dizzy dame lets us cool it more often."

It seems so long ago that my mother said, "Dance hard, Lucille. Someday you may have to support us both."

And dance I did . . . thousands and thousands of miles and all the way into a strange and wonderful destiny. I was so lucky to have been a part of Hollywood's Golden Era. I treasure my memories but I do not waste time looking back. The days of opulence are over. The movie folks are no longer the godlike figures they once were. There is still a big future for me, a new career for me to think about.

I do not delude myself. There is no place for me in most of the films being made now. But I feel about it like Clark Gable felt about it when he said to Vivien Leigh in *Gone With the Wind*—"Frankly, my dear, I don't give a damn."

Gone are my days of reaching for the gold ring of the Hollywood merry-go-round. There are other fish to fry and rings to reach for.

Mame opened a new window in my life and my career. Live, live, live. That's exactly what I plan to keep doing for a long while to come. I was teethed on caviar and champagne, I still love them, and I intend to have a lot more.

I'm on the threshold of fifty now, but age has nothing to do with anything. In *Mame* I sang and danced "How Young I

Feel." You're only as old as you feel and I feel eighteen. I've just had a nice long rest and I'm a-rarin' to go again, as they say in Texas. I have so much yet to do and to learn.

For me, life begins at fifty, all over again, and I know there's a whole new world out there just waiting for me to swing it by the tail. So play me no taps nor put me to pasture. I have no intention of being put out to pasture—at fifty, sixty, or any other age.

As I've mentioned, people remind me of animals, and the reason I think of myself as a race horse is that dancers and race horses have much in common. They're treated the same way. They both have "trainers." They both have to "work out" regularly and get plenty of rest. And the financial upkeep on both dancers and race horses is rather astronomical. I remember Louis B. Mayer telling me once, "You could keep four mistresses in great style with what it costs to own one champion race horse."

Dancers and race horses are always petted and pampered by their owners. They have their own "star" dressing rooms and stalls where they are massaged and curried and fed daily like royalty.

Dancers and race horses are vain. They like to look their best. They enjoy all the attention and applause from their adoring fans.

When a race horse breaks a leg, sometimes they shoot him, sometimes they try to mend the leg, sometimes they put him out to pasture to breed. I've retired to the pasture three times in marriage, but always jumped the corral and came back to the welcome clamor of show biz.

How many times have I heard someone call out as I went on stage, "Hey there, break-a-leg, Annie." It always made me wince because it reminded me that I'm a race horse and I would think to myself, "Gee whiz, what if I really did break a leg and they'd have to haul me off the track in a truck and shoot me."

I've seen horses run in a race with a sore leg or foot because their greedy owners kept them running and wouldn't give them time for the wounds to heal properly.

I've danced with toe nails broken and bleeding, with sore swollen feet, blood clots in my leg, my back in a brace—and in pain. Not all at the same time, of course. But I always remembered to screw my earrings so tight that my ears hurt, and this helped me not to feel the pain in my feet.

Being a race horse or a dancer is rough hard work. Sometimes I think when I'm reincarnated again I'd rather come back as a spoiled and pampered French poodle. Now there's the life. But no, not really. Being a race horse or a dancer may be grueling work—but nothing in the world is more exciting than being a winner on a race track. Or on Broadway.

If a race horse loses too many races, his owner sells him or auctions him off to the highest bidder. The same in Hollywood. When a star begins to lose money at the box office, the studio either tries to sell him to a lesser studio, or doesn't pick up his option. Sometimes the old-time stars wind up as extras or bit players in their later years, like the old race horses at Caliente—still running. I've seen many well-known old horses still running at Caliente and die from a broken heart on the track. They're shot and put in a big truck and hauled away. Their past track records are forgotten.

How many times I've said to myself, Please God, don't let me die like that. I want my track record to be remembered. Maybe that's why I'm writing this book.

Come to think of it, maybe the title of it should have been *Native Dancer*. Because that was the name of my most all-time favorite race horse—Native Dancer. I saw this black beauty win many races, and I loved watching him strut past the judges to the winner's circle and take a bow, while the horseshoe wreath of flowers was slipped over his neck. The gold cup was presented. And then with a crown of flowers on · his neck, he would slowly strut off to his stall—his head high, his tail arched, his ears up, so proud and vain and beautiful. He was a magnificent animal, the champion of champions. I wept when Native Dancer died, and I thought to myself, how great if I could be like Native Dancer, a champion to be proud of, a winner till the end . . . His owners sent me a color photograph of him which has its special place of honor in my den and is one of my most treasured possessions.

Mame opened new doors for me. For the first time I was recognized as more than a dancer—as a singer and actress as well. But deep down I know that I'll always keep dancing because I am a Native Dancer at heart in the sense that I was born to dance, it was my destiny, it was meant to be. Every seer I've ever consulted has told me this, and they've all said I was a dancer in my previous lives.

There's another reason I'll never stop dancing. I'm never lonely or alone when I'm dancing. There's always a dreamlike feeling that someone else is up there with me dancing. Looking back now my whole life takes on a dreamlike quality. How can you tell where reality begins and the dream ends?

Sometimes when I'm dressing to go out for the evening I look at all those wardrobes and closets and I thank God and Mama-Kat for the happy memories they hold.

I look at the racks of clothes and they remind me of the high life and good times I've had all over the world.

And sometimes I laugh when I look at that $10,000 worth of negligees and night gowns I bought for Arthur Cameron—still hanging there, never used, because he didn't like night gowns. I think of them as forlorn puppies hoping to be adopted. Sometimes I talk to them. I say, "Hey now, hang in there, old beans, you beautiful things. Don't give up hope. All is not lost yet."

I still have my shortie night gowns from my Bill Moss era with the name "Twink" embroidered on them. He always called me "Twinkle Toes," but "Twink" for short.

My "Twink" gowns always remind me of our wedding in La

Jolla and the telephone ringing and Bill O'Connor begging me to call off the wedding.

Yes, I still dream of a Prince Charming who won't fall off his horse. One is never too old to dream and dreams do come true. But, please, God, next time just give me a plain boy with no family fortune to weigh him down.

Only the other day another psychic told me that my next husband is going to be in politics. She also saw a new career unfolding for me. She said, "You have never been free. I see the sadness, the imprisonment you have felt. A door is opening for you. I see a bright colored rainbow in front of you and you are swinging from the rainbow. You are going to be free, my child, not only in this life but forevermore."

I hope she meant that is the end of my karma.

As I write this, I am looking out from my den upon our pretty tree-shaded green lawn and garden in Beverly Hills. I feel so alive. Spring is here. Babies are still being born. There is music all around me . . . the Good Humor ice cream truck tinkles down the street.

I know it is true that if you just sit still and listen you can see your own future. So I went out in our garden and sat there a while and just listened. I saw a rainbow with a little girl named Johnnie Lucille Collier swinging on it. I heard a voice say, "Annie, you haven't even commenced yet. There's a brand new future ahead of you."

I answered, "Fine. And I want this one to be the greatest experience of my life."

Copy 1.   B
                                 Miller
Miller, Ann
    Miller's high life.